GCSE

BUSINESS STUDIES FOR CCEA

Hope Kerr

Hodder & Stoughton
A MEMBER OF THE HODDER HEADLINE GROUP

Orders: please contact Bookpoint Ltd, 130 Milton Park, Abingdon, Oxon OX14 4SB. Telephone: (44) 01235 827720. Fax: (44) 01235 400454. Lines are open from 9.00–6.00, Monday to Saturday, with a 24 hour message answering service. You can also order through our wedsite: www.hodderheadline.co.uk.

British Library Cataloguing in Publication Data
A catalogue record for this title is available from the British Library

ISBN 0 340 85843 5

First Published 2003
Impression number   10 9 8 7 6 5 4 3
Year   2008 2007 2006 2005 2004

Typeset by Pantek Arts Ltd, Maidstone, Kent.
Printed in Dubai for Hodder & Stoughton Educational, a division of Hodder Headline Plc, 338 Euston Road, London NW1 3BH.

CONTENTS

ACKNOWLEDGEMENTS

My sincere thanks are due to my husband Robert for his support and encouragement throughout the writing of this book. In addition, he took on the onerous task of proofreading the entire work, which I greatly appreciate.

I also gratefully acknowledge the advice so willingly provided by Alexia Chan and Pete Keogh, as well as the practical help from the technical team at Hodder and Stoughton.

Hope Kerr

The author and publishers would like to thank the following for permission to reproduce copyright material:

Advertising Standards Authority p. 241; Balcas pp. 59, 275; Ballygally Castle Hotel p. 83; © R D Battersby pp. 214, 250, 263, 273, 290, 316; *Belfast Telegraph* pp. 9, 11, 112, 114, 144, 165, 232, 233; Belleek Pottery p. 201; Brian Morton and Co. p. 11; © Brownie Harris Productions/CORBIS pp. 73, 151; Castelreagh Borough Council pp. 40, 41; Citizens' Advice Bureaux p. 268; © Charles Gupton Photography/CORBIS p. 145; Charter Mark and Beacon Scheme Unit p. 205; © Chuck Savage/CORBIS p. 147; Culloden Hotel pp. 10, 47; Diamond Recruitment p. 125; Doctor's Associates Inc. (The SUBWAY logo is a registered trademark of Doctor's Associates Inc.) p. 31; Dungannon and South Tyrone Borough Council p. 117; Eadie, McFarland and Co. p. 11; Equality Commission for Northern Ireland p. 134; Eric K. K. Yu/CORBIS p. 327; European Foundation for Quality Management p. 207; © Image 100/Royalty-Free/CORBIS p. 141; © The Image Bank/Getty Images p. 72; Independent Television Commission p. 242; Invest Northern Ireland p. 89 (The Northern Ireland Business Start Programme is funded by Invest NI, the twenty six councils in Northern Ireland and the European Union.); Investors in People p. 208; © Jim Zuckerman/CORBIS p. 127; © Joaquin Palting/CORBIS p. 140; © Jose Luis Pelaez, Inc./CORBIS p. 85; Labour Relations Agency p. 167; © Michael Keller/CORBIS p. 224; © Michelle Garrett/CORBIS p. 177; Mivan Ltd. p. 233; NASUWT p. 161; Northern Ireland Council for the Curriculum, Examinations and Assessment p. 206; Office of Fair Trading p. 242; © Paisley Museum & Art Galleries, Renfrew District Council p. 108; © Paul Russell/CORBIS p. 253; Phoenix Natural Gas pp. 47, 50, 86, 204, 253; Prontaprint Limited p. 31; Raymond Humphreys Photography p. 70; © Roger Ressmeyer/CORBIS p. 191; © Roger Wilmshurst; Frank Lane Picture Agency/CORBIS p. 203; J Sainsbury p. 221, 234; © Ted Horowitz/CORBIS p. 184; Trades Union Congress p. 169; Ulster Property Sales p. 11; Ulster Teachers' Union p.161; Unilever Bestfoods UK/Colman's p. 255; Which? (published by Consumers' Association, 2 Marylebone Road, London NW1 4DF; for further information please phone 0800 252 100) p. 267; Wimpy International p. 11.

Every effort has been made to trace and acknowledge copyright. The publishers will be happy to make arrangements with any copyright holder whom it has not been possible to contact.

INTRODUCTION

This textbook has been written especially for the new Northern Ireland GCSE Business Studies specification which is due to be examined for the first time in May 2003.

It is based totally in Northern Ireland, drawing on examples from local businesses and providing photographs of areas with which students already will be familiar. In addition, the book provides up-to-date and comprehensive coverage of agencies and legislation which operate in Northern Ireland and which may differ from those operating in other parts of the United Kingdom. For these reasons, students and teachers will find it a valuable resource in preparing for the examination component of CCEA Business Studies at GCSE level.

This new textbook accurately follows the order of the specification but, in the interests of simplicity, it combines sections where there is overlap in the specification. Like the specification, the book is divided into five main sections which, in turn, are divided into units to provide the coverage of the necessary material. This in no way aims to dictate the order in which the specification should be approached.

Adapted questions have been selected from recent CCEA Business Studies examination papers and included at appropriate points throughout the book. These questions have been accompanied by tips for answering them, and are intended to familiarise students with the style and requirements of the papers and to build confidence. As Chief Examiner, the author understands that many candidates do not answer questions appropriately because they fail to recognise the requirements of the command words used in questions. For this reason, a section on Command Words is included at the end of the book.

In addition, each unit includes activities which have been designed to reinforce learning and to make the student think further about the knowledge-based material provided, as well as to give opportunities to develop the skills of application, analysis and evaluation. The author is aware of the wide range of ability in the candidature for this particular examination, so activities have been designed to cater for these varying abilities. It has to be understood, therefore, that some activities will be too easy for some candidates while some activities will be too difficult for other candidates.

The effectiveness of these activities and examination questions is largely dependent on the skill and expertise of the business studies teacher and the book acknowledges the vital role which the teacher plays. Only the teacher can know the individual students and cater for their individual needs.

Each unit ends with an indication of the key facts which should be understood at that stage, and the Glossary provides an easy reference for revision.

Hope Kerr

HOW TO USE THIS BOOK

This book is divided into five sections to correspond with the CCEA specification for GCSE Business Studies. Each section is further divided into units, breaking down the material in order to make it more manageable.

The order in which the sections are approached will be decided by your teacher, but the author recommends that all the units within each section are completed in the order shown in the book.

Diagrams and local examples have been used frequently in this book and almost all the photographs have been taken in Northern Ireland. These should be studied carefully by students to make the subject matter meaningful and alive; they serve to demonstrate that the subject of Business Studies is happening all around.

ACTIVITY

The large number of activities should be worked on as they arise in the units. Although some are more difficult than others, they are deliberately not graded and are suitable for being attempted by all candidates of the examination. The working of the activities is important if you are to understand and apply the knowledge contained in the units. Most are suitable for being worked on as either classwork or homework exercises.

Some of the activities are designed in the form of short case studies. These provide simple examples which will help you to prepare for the compulsory case study in the examination.

Class discussion

A number of discussions and debates are included. These usually involve groupwork and should be carried out in class.

EXAMINATION QUESTION

Nearly every unit contains actual examination questions selected from recent papers at both foundation and higher levels. If you complete these on your own as they arise in the book, they will help you to become familiar with the style and language of the GCSE examination. Work on actual questions should also help you to choose the appropriate level of entry for the examination.

Tips for answering this question:

Each examination question is accompanied by 'tips for answering' it. Pay attention to the tips because they are written to guide you on the most appropriate responses to the questions. Marks are indicated in order to help you to manage your time well and to prevent you from spending a long time on a question for few marks.

REVISION

Each unit concludes with a revision section which highlights the most important concepts in the unit, and shows what you are expected to have learned at that stage. If you are still unsure, you should look up the terms in the glossary at the end of the book.

SECTION ONE

Business Aims, Types and Organisations

Learning Objectives

To develop a knowledge and critical understanding of

- the context within which business is organised
- the aims of business
- the different types of business
- how businesses are organised
- how businesses grow
- the resources and assistance available to businesses
- business planning.

To develop an appreciation of

- the ethical and moral issues associated with business aims
- social and moral issues of the growth of large firms.

Business Context

Before we really get into the subject of Business Studies, this section aims to give a broad overview of the business world. Firstly, you should be aware that various countries allow businesses to operate in different ways. There are three main economic systems – planned, market and mixed.

Economic Systems

In some cases, the government plays a very prominent role and plans how much will be produced and how much resources will be used. That is known as a **planned economy**. In other cases, the government plays a less prominent role, leaving business decisions to the business people. That is known as a **market economy**. In other countries a mixture of these two systems operate and that is known as a **mixed economy**.

Let's look at these three types of economy, now in slightly more detail.

Planned economy

A planned economy is also sometimes called a **command economy**. This type of economy once was operated in all countries which were under a Communist regime, however it is now very rare and Cuba and North Korea are probably the only examples left.

In a planned economy there is public ownership, which means that the government owns all the land and property. There is no private property in a planned economy

Figure 1.1

and everybody works for the government, which has total control and makes all the major decisions.

The government would decide, for example, which crops would be grown and how much land would be devoted to their use. It would also decide what would be produced, where individual people would work and how much they would be paid, how many people would be employed in each industry or service and which countries would be traded with. There is little variety of goods in the shops and no competition between shopkeepers.

A planned economy has both good and bad points:

Advantages	Disadvantages
Producers are told exactly what to make so there is no overlap or waste	Nobody can own any property so the workers have little ambition
The government regulates employment so there is work for everyone	Workers could be difficult to motivate as there are few rewards
People are not competing against each other and therefore everyone is equal	There is no variety of goods and consumers cannot buy luxury goods

ACTIVITY

Try to imagine that you are in school in Cuba and are just about to go to work. Write a short description of how you think that the planned economy in the country would affect you.

Market economy

The market economy is the direct opposite of the planned economy. In a market economy there is total private ownership which means that private people and business own all the land and property. The government plays a very small role in business, while the owners have control of their own affairs and make all their own decisions regarding how many they will employ, where they will locate their businesses, what they will produce in their factories or sell in their shops, and regarding the prices they will charge.

In a market economy there is great competition between producers and between shopkeepers. Their decisions are, therefore, guided by consumers – their market. They all are anxious to satisfy the market and encourage consumers to buy their particular goods so they price their goods at a level which will achieve the most sales and the highest profit.

As a result of this competition, there is a great variety of goods in the shops.

Figure 1.2

America and the Philippines are the nearest examples of the market economy which exist in the modern world, although, even in those countries, the government does exercise a lot of authority over their economic affairs.

A market economy has both good and bad points:

Advantages	Disadvantages
Consumers dictate what is produced so their needs are satisfied	Businesses are motivated by profit so they will not produce goods which are not profitable
Business is efficient because it aims to make the maximum amount of profit	There is a great difference between the rich and the poor
There is strong competition so producers are keen to produce exactly what is needed	The government does not provide services such as education or health. This means that these services are available only to those who can afford to pay for them
Competition keeps prices lower	
There is a great variety of goods on offer so the consumer has a vast choice	
Employee motivation is high and workers are rewarded for hard work	

ACTIVITY

If you were living in America or the Philippines you would benefit from the additional competition there is in a market economy. State one advantage which you would gain as a consumer in those countries because of the high level of competition.

Mixed economy

A situation where privately owned and publicly owned businesses both exist is known as a mixed economy. This is the most popular type of economy since it permits free enterprise but, at the same time, ensures that the basic needs of all citizens are met. We have a mixed

Figure 1.3
An example of publicly and privately owned businesses existing alongside each other in Enniskillen

economy in Great Britain and Ireland where the majority of businesses are privately owned and exist alongside other businesses which are publicly owned and run by the government.

This type of economy has all the features of the market economy with the government involving itself in business only in order to ensure that Health and Safety regulations are carried out and that consumers are treated fairly. However the government does provide public services, such as health, fire, education, public transport, water supply, electricity supply and defence, which must be available to everyone living in the country. These services are partially financed by rates and taxes which are taken from everyone, and partially by central government funds.

A mixed economy provides the best of both worlds, although it has its critics:

Advantages	Disadvantages
All the benefits of competition exist as in the market economy which keeps prices lower and provides a great variety of goods	Demand for health services in particular is so high that waiting lists are very long and the service is often slow
Employee motivation is high because employees are rewarded for hard work	This means that many people still pay for their treatment while others cannot afford to do so
There is good opportunity for enterprise	
Public services are provided for everyone	

ACTIVITY

In this country the government provides the services of education, health, fire control and electricity. Copy the following table and complete the spaces to show the advantages and disadvantages of these services being provided by the government.

Service	Advantage	Disadvantage
Education		
Health		
Electricity		
Fire		

ACTIVITY

Trace or photocopy a map of the world. Label two countries which have a planned economy and colour them red. Next, label two countries which have a market economy and colour them green. Finally, label two countries which have a mixed economy and colour them yellow.

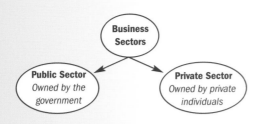

Sectors of Business

We have just seen how some businesses in the mixed economy are owned and run by private people and some are owned and run by the government.

Those businesses which are owned and run by private individuals are said to be in the **private sector**. Those businesses which are owned and run by the government are said to be in the **public sector**.

Figure 1.4

Examples of public-sector and private-sector businesses in Northern Ireland

ACTIVITY

Make a list of six privately owned businesses and two publicly owned businesses in your nearest town. Write the names of the businesses in your notebook.

These two main divisions, or sectors, of business are differently organised and financed and their aims are also different. These differences are dealt with in detail later in this book in Unit 1.2.

Significance of small- to medium-sized enterprises (SMEs)

What are SMEs?

An SME is a business which has fewer than 250 employees. In 1996 the European Union issued the

A micro business has fewer than ten employees
A small enterprise has a maximum of 50 employees
A medium-sized enterprise has a maximum of 250
A large enterprise has more than 250 employees

definitions on page 6. At the time of writing, these definitions are still being used but are to be updated in the near future.

Importance of SMEs

The following statistics illustrate the importance of SMEs. Altogether in the United Kingdom it is estimated that there were 3.7 million businesses at the start of the year 2000. 99% of those businesses were small, often without any employees at all. 25,000 of those businesses were medium-sized, with between 50 and 250 employees each. Seven thousand of the total number of businesses were large, employing more than 250 people.

Number of Businesses	Number of Employees
3,668,000	Less than 50
25,000	50–250
7,000	More than 250

Almost half of all employees work in small businesses. Northern Ireland is a small-business economy with the majority of businesses falling into this category. In the year 2000 alone, there was an increase of 300 businesses in Northern Ireland and the province has the highest business survival rates of any region in the United Kingdom. For example, 70.1% of firms which registered in Northern Ireland in 1996 were still in business three years later, compared with 62.4% in England, 63.1% in Wales and 61.2% in Scotland.

This success is largely due to the high level of government support which is given to SMEs through agencies such as Invest Northern Ireland as well as the former Local Enterprise Development Unit (LEDU). People who cannot find other work are encouraged to use their business ideas to start a new business. Training and ongoing support are given to such businesses.

The government is supportive of SMEs and encourages their development because they:

- provide a key source of local employment
- create local economic development
- improve the standard of living for the local community
- promote an enterprise culture
- increase competition
- lead to greater consumer choice.

ACTIVITY

Many businesses remain small by choice. Consider the following case study and answer the questions at the end.

Sandra was excellent at ICT at school but could not find suitable work when she left school. She owned a very good computer and other equipment and decided to work from home as a word processor and printer. She advertised locally and soon got lots of work processing theses for university students and undertaking office overload work for local businesses.

The quality of her work was first class and many people were advising her to open new premises and employ some people to help her.

Activity continues overleaf

Although the idea was tempting, Sandra decided to remain as she was.

1. Name two advantages which Sandra has in her present work.
2. List two disadvantages which Sandra has in working on her own.
3. Sandra was tempted to expand her business. What benefits would she have gained by employing other people to work for her?
4. Sandra's prices are very reasonable, according to her customers. How, and why, might her prices have altered if she had enlarged her business?

Potential and Implications of E-commerce for Business

What is e-commerce?

E-commerce (short for electronic commerce) is a very up-to-date method of buying and selling goods using the Internet. This method is being adopted by most businesses and gives them access to customers all over the world. This is known as the global market.

The system is very simple to operate. The business designs a website which describes its product or service, giving all necessary details such as price, colour and dimensions. Obviously, it is important that the home page is attractive in order to encourage customers to view the contents of the site.

The customer selects the goods which he/she wishes to purchase and gives the details of his/her credit card. On receipt of the order, the business prepares the goods for despatch and debits the customer's credit card as payment.

The use of the Internet in business has become very sophisticated. For example, customers using the worldwide delivery firm DHL can place their orders, then pay and track the progress of a delivery on-line.

There are many advantages for both customers and suppliers in using e-commerce, as well as some disadvantages:

Advantages of e-commerce for a business

- Having access to a global market makes the business better known
- This wider market gives the business the opportunity to be ahead of its competitors
- E-commerce increases sales which usually leads to increased profit for the business
- Expensive showrooms and premises are unnecessary which is a major saving
- Advertising costs are kept to a minimum
- Increased sales and production enable the business to take advantage of economies of scale
- The business is always open so there are opportunities for sales at all times.

Advantages of e-commerce for customers

- Customers have a much wider range of goods from which to choose
- It is easy for customers to 'shop around' a number of websites and get the best bargain available

- Prices are frequently lower on the Internet because the expense of advertising is reduced and business have been able to take advantage of economies of scale
- Customers can shop at any time they find suitable
- It avoids traffic congestion in towns.

Disadvantages of e-commerce for a business

- Being part of the global market brings the business into competition with a large number of others
- Designing and updating the website is expensive since specialists usually have to be employed
- Market research needs to be very detailed in order to assess the requirements of customers in such a wide market

Figure 1.5

- The business has to pack products very carefully and distribute them over a wide area. This is very expensive. Distribution is also dependent on the services of either the Post Office or private carriers
- Certain groups – such as the elderly – find computers intimidating. Since customers need to have access to the Internet this makes e-commerce unsuitable for goods such as walking aids or other products designed for the elderly.

Disadvantages of e-commerce for customers

- The customer must own, or have access to, a computer and be on-line.
- The service is very impersonal and it is difficult to make further enquiries about the goods
- In reality, the goods may look different from the impression given on the screen. It is also impossible to gauge the quality of items such as clothes or fabrics
- Returning unsuitable goods can be inconvenient
- Payment is generally by credit card so e-commerce is not available to any customer who does not use this method of payment
- There is a security risk attached to giving credit card details, although this problem is being reduced.

Here are three examples of very different businesses, all of which use e-commerce.

Figure 1.6
The Culloden Hotel, Cultra

The five-star Culloden Hotel in Cultra is one of the Hastings Group of hotels and a member of the exclusive Small Luxury Hotels of the World.

The hotel's website gives a full description of the hotel and its facilities as well as a picture gallery of its interior and exterior. This serves as one of the Culloden's marketing methods.

Until recently, the Culloden Hotel had taken its bookings either over the telephone or through the Global Distribution System. The latter system was very expensive because the hotel was charged commission on each reservation made. Recently the hotel introduced on-line bookings which saves this charge. Now visitors can log on to the hotel's website, give the details of their accommodation requirements, learn if the accommodation is available and make the booking straight away.

Figure 1.7
The Culloden Hotel's on-line reservations page

ACTIVITY

Answer the following questions in your notebook.

1. Justify the commission charge which is made by the Global Distribution System.
2. What effect is the gallery of pictures of the hotel likely to have on bookings?
3. Give one benefit to visitors of being able to make their hotel reservations on-line.
4. State one possible disadvantage of the on-line reservation system to visitors.
5. What effect is the changeover to on-line bookings likely to have on the hotel staff?

The National Association of Estate Agents (NAEA) says that approximately 86% of estate agents have their own websites and report that people selling their homes now expect to see their homes displayed on the Internet.

The NAEA has estimated that the Northern Ireland based site 'propertynews.com' is getting more than 32,000 hits per day and that the Internet now accounts for 14% of all enquiries from people wishing to move house in the province.

This method enables buyers quickly to find homes which would be suitable for them. They then can contact the agent concerned instead of spending time unnecessarily visiting a number of estate agents and viewing a large number of houses.

Figure 1.8
A selection of Northern Ireland estate agents' logos

ACTIVITY

Read the report from the National Association of Estate Agents and answer the following questions:

1. State one advantage of using the Internet for someone selling a house.

2. State one advantage of using the Internet for someone buying a house.

3. Name one possible disadvantage of using the Internet for someone buying a house.

The *Belfast Telegraph* carried the following report of another business which is successfully trading via the Internet:

Wheel dealers do wonders on the web

ANTRIM-based firm Toshe Trading is the BT Northern Ireland/Belfast Telegraph e-Xcellence Award winner for April.

The company scooped the award after impressing the judges with its website www.performancealloys.com.

Toshe Trading has taken advantage of the opportunities available on the internet and prides itself in being the number one website for alloy wheels in Ireland and the UK.

Rory McLornan, sales manager for Toshe Trading, explained: "The internet enables product viewing and ordering 24 hours a day around the world. People can access our site at their convenience, regardless of differet time zones at any time of the day or night.

"The traditional method of new market entry via agents and distributors would have been condiserably more costly in terms of time and money for us."

He said the site enables its customers to view more than 500 different alloy products.

"We save the customer time by allowing them to inspect all the alloy wheels which will fit their car.

"They then have the ability to price wheels and tyre packages in different sizes. Customers can receive their order within the UK and Ireland free in an extremely short time span." ...

Tony McLornan, managing director of Toshe Trading, said: "...The company is excited about the opportunities that the internet offers and is keen to take advantage of these."

Performancealloys.com receives numerous unique visitors per day and it has customers all over the world, from Hong Kong, Singapore, America, Canada and Armenia to the United Arab Emirates and the Seychelles.

ACTIVITY

Read the newspaper article 'Wheel dealers do wonders on web' and answer the following questions:

1. Where does Toshe Trading have customers?
2. List three advantages which Toshe Trading has found in using the Internet.
3. Which disadvantages did the traditional method of working through agents and distributors have?
4. How has the business been able to save money by using e-commerce?

Types of Production

Before you started to study the subject of **Business Studies** you may have thought that 'production' referred only to making goods. That interpretation is too narrow – the word 'production' more accurately refers to the creation of either goods or services. The teachers in your school, for example, are involved in production – they produce the service of education.

Production may be divided into three types: primary, secondary and tertiary. You are already familiar with these three words in connection with school. You started your education in a primary school – that was the first stage. You are now at the secondary level of education and if you continue into college or university, you will enter the tertiary level – the third stage.

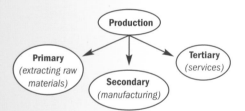

Similarly, each industrial and business activity falls into a primary, secondary or tertiary stage.

Primary industry

Primary industry is the getting of raw materials from the ground or from the sea. It is also using the earth's resources to grow items such as crops, fruit, flowers and trees.

Forestry by a Fermanagh firm

Fishing in Kilkeel

Figure 1.9

Examples of primary production in Northern Ireland

Primary industries include farming, fishing, mining, quarrying, forestry and oil drilling.

Farming is particularly important in Northern Ireland. There are approximately 30,000 farms in the province and their average size is 88 acres. In percentage terms, there are 3.5 times more people working in agriculture in Northern Ireland than in the rest of the United Kingdom. In the Republic of Ireland, there are almost 144,000 farms and their average size is 72 acres.

Secondary industry

Secondary industry takes the raw material produced by the primary industries and works on it to manufacture finished goods. For example, wood produced by a primary industry would be manufactured into tables and chairs by a secondary industry.

Tertiary industry

Tertiary industry provides services to all the other industries and members of the public. These services include commercial services such as banking, marketing, insurance, transport, and retail trading. It also includes all professional services such as entertainment, hospitality, education, and legal, religious and medical services.

Figure 1.10
Examples of services provided by tertiary industry

The Chain of Production

Each stage of production is dependent on the other two in order to get the finished product to the consumer.

The production of Tayto Potato Crisps in Tandragee illustrates the chain of production very well and shows how all three stages of production work together and are required in order to get the crisps to the consumer.

Figure 1.11
Tayto Crisps

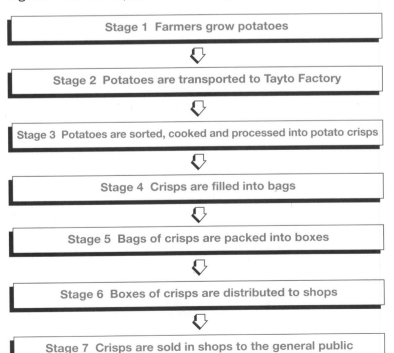

Stage 1 Farmers grow potatoes

⇩

Stage 2 Potatoes are transported to Tayto Factory

⇩

Stage 3 Potatoes are sorted, cooked and processed into potato crisps

⇩

Stage 4 Crisps are filled into bags

⇩

Stage 5 Bags of crisps are packed into boxes

⇩

Stage 6 Boxes of crisps are distributed to shops

⇩

Stage 7 Crisps are sold in shops to the general public

ACTIVITY

You should now copy the stages involved in manufacturing potato crisps. Beside each stage, in the spaces provided on the right hand side, write down whether it is primary, secondary or tertiary

Farmers grow potatoes ....

Potatoes are transported to Tayto Factory ....

Potatoes are sorted, cooked and processed into potato crisps ....

Crisps are filled into bags ....

Bags of crisps are packed into boxes ....

Boxes of crisps are distributed to shops ....

Crisps are sold to the general public ....

ACTIVITY

In this activity you are asked to think of any five adults you know. They may be members of your own family, or they may be friends or neighbours. Copy the following table and use it to fill in the appropriate details of the work they do.

Name of Person	Occupation	Sector of Industry
....	....	....
....	....	....
....	....	....
....	....	....
....	....	....

ACTIVITY

Copy the following table on your computer and complete the spaces to show which type of production each one is involved in.

Occupation	Primary, Secondary or Tertiary
Insurance agent	
Fisherman	
Furniture manufacturer	
Teacher	
Farmer	
Shopkeeper	
Market gardener	
House builder	
Solicitor	
Coal miner	

Stakeholder Groups Involved in Business

> Throughout your Business Studies course you will hear of many different groups of people all of whom have an interest in the business world. Any one with an interest in business is called a stakeholder.

The following are the main stakeholders in business:

Owners

The owners of a business are those who have invested money in it. They may have contributed the total capital for the business, as in the case of a sole trader or a partnership. In a small business, the owners may also manage and run the business.

Owners have the greatest interest in the progress of the business since a large part of their money is invested in it and, in the majority of cases, the owners depend on the business for their livelihood.

The reward which owners get from the business is in the form of profit but they also risk having to bear any loss incurred in the business.

Shareholders

Shareholders are those people who invest money in a business which is a limited company. Their investment is in the form of shares and this makes them part owners of the company. Shareholders do not take any part in the management of the company although they are entitled to attend the annual general meeting and vote for the Board of Directors.

The reward which shareholders receive from the business is in the form of a dividend which is a share of the annual profit. If the company is not in a profit-making position, the shareholders risk losing their shares. However, they have limited liability which means that their loss is limited to the amount they invested in the shares.

Directors

Directors are appointed to the Board of a limited company and their function is to be responsible for the overall running of the company. Directors make the policy decisions and have the ultimate power in the company. It is usual for a company to have a managing director and a number of other directors each of whom looks after a certain area of the business's operation, for example sales, finance or production.

The reward which a director receives from the business is in the form of a salary although it is possible for directors also to be shareholders, in which case they would also receive a dividend.

Managers

Managers are the second layer of authority below the directors, and they have responsibility for the day-to-day running of the business. Managers oversee the work being done in the company, and the workers and supervisors report to them.

Managers are rewarded with a salary and they have a great interest in the success of the business since their employment depends on it.

Producers

Producers of materials to a business also have a stakeholding in it and want to see it succeed. This is because producers do not want to lose any of their customers but want to ensure that they are prosperous and able to pay their accounts.

Producers are rewarded by high levels of sales which adds to the profits of their own businesses.

Consumers

Consumers are the business's customers and are therefore vital to its success. The business depends on consumers for its income and needs them to purchase its goods or services. If consumers do not buy its product, the business will experience a loss and may eventually have to close.

Consumers have a stake in a business since it probably is situated in a convenient place for them and they will support it if it supplies goods at suitable prices. They also have an interest in seeing that the business succeeds because they have a greater number of firms to deal with which improves the competition and the variety of goods on offer.

Taxpayers

Taxpayers have an indirect stakeholding in business and therefore wish to see general business prosperity. Everyone pays tax in some way. Those who are earning pay income tax and we all have to pay value added tax (VAT) on most purchases. If businesses are successful, there is full employment in the country so workers have more money to spend. This, in turn, keeps down government spending on items such as unemployment benefits and therefore the government has less need to increase taxation.

Trade unions

A trade union is an organisation which represents the interests of the workers in the business and negotiates with management on their behalf. The trade union has an interest in seeing a business succeed because it ensures the safety of its members' jobs. If the business loses profit or fails altogether, it will have to make workers redundant. Those workers would then depend on the trade union to try to save their jobs or find them work elsewhere.

Employers' organisations

An employers' organisation represents the owners and bosses in the business, and speaks on their behalf to central government and to local authorities. The employers' organisation is anxious for the success of the business because its failure would have a bad effect, not only on that particular business, but also on other businesses, as well as on the local community in which it is situated.

ACTIVITY

Complete the following table to show why each stakeholder would have an interest in a business.

Stakeholder	Interest
Owners	
Shareholders	
Directors	
Managers	
Producers	
Consumers	
Taxpayers	
Trade unions	
Employers' organisations	

REVISION

At this stage you should understand:

Planned economy	Market economy	Mixed economy
Private sector	Public sector	e-commerce
Primary production	Secondary production	Tertiary production
Chain of production		

As revision, look each one up in the Glossary at the end of the book.

Types of Business Organisation – Private Sector

Introduction to Private Sector Businesses

> **Any business which is owned by private people is known as a private sector business.**

Some of these businesses may be small and owned by just one person – that person is called a sole trader. In some cases the business may be slightly larger and two or more people may have put money into it and perhaps joined together to work in the business. That is an example of a partnership.

Other businesses may be even larger and money would be needed from many people to keep them going. A large business would be organised as a private limited company, and the largest business of all would be organised as a public limited company.

There are two other types of businesses in the private sector: a franchise and a workers' co-operative.

In this unit we shall study each one of these types of business organisation in turn. At this stage, it is important for you to remember that private sector businesses are owned and controlled by private people who aim to make a profit from the money they have invested in the businesses.

Private sector businesses

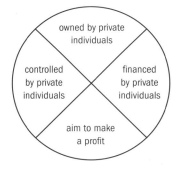

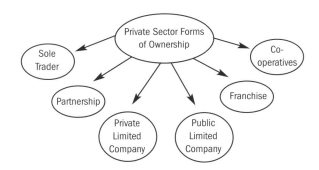

Sole Trader

This is the most common form of business ownership. Sole traders are found in every town and district throughout Northern Ireland, running small and medium-sized shops as well as providing services such as hairdressing, plumbing, dressmaking, painting or electrical work.

It is a popular form of business organisation because sole traders are their own bosses and own the businesses themselves. For this reason, they are also sometimes called sole proprietors.

Sole traders' businesses are easy to form as they do not have to provide a lot of involved legal documentation before they can be established. All the sole trader has to do is to get a licence to trade from the local authority and perhaps planning permission if the building is to be altered. The business has to registered for VAT with Customs and Excise and then it is ready to open.

Sole traders provide the entire capital for setting up their businesses and usually work in their own shops or businesses. Their major aim in running the business is to make a profit and to expand. Depending on the size of the business, they may employ others to help with the work.

Sole traders are entitled to keep any profits made but also are responsible for losses incurred. They have unlimited liability which means that if they do not have enough money in their businesses to pay their debts, they have to use their private funds to meet them.

Figure 1.12
A sole trader's shop in Tyrone

Advantages of a sole trader

- The business is cheaply and easily formed without involved legal procedures
- The owner can keep all the profits made in the business
- The owner can make all the decisions and can make them quickly without having to call committee meetings
- Because the business is usually small, the sole trader has very close links with the customers and employees
- The financial affairs of the business do not have to be published, although tax authorities must have access to them.

Disadvantages of a sole trader

- The major disadvantage is unlimited liability. This means that if sole traders do not have enough money in their businesses to pay their debts, they have to use their private money to meet them. This could have serious consequences because, in extreme circumstances, their cars, houses and other private possessions might have to be sold
- Sole traders are responsible for all the losses in the business
- Sole traders have to raise all their own capital
- The amount of capital which sole traders have is limited, so their businesses are likely to be small
- Because their businesses are small, banks are less willing to lend money to sole traders than they would to large businesses
- Being limited, it is more difficult for sole traders to compete with the large business organisations as they cannot take advantage of economies of scale
- The business is very dependent on one person. The sole trader in a shop, for example, is expected to have expertise in sales, purchasing, advertising, accounting, window dressing, deliveries and stocktaking. This means they work very long hours
- If the sole trader becomes ill or is on holiday, there is often no one to call on to cover for him/her
- The sole trader frequently does not have anyone with whom to discuss business problems.

ACTIVITY

Read the following short case study and answer the questions which follow.

Gillian is an excellent hairdresser who has been working at 'Best Cuts' – a very good hair salon in Newcastle. She loves her job but has always dreamed of setting up her own salon. For several weeks she has noticed an empty shop which has a notice in the window saying it was available for renting.

Her mother helps her to clean and paint it. Her father puts up some mirrors, installs basins and builds shelves and cupboards. Gillian has saved enough to be able to buy dryers and other necessary items of small equipment. Her brother offers to lend her money, if necessary.

On 1st October Gillian opens her new business, which she names 'Hair for You'.

1. Outline the difficulties she might have in her new business.
2. State the advantages which Gillian will have as a sole trader.
3. How might Gillian use extra money in the business?

EXAMINATION QUESTION

Samuel has started to work in a local news agency owned by his uncle.

a   **What type of business organisation is the news agency?**
(1 mark)

b   **Explain the type of liability Samuel's boss has.**
(2 marks)

c   **Outline two aims the news agency might have.**
(4 marks)

(Adapted from CCEA Business Studies, GCSE, Paper 2 Foundation Tier, 2001)

Tips for answering this question:

Part A is a straightforward, knowledge-based question. For 1 mark you should simply name the type of organisation – without any explanation.

Part B asks you to 'explain' so here you must name the type of liability (for 1 mark) and then, for the second mark, briefly say what that type of liability means.

Part C would be approached in a similar way to Part B. Here you should name two aims (for 2 marks). To 'outline' means that you are asked to write a very short description. In this question you should write a short sentence on each of the aims you have named, to show that you understand them.

Partnership

Partnerships are most frequently found in professional businesses such as doctors, dentists, veterinary surgeons, accountants and solicitors. Just think of the doctor, dentist or vet you go to – do they work on their own or in partnerships? If you are unsure, have a look at their nameplates outside their doors, or on their headed paper. If they show a number of names, then the business is a partnership.

Partnerships are also commonly found in trades such as plumbers, hairdressers and electricians. They are popular in all of these businesses because expertise can be shared and each doctor or solicitor can take responsibility for one area of work.

Figure 1.13
Name plates of partnerships

A partnership consists of a minimum of two people (partners) and a maximum of twenty who jointly own a business. On some occasions an additional partner may be brought in to contribute capital but not to work in the business or to take any part in its organisation. This person is known as a 'sleeping partner'.

The partners:

- agree between themselves how they will run and organise their business
- are jointly responsible for any debts incurred in the business
- provide the entire capital for setting up their business
- aim to make a profit and to expand
- are entitled to keep any profits made but also are responsible for losses incurred.

Like the sole trader's business, a partnership is easy to set up and requires only the agreement of the partners about how their business would be organised.

Partnership Act 1890

The partnership is governed by the Partnership Act 1890 which states that:

- any profits or losses made in the business will be equally shared between them
- no partner will be paid a salary.

The Partnership Act, however, does not take into consideration the individual situation in each business. For example, one partner may have contributed much more capital to the business than the others, so it would be only fair to give that partner more of the profits. The other way of rewarding that partner would be to pay him/her interest on capital. One partner may work full time in the business while the other partners may carry on their careers elsewhere. In this case it is unfair that the partner working full time cannot be paid a salary.

Deed of partnership

For all of the above reasons, the partners are advised to draw up a deed of partnership which is a legal document setting out the terms and conditions under which that particular business would operate.

If a deed of partnership is drawn up, it takes the place of the rules in the Partnership Act for that business and states:

- how the profits and losses are to be shared
- the amount of capital which each partner would contribute
- if salaries are to be paid and the amount to be paid

- whether interest on capital is payable
- how the duties and responsibilities are to be shared
- how new partners might be introduced to the firm
- how the partnership could be dissolved and, in the event of this happening, how the assets would be shared.

Figure 1.14

Darren and Jamie were good friends who both loved working with cars. Even before they left school they had earned pocket money for themselves by washing cars in the large yard at the side of Jamie's home. They quickly built up a good reputation as very capable workers and their business was increasing all the time.

The boys realised that their hobby could be turned into a profitable business so, soon after leaving school, they decided to open a car wash and valeting business in Garvagh.

Market research had shown that there was no local competition and they had proved that there was a demand for this service.

Darren had a substantial sum of money which he had inherited from an uncle and he was willing to invest some of it in the new business. Jamie was able to borrow £2,000 from his father and the boys were allowed to continue to use the yard at Jamie's house for a small rental.

They consulted a business adviser who helped them to plan the details of their business and also drafted their deed of partnership (opposite). Darren and Jamie thought the deed was unnecessary since they were such good friends, but the business adviser insisted.

Advantages of a partnership

- There is more capital in the business which allows it to expand
- Specialisation is possible as the partners may bring different skills to the business
- The owners can share responsibility for decision making and discuss the problems which occur in the business
- If one partner is ill or on holiday the business can carry on
- The financial affairs of a partnership do not have to be published although tax authorities must have access to them.

Disadvantages of a partnership

- As in the case of the sole trader, the major disadvantage in a partnership is unlimited liability. This means that if the partners do not have enough money in their business to pay their bills, they have to use their own private money. This puts their private possessions at risk. Each partner is liable in this way, even if the debt was created by one of the other partners

DEED OF PARTNERSHIP
BETWEEN
DARREN ALDERS
AND
JAMIE MOORE

TRADING NAME OF THE BUSINESS:

Garvagh Car Valet Service

THE FUNCTION OF THE BUSINESS WILL BE TO PROVIDE THE SERVICES OF:

- Power washing and waxing all road vehicles
- Cleaning vehicles in preparation for Motor Vehicle Testing
- Valeting vehicle interiors

BUSINESS CAPITAL:

- The total capital of the business will be £4,000
- Each partner will contribute £2,000

SHARE OF PROFITS OR LOSSES:

All profits or losses will be shared equally by Darren Alders and Jamie Moore

WAGES AND INTEREST PAYABLE:

- Each partner will be entitled to draw equal wages from the partnership as agreed annually between them
- No interest will be payable on capital

BANKING

- The bank account will be in the name of Garvagh Car Valet Service
- Each cheque must be signed by both Darren Alders and Jamie Moore

THE DUTIES OF THE PARTNERS WILL BE AS FOLLOWS:

- Darren Alders will undertake all accounting and banking
- Jamie Moore will undertake all purchasing of materials and machinery
- Both partners will share equally the work of washing, waxing and valeting

DISSOLUTION OF THE PARTNERSHIP

- The partnership may be dissolved by mutual consent between the two partners
- In this event, the assets will be shared equally between the two partners

- If one partner is dishonest or inefficient, all partners are held liable for that partner's actions or decisions. It is important, therefore, that partnerships are formed only between people who know each other well and trust each other totally
- The partners have to raise their own capital
- When compared to a large company, the amount of capital in a partnership business is small. They have the same difficulty as a sole trader in borrowing money from banks and cannot take advantage of economies of scale
- There is the possibility of conflict between the partners
- The death or bankruptcy of one partner may cause the break-up of the business. Otherwise the remaining partner has to 'buy him out'. This is known as 'lack of continuity'.

ACTIVITY

Either use the *Yellow Pages* or do field research to discover the names of all the doctors, dentists, veterinary surgeons, accountants and solicitors in your town or local area.

Write down their names and work out the percentage of them who are organised as partnerships.

ACTIVITY

Gillian's hairdressing business in Newcastle, 'Hair for You', has been very successful. She now employs two juniors to do shampoos and act as receptionists, and her own skills as a hairdresser are in great demand.

However, Gillian is annoyed at having to turn away customers because she is too busy. She knows there is enough work for two qualified hairdressers and has thought of employing another one to work with her. The difficulty is lack of space and she does not want to borrow money in case she could not repay it.

Gillian's friend Charles, also a qualified hairdresser, has discussed the possibility of forming a business partnership with her. Eventually, they decide to go for it. They also decide to retain the name 'Hair for You', to make it a unisex salon, to keep the two juniors and to move to larger premises which are available in the town. They have agreed to contribute £10,000 each as capital and wish to draw up a deed of partnership.

a   Design a deed of partnership suitable for Gillian and Charles.
b   Name any advantages which Gillian will gain by moving into a partnership.
c   What new problems may arise for Gillian in the new business arrangement?

EXAMINATION QUESTION

Jonathan and Michael formed a partnership to set up a pizza restaurant, 'Pizza Point', several years ago. The business is now doing so well that they have decided to buy a van and start a delivery service. To help to finance this, they decide to take on a sleeping partner, Caroline, one of their friends, who is interested.

a   Explain why a partnership is a suitable form of ownership for a restaurant.

(2 marks)

b   Jonathan and Michael have unlimited liability. Explain how this might affect them.

(2 marks)

Question continues on the next page

Tips for answering this question:

In both Part A and Part B you are asked to 'explain'. This means that the examiner wants you to show that you understand why a partnership is a good form of ownership for a restaurant and how limited liability might affect the owners. However, you should look at the number of marks allocated to each question. There are 2 marks in each of Parts A and B so you should explain just one reason in each case.

Tips continues on the next page

EXAMINATION QUESTION

c   **Discuss two reasons why Caroline is interested in becoming a sleeping partner in the firm.**

(4 marks)

(Adapted from CCEA Business Studies, GCSE Paper 2 Higher and Foundation Tiers, 2000)

Tips continued

In Part C you have to 'discuss' two reasons. To do this, you must first name two reasons why Caroline might be interested in the business, but then you must put forward both good and bad points for Caroline in being a sleeping partner. At the end of a question in which you are asked to 'discuss', you should give a conclusion – in this case, you could say whether you feel Caroline is wise or unwise to become a sleeping partner.

Limited Companies

It is legally possible to form a company with as few as two shareholders and one director, and there is no limitation on how large it may become. While there are many small companies in Northern Ireland, there are also many which are extremely large. Businesses on this scale could not possibly raise the amounts of capital required if they remained as sole traders or partnerships.

A company is a group of people who have joined together to form a business. You may be thinking that that sounds like a partnership. Right so far – but read on to see the differences between companies and partnerships.

Figure 1.15
Tesco - one of the large limited companies operating in Northern Ireland

Shares and shareholders

In order to raise the vast amount of capital required, members of the public are invited to become members of the company and invest money in it. They do this by buying shares on the Stock Exchange. This makes them shareholders – or part-owners – in the company. From the company's point of view this has the advantage of providing large amounts of capital and the shareholder benefits by becoming a part owner of the company and being entitled to a share of its profits at the end of the year.

There are two types of shares:

- **Ordinary** shares   Ordinary shares are not guaranteed a dividend (share of the profit) at the end of the year. Whether they get a dividend depends on how successful the company has been during the year.

   Owners of Ordinary shares are given voting rights in the company which gives them a say in the election of the Board of Directors.

- **Preference** shares

Preference shares are very safe because they are guaranteed a fixed dividend out of the profits before any payment is made to the ordinary shareholders.

Preference shareholders are not given voting rights in the company because their investment is not at risk and they have a guaranteed dividend.

ACTIVITY

Rita has £1,000 which she has decided to invest in shares. Unfortunately, she has no experience of buying shares and needs your advice. She wants to know whether she should go for ordinary or preference shares.

Write down one advantage and one disadvantage of each type of share and say which type you would buy if you were Rita.

Ownership and control of a company

Although the shareholders are the owners of the company, obviously it is impossible for them to run the company. The shareholders are entitled to attend the Company's Annual General Meeting to elect a Board of Directors who run the business on their behalf. In practice, few shareholders actually attend the Annual General Meeting.

Although the Board of Directors has overall responsibility for the running of the company, they employ managers to undertake its day-to-day running. This situation is often referred to as a 'divorce of ownership and control', because the people who own the company do not control its running and the people who run it may not be its owners.

ACTIVITY

a   Explain the phrase 'divorce of ownership and control'.
b   Explain the effect this might have on the company.

Main features of limited companies

Apart from the increased capital you have already learned about, companies have two other important advantages over sole traders and partnerships. They are:

1. Limited liability
   The most significant feature of the limited company is that it has limited liability. This means that people who invest in a company cannot lose any money other than the amount they put into it. If the business should fail, the shareholders' liability is limited to the amount of their

original investment – their private possessions cannot be taken. (You will remember that sole traders and partners risked losing everything if their businesses failed.)

2. Separate legal existence (incorporation)
   In law, a limited company is considered to be quite separate from its owners – it is said to be incorporated. Being incorporated gives creditors the right to sue the company without affecting the owners of the company. Equally, the company could sue its debtors if the need arose. This is very different from the situation of the sole trader or partners who could be taken to court as owners of the business.

Forming a limited company

Setting up a limited company is a lengthy legal procedure and the company must be registered with the Registrar of Companies. The following documents have to be completed before trading may commence:

Memorandum of association
The memorandum of association has six clauses which state the official name of the company, the country in which the company will be situated, the work the company will be doing, and the amount of capital with which the company is to start. The memorandum also has a liability clause which states that members' liability is limited and an association clause which is a declaration by at least two people that they wish to form a company.

Articles of association
The articles of association show the voting rights of the shareholders, the method of election of directors, how profits will be divided, how meetings are to be conducted and the duties of the directors.

Certificate of incorporation
This certificate is issued to show that the company has a separate legal existence from its owners, and can act independently from them.

Prospectus
Before shares can be sold, the company issues a prospectus which gives details of the company's plans and its hopes for the future. Possible investors will read the prospectus and use it to decide whether or not the company is a worthwhile investment.

Trading certificate
After the company has sold shares and raised enough capital to be able to trade efficiently, a trading certificate will be issued, showing that the Registrar is satisfied that the company is in a position to begin trading. At that stage, the company may begin to trade.

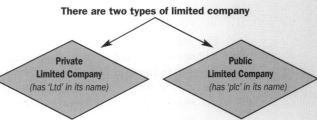

Private limited company

A private limited company is called 'private' because its shares cannot be bought by members of the public. Instead shares in a private limited company are held by a small group of people (very often members of one family) who are able to keep control of the business. Shareholders in a private limited company may only sell their shares privately and with the consent of the other shareholders. Each year the shareholders are entitled to a share of the profits which is paid in direct proportion to the number of shares each one holds.

A private limited company is attractive to shareholders because they retain control of the business while, at the same time, enjoying the benefits of limited liability. This gives them all the advantages they would have had in a partnership but with the added security of limited liability. You can now see why the partnership is less popular to trading businesses. The official name of the company includes either 'Limited' or 'Ltd' in it to indicate that the liability of the owners is limited.

Advantages of a private limited company
- The amount of capital available is much greater than to sole traders and partnerships
- Because the business is on a larger scale, it is easier for it to borrow money
- As a larger business, it can benefit from economies of scale
- It has limited liability
- The business has a separate legal identity from that of its owners and may take legal action on its own behalf without involving the owners
- The business has continuity. This means that if one shareholder dies the business is not affected
- There is a number of directors and managers in the business, so responsibility and workloads are shared
- There are opportunities for specialisation and division of labour
- Control of the business is retained by a small group of shareholders.

Disadvantages of a private limited company
- Some of the financial information of a private limited company must be available for inspection by members of the general public. This may give competitors valuable insights into the affairs of the business
- Shares are not available for wider sale, so expansion may be difficult
- Shareholders are entitled to receive a share of the profit in the form of dividends
- The process of forming the company is more involved than it is in business organisations such as sole traders and partnerships.

EXAMINATION QUESTION

Sandwich Ltd has been established for over 10 years. Originally, it was a partnership with only one shop in Belfast which prepared sandwiches to be delivered to offices. Due to its success, the owners extended the premises and opened a coffee shop.

Five years ago the business became a limited company and opened four new outlets. The company has gone from strength to strength and has a reputation for high quality.

a   Identify the main differences between a partnership and a limited company.

(4 marks)

b   Explain the reasons why this business may have decided to become a limited company.

(4 marks)

c   Explain two aims which this business may have.

(4 marks)

(CCEA Business Studies, GCSE Paper 2 Higher and Foundation Tiers, 2002)

Tips for answering this question:

Part A is a straightforward question to find out if you understand the two types of business. Name two differences and show both sides. Suitable wording would be 'A partnership is .... whereas a limited company is .... Show two differences between them.

Parts B and C ask you to 'explain' so in Part B you must give details of two reasons why the business became a limited company and in Part C you have to give details of two aims. For full marks in Parts B and C it is necessary to show that you understand the reasons and aims – not simply to name them.

Public limited company

A public limited company is the largest type of private sector organisation, and must have a minimum capital of £50,000. Shares in a public limited company (plc) may be sold to members of the public – that is how it gets its name. Shares are bought and sold on the Stock Exchange all the time, but although ownership of the shares may change, the actual amount of capital in the business does not alter. The value of the shares rises and falls according to how successful the company is being at that particular time, and according to the general economic conditions in the country.

A public limited company may have thousands of owners, although the number of shares owned by each person may be quite small. However, the total capital in the company is very large. The liability of the shareholders is limited to the amount which they invested in the firm and they have the confidence of knowing that they cannot lose more that than that. Each year a dividend is declared, and shareholders are paid a share of the dividend in proportion to the number of shares they own.

The official name of the company includes the initials 'plc' to indicate that the liability of the owners is limited.

Figure 1.16 is an extract from a published list of share prices. It shows the current prices for food retailers and general retailers. The first column shows the name of the company, the second shows the present price of each share in pence, the plus or minus sign shows whether the price has risen or fallen from the previous day, and the final column shows the number of pence by which the price has risen or fallen.

FOOD RETAILERS			
Safeway	310	+	6
Sainsbury	402 1/2	+	2 1/2
Tesco	260 1/2	–	2 1/2

GENERAL RETAILERS			
Ashley L.	19 1/4	–	3 1/2
Boots	707	–	3 1/2
Debenhams	395 1/2	+	3 1/2
Dixons	229 1/2	+	2 1/2
GUS	628	+	4
M&S	398	+	1
Mothercare	255		
Next	1037 3/4	–	2 3/4
WH Smith	449	+	1

Figure 1.16

ACTIVITY

Answer the following questions in your notebook. They are all based on the list of share prices in food and general retailers.

1. You are considering buying some shares in retailers. On the basis of the above extract, which is the best business to invest in today?
2. Which business has had no change in its prices?
3. What do the above figures tell you about the performance of Next stores?
4. If you had £50 to invest in Laura Ashley, how many shares could you buy?
5. How many Marks & Spencer shares would you be able to buy for £100?
6. Why would it not be wise to make investment decisions on the basis of this single list? What would it be better to do?

Advantages of a public limited company

- Public limited companies are very powerful organisations, with great influence in the market
- Shareholders have limited liability
- The capital available is very large which gives the business all the benefits of easier borrowing and economies of scale
- A public limited company has the resources necessary for growth and expansion
- Because the business has a separate legal identity from that of its owners, it can take legal action without involving the shareholders

- The business has continuity and shareholders may buy and sell their shares without affecting the business
- Each director and manager has his/her own area of responsibility in the business, giving the benefits of specialisation and division of labour.

Disadvantages of a public limited company
- The shareholders are the owners of the business but the directors and managers make all the decisions. Therefore the owners of the company have no real say in its running
- The formation of a public limited company involves a lengthy legal procedure
- The financial information of a public limited company must be published for the information of the general public
- In some public companies top management and employees feel out of touch with one another
- Decision-making in large companies is frequently slow because a series of meetings have to be held and numerous people consulted.

ACTIVITY

The following extracts from letterheads indicate the type of business organisation in each of the businesses. Study the letterheads and complete the questions for each business.

1
JONATHAN LOWRY
Plumber and Electrician
88 Middle Street
CRUMLIN
Co Antrim

2
MARIE LONG & KIM SHORTT
QUALIFIED HAIRDRESSERS
101 Top Road
DROMORE
Co Down

3
PREMIER PRINTERS LTD
PREMIER PRINTERS LTD
66 Low Avenue
MARKETHILL
Co Armagh

4
ALPHA MUSIC MAKERS PLC
15 Beta Drive
CASTLEDERG
Co Tyrone

1. The business organisation is _____

2. How many people might it be owned by? _____

3. What, in your view, is the greatest advantage of this type of organisation?

_____

4. What, in your view, is the greatest disadvantage of this type of organisation?

_____

Franchise

A franchise is an excellent way for someone to set up in business. This method gives the person the opportunity to sell a well-known set of products, but without the risks attached to opening as a sole trader and having to start from scratch.

Franchising originated in America and has become popular all over the world. It is a system through which successful business ideas can be hired out to other businesses. A franchise gives permission to the franchisee (person who is buying the franchise) to set up a business, using an established business name and idea. The business can also use the established trade mark and image. A franchisee's liability depends on whether the business is organised as a sole trader, partnership or limited company.

You will be familiar with and may well use many of these franchised businesses:

Figure 1.17
McDonald's is a favourite franchise

Some of the other franchises operating in Northern Ireland are:

Another of the well-known franchises in Northern Ireland is Benetton – you probably shop there yourself!

Just imagine that, at some time in the future, you are setting up a new Benetton shop in your local area. Very simply, you would reply to an advertisement and apply to Benetton for a licence to sell their goods and operate a business using their name.

Benetton would consider your application – for example, they have to be sure that you have the experience and qualifications to run one of their retail outlets, and that the new outlet would not be too close to one of their existing shops.

If your application were to be successful, you (the franchisee) would pay an agreed sum of money as capital for the use of the Benetton trademark and image, and Benetton (the franchiser) would provide shop fittings, stock, premises and design. They would also train you in the techniques which they apply to selling their products.

You would be expected to buy an agreed percentage of goods solely from Benetton, to reach a certain sales target and to organise the business according to the Benetton guidelines. In addition, you would have to pay a royalty to the franchiser – this is really a share of the profit made, and would be a set percentage.

Advantages of a franchise

The franchisee gains:

- from having reduced risks and capital investment
- the sole right to sell a well-known set of products and brand in that particular area
- increased sales as consumers know the quality of that particular established brand
- use of a brand name
- training provided by the franchiser
- the right to be his/her own boss in the shop
- the benefits of national advertising and promotions
- continuous support from the franchiser
- increased borrowing power from the bank because franchised businesses are usually profitable.

The franchiser gains:

- increased opportunities for expansion
- further benefits from economies of scale
- a percentage profit from all sales in that particular shop
- another retail outlet which is run without any increased capital investment
- by having the retail outlet run and managed for them.

Disadvantages of a franchise

The franchisee loses:

- any individuality. All shops are decorated and organised in the same way in order to be instantly recognisable by the public
- independence, as he must organise the business according to the rules given by the franchiser. In many ways, he could be seen more as a manager than an owner
- the right to sell the business without approval from the franchiser
- the right to buy stock from other sources which may be cheaper

- royalties which must be paid annually to the franchiser.

The franchiser loses:

- management of the day-to-day running of the shop. If the local service is poor, the reputation of the franchise is damaged.

EXAMINATION QUESTION

Sandwich Ltd prepares sandwiches to be delivered to offices, and runs a total of five coffee shops in Belfast.

It has been suggested that the owners of Sandwich Ltd might consider expanding further by appointing franchisees.

a   Discuss two reasons why someone might be interested in becoming a franchisee of Sandwich Ltd instead of setting up a small independent business.

(6 marks)

b   Would you advise Sandwich Ltd to franchise the business? Give a reason for your advice.

(3 marks)

c   Discuss the personal qualities Sandwich Ltd would be looking for in the franchisee.

(6 marks)

(Adapted from CCEA Business Studies, GCSE Paper 2 Higher and Foundation Tiers, 2002)

Tips for answering this question:

Part A is a discussion question. This is more difficult and therefore carries 6 marks. You should answer it by giving two reasons why someone may want to become a franchisee instead of starting his own business – this is really asking for two advantages of becoming a franchisee. At the end you should say whether you think franchising or sole ownership is better – with your reason.

In Part B you must make a judgment as to whether franchising is advisable in this case. Your judgment, either for or against franchising, is acceptable (for 1 mark) but you must justify your decision to gain the other two marks.

Part C is another discussion question. You should give details of two to three personal qualities which a franchisee would need to have to run a shop for the business. For full marks, you need to say why those qualities would be necessary.

ACTIVITY

The following people all want to set up in business and ask you to tell them which type of business organisation is best suited to their needs. Complete the following table with the appropriate names.

Activity continues overleaf

Person	Individual Needs	Suitable Type Of Business Organisation
Phillip	I want to be my own boss	
Peter	I want to run a McDonalds fast food restaurant	
Brian	I want to operate a fleet of 10 jets	
Lawrence	I want to go into business with my cousin	
Barbara	I need to have limited liability	
Olive	I want to be part of a really big business with lots of capital	
Dorothy	I would love to open up a little home bakery and do the work myself	
Florence	My sister and I could set up a dressmaking business. We work well together	
Christopher	I dream of owning a leisure centre with my four friends but I do want limited liability	
David	I want to open an outlet for Socks Shop	

Workers' Co-Operatives

Co-operatives often are formed by workers because a business has failed and is closing down. The employees, in an effort to save jobs, form a co-operative to try to keep the business open.

The basic feature of a workers' co-operative is that all workers in the business partly own it and each worker has one vote in making decisions about its management. Therefore the workers are the managers which could be a problem in situations where there are large numbers of workers and agreement may be difficult to achieve. It is also difficult to hold meetings of all workers frequently enough to discuss all management decisions.

The profits or losses of the business are equally shared amongst all workers, and each one is jointly responsible for its success or failure.

If the business is very small and was originally established as a sole trader or a partnership, the workers' liability will be unlimited. Liability would be limited if the business was formed originally as a company.

If the business should require additional funding, it would have to come from the personal resources of the workers. Indeed, many workers' co-operatives are set up using the redundancy money which the workers were given when the business first closed down.

Advantages of a workers' co-operative

- Since the workers own the business, there is a high level of motivation to succeed
- Control is shared and no single person could take control
- Local unemployment is prevented
- It is very democratic
- There is a high degree of loyalty and support in the local area
- Workers feel very responsible for the business.

Disadvantages of a workers' co-operative

- Workers may not always have the necessary management skills to plan, run and control the business
- The business sometimes suffers from a lack of capital – this may prevent it from bringing in experts
- Differences of opinion can arise which causes delays in decision making
- There is a high failure rate in this type of business
- Most co-operatives are small so the business could not benefit from economies of scale
- There is little, if any, opportunity for career promotions.

ACTIVITY

Copy and complete the following table to show details of businesses in the private sector

	Type of liability	Source of capital	Use of profits	Who controls the business?
Sole trader				
Partnership				
Private limited company (Ltd)				
Public limited company (plc)				
Franchise				
Workers' co-operative				

R E V I S I O N

At this stage you should understand:

Sole trader	Partnership	Private limited company
Public limited company	Franchise	Workers' co-operative
Unlimited liability	Partnership Act 1890	Ordinary share
Preference share	Memorandum of association	Articles of association

As revision, look each one up in the Glossary at the end of the book.

Types of Business Organisation – Public Sector

Introduction to Public-Sector Forms of Ownership

> Any business which is owned by the country as a whole and run on behalf of the people is known as a public sector business.

Some public-sector enterprises are run by the central government of the country, either in Westminster or by the Northern Ireland Assembly in Stormont. Others, known as municipal undertakings, are run by local authorities (councils).

Although the government or local authorities run and control public-sector businesses, they are owned by the country.

Figure 1.18
Parliament Buildings, Stormont

The finance for public-sector businesses is found by either central or local government, and their aim is to give a service either for the people of the country as a whole or for those who live in the local authority area.

Differences between public- and private-sector businesses

Public sector businesses differ from private sector businesses in several important ways:

Public Sector Businesses are:

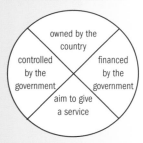

- Firstly, private-sector businesses are owned by private people but public-sector businesses are owned by the country as a whole. There are no individual owners in the public sector
- Secondly, private-sector businesses are controlled by the people who own them or by directors and managers appointed to do so, but public-sector businesses are controlled by the government or local authority
- The third difference is the method of raising capital. In private-sector businesses, the capital is invested by private people but in public-sector businesses the capital is either borrowed from the Treasury or taken out of the local rates
- The fourth major difference is the way in which the profits of the business are used or losses are met. In private-sector businesses, at least some of the profits are distributed to the owners and they also bear the losses, but in public-sector businesses, any profits are handed back to the government and their losses are offset by the Treasury
- The final very important difference between businesses in the two sectors is what they aim to do. Private-sector businesses aim to maximise profits for their owners. In public-sector businesses, however, the aim is to give a service to the people and less emphasis is placed on profit making, although they are expected to break even.

This information is summarised in the following table:

	Private sector	*Public sector*
Ownership	Private individuals	Country or state
Control	Private owners or directors and managers working on their behalf	National government or local authority

Capital	Raised by private owners	Comes from Treasury or from rates
Use of profits	Distributed to owners	Handed back to government or local authority
Aim	To make profit	To give a service

Public Corporations

Public Corporations are defined as government-controlled market bodies. (A market body is one which produces goods and services for sale, and at least 50% of its income comes from sales.)

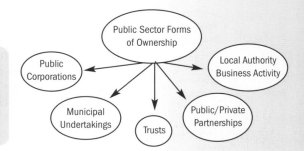

Examples of public corporations in the United Kingdom

- British Nuclear Fuels
- Bank of England
- British Coal Corporation
- British Broadcasting Corporation
- Civil Aviation Authority
- Royal Mint
- Railtrack
- British Shipbuilders
- British Waterways Board
- Port of London Authority
- Manchester Airport
- The Stationery Office
- Oil and Pipeline Agency
- National Blood Authority

Public corporations are set up by Acts of Parliament in order to run a certain industry or service. They may have been created by government to fulfil a given function or they may have been in the private sector at one time and then were taken over (or nationalised) by the government. In the latter case, they are known as nationalised industries.

Nationalisation was undertaken frequently after World War II when many of the country's services, such as the railways, were very run down. Private owners did not have the vast amounts of capital required to restore the services so the government had to step in if they were to be kept going.

The United Kingdom had a large number of nationalised industries through to the 1970s when the Conservative government, with Margaret Thatcher as Prime Minister, began the process of returning them to private ownership.

Today there are comparatively few public corporations left.

There are several reasons why these industries have been nationalised

- Some services are essential and must be provided, but their costs are so high that a privately owned firm would not be interested in them because they would not make profit
- In many cases the capital investment needed would be too great for any privately owned business to afford
- It would be unsafe for private people to run dangerous industries such as the provision of atomic energy
- Nationalisation prevented large, powerful, privately owned monopolies from existing and being able to set very high prices for their services
- In some instances, the business was failing, so the government took it over in order to save jobs
- There are examples where it would be wasteful to have several organisations duplicating services.

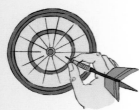

Aims of public corporations

The overriding aim of a public corporation is to give a service. At one time little or no emphasis was placed on profit making, however that situation has changed and nowadays public corporations are expected to break even at least.

Financial targets are set by the government and the corporations are now expected to meet those targets and to be able to pay for any new investment they may require.

Public corporations are controlled in the following way

The government has overall control of the corporation and appoints a government minister to take responsibility for it. The minister appointed would be the one whose department is most closely linked to the work of the corporation. For example, Railtrack is accountable to the Minister of Transport. The minister would oversee the appointment of a chairman and board of directors and they would become responsible for the day-to-day running of the industry.

The chairman of the Board of Directors must report annually to the minister who, in turn, presents the report in Parliament where it is publicly debated and later published for the information of the general public.

Public corporations are financed in the following way

- Most of the money for public corporations comes through grants from the Treasury which is the government department responsible for the country's finance
- In addition, the corporation may borrow from the Treasury
- If the corporation makes profit from its activities, some may be ploughed back into the business
- Public corporations get revenue from charging for the services they provide.

Advantages of public corporations

- The government ensures that the country's essential services are provided
- The government is in a good position to plan the overall provision for the country
- Services are not duplicated and resources are not wasted
- Any profits made could benefit taxpayers by reducing the level of taxation.

Disadvantages of public corporations

- Public corporations are very large, which can lead to inefficiencies
- It is difficult to motivate employees in an impersonal organisation such as this
- The taxpayer has to meet higher tax payments if the corporation makes a loss
- The running of the corporation could be politically influenced.

ACTIVITY

In the following table, link the first part of the sentence with its correct ending. The first one is done for you as a guide.

Activity continues on the next page

A public corporation is	nationalised industries
Public corporations are sometimes called	that it may be inefficient
One advantage of a public corporation is	to give a service
A disadvantage of a public corporation is	by the Treasury
Public corporations aim	that services are not duplicated
Public corporations are financed	controlled by the government

Municipal Undertakings

> The word 'municipal' refers to local government, so municipal undertakings are activities organised by the local councils.

There are 26 local councils in Northern Ireland and each one looks after its own area. The following map shows the area covered by each one, and you can check which district council is responsible for your area.

The councils in Northern Ireland are

1. Antrim Borough Council
2. Ards Borough Council
3. Armagh City and District Council
4. Ballymena Borough Council
5. Ballymoney Borough Council
6. Banbridge Borough Council
7. Belfast City Council
8. Carrickfergus Borough Council
9. Castlereagh Borough Council
10. Coleraine Borough Council
11. Cookstown District Council
12. Craigavon Borough Council
13. Derry City Council
14. Down District Council
15. Dungannon and South Tyrone Borough Council
16. Fermanagh District Council
17. Larne Borough Council
18. Limavady Borough Council
19. Lisburn Borough Council
20. Magherafelt District Council
21. Moyle District Council
22. Newry and Mourne District Council
23. Newtownabbey Borough Council
24. North Down Borough Council
25. Omagh District Council
26. Strabane District Council

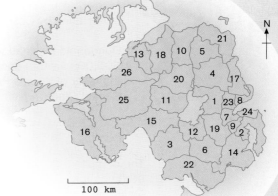

Figure 1.19
District Council areas in Northern Ireland

Each district council has elected representatives who have been voted on to the council to represent the people and to work with the council staff to provide and maintain key services throughout the area.

The services for which local authorities are responsible may vary slightly from area to area, but all are expected to provide:

- refuse collection and disposal
- street cleaning
- health and environmental services
- parks and recreational facilities
- local housing
- parking areas
- maintenance of local roads.

In addition, they support:

- the arts
- tourism
- economic development.

Figure 1.20
Refuse collection

Main sources of finance for municipal undertakings

1. **Government grant**

   The government gives a capital grant to the local authority to assist it with essential building work. It is unusual for the government to finance the project any further.

   2. **Rates**

      Some of the money required to run local government enterprises comes from the rates. Rates are paid by each householder and each business in the area according to the size of their properties.

   3. **Charge for the activity**

      An entrance fee is charged to each person using the facilities provided by the council in the area – for example a swimming pool or leisure centre.

Activities undertaken by Castlereagh Borough Council

Castlereagh Borough Council provides a wide range of community and leisure services.

Many of you will have visited Dundonald Ice Bowl. It is one of the business activities undertaken by Castlereagh Borough Council.

Dundonald International Ice Bowl is Northern Ireland's busiest leisure complex, with 500,000 visitors each year. To date it has been visited by nearly six million people. The manager of the Ice Bowl attributes its present massive business to the popularity of the Belfast Giants which has created a desire in members of the public to learn to skate.

The Ice Bowl, which was opened in 1986, caters for ice skating, ice hockey and ten-pin bowling.

The complex is owned by Castlereagh Borough Council. The council is responsible for its staffing, upkeep and financing and makes a charge to the public for the use of its facilities. A sample of its charges are:

Figure 1.21
Dundonald Ice Bowl

Ice skating Adults £4
Concession £3
Family ticket £15
Skate hire £1

Some of the other leisure and community activities operated by Castlereagh Borough Council are:

The Robinson Centre

Gilnahirk Golf Course

Lough Moss Centre

ACTIVITY

This activity is based on your own local authority. You should arrange for one member of your class to contact the local authority in order to find the necessary information. Alternatively, if you have access to the Internet, you could find some information there.

Activity continues on the next page

Write the answers to the following questions in your notebook.

1. Give the name of your local authority.
2. Write down the address of its main offices.
3. Find out the name of the Chief Executive of the council.
4. Find out the name of the councillor who is responsible for the area where you live.
5. Paste a copy of your council's crest into your book.
6. Make a list of the business activities your local council undertakes.

EXAMINATION QUESTION

Frances has recently got a part-time job with the local council. Part of her job is dealing with a local municipal undertaking.

a   Define a 'municipal undertaking'.
(2 marks)

b   Describe two activities that the local council might be involved in.
(4 marks)

(Adapted from CCEA Business Studies, GCSE, Paper 2 Higher Tier, 2001)

Tips for answering this question:

Part A is simply asking for a straightforward definition and is a knowledge-based question. Write a brief definition beginning with the words 'A municipal undertaking is …')

In Part B you should choose any two things which the council does – this would earn 2 marks. The other 2 marks are awarded for a brief (one-sentence) description of what is involved in the two activities you have chosen.

Public Private Partnerships (PPP)

A public private partnership is a collaboration between a public body, such as the government or local authority, and private companies.

Figure 1.22
Drumglass High School, Dungannon

Public private partnerships are those where finance from the private sector is introduced in order to help public funds and to spread the costs involved in some major capital projects. The scheme includes the Private Finance Initiative (PFI).

The private investors undertake to build the new public-sector building such as a hospital or school and then they charge the health authority or education authority for its use during an agreed number of years – usually 25. In this way, the private businesses recover their expenses while the public authority can continue to provide a service without a major capital outlay.

The overriding argument in favour of public private partnerships is the fact that most of the new facilities would not have been built otherwise because public money was simply not available. However, the system has advantages for both the public and private partners. The private partners find new business opportunities and a good return on investment but take the risks. On the other hand, the public partners get value for money in a high-quality service, and benefit from the skill and experience found in the private sector.

Nevertheless, public private partnerships have their critics who estimate that the profit gained by the private sector is huge. For example, it is claimed that the cost of building Fazackerly Prison in Liverpool was repaid within two years, leaving 23 years of profit making for the private contractors.

The present government is committed to public private partnerships, and the Prime Minister is keen to expand the range of partnerships because he believes they offer the best way to provide the improvements required in the public services.

Figure 1.23
St Genevieve's High School, Belfast

Public private partnerships are gaining in popularity, especially in England where approximately 50 deals have been signed so far. These contracts were for the building of new airports, hospitals, prisons, schools and roads.

The system is still relatively new in Northern Ireland but is growing. The first school in Northern Ireland to be financed by this system was Drumglass High School in Dungannon which was opened in September 2000. Since then three other schools have been built in Belfast in public private partnerships. They are St Genevieve's High School, Balmoral High School and Wellington College.

Figure 1.24
Balmoral High School, Belfast

Advantages of public private partnerships

- The largest hospital and school building programme in living memory has been made possible through public private partnerships
- Modern, high-quality buildings are provided, with advanced equipment
- There are performance-related penalties built into contracts so quality is maintained
- Improved services are secured without an increase in taxes
- Government spending is reduced at the beginning and public-sector finance is boosted
- Payments for the use of the building can be spread over a long period of time
- The government is enabled to draw up more accurate budgets for the future
- All risks are taken by the private-sector partner who is better equipped to manage them
- The public sector can benefit from the business expertise of the private sector
- Use is made of practical ideas from private investors.

Disadvantages of public private partnerships

- The private sector has no experience of the unique requirements of public sector buildings such as schools or hospitals
- The public sector is likely to have to pay a larger sum overall even though it is spread over a long time
- Critics feel, therefore, that future taxation will be increased
- There is union opposition to public private partnerships because the unions fear for their members' job security
- Some feel that the private sector gains a huge profit at the expense of the public sector
- Such partnerships would not be suitable for all public services.

Hospital Trusts

Hospitals and other health care providers can now be given trust status which makes them independent. Hospital trusts are self-governing but remain within the National Health Service (NHS). They are run by boards (which have some local representatives) and report directly to the Secretary of State. Trusts manage their own budgets, employ their own staff and can make decisions on all aspects of the day-to-day activity in the area under their control.

The original idea in creating National Health Service Trusts was to raise standards of care in the health service by allowing hospitals to take responsibility for their own affairs.

Each trust provides a range of health care services within its area which local doctors (general practitioners) and other health organisations purchase from it.

Advantages of trusts

- They are allowed to work out their own management structure
- Trusts can purchase their own assets. This allows them to have the equipment they feel is most appropriate for their needs
- Trusts are allowed to keep any profit they make so they have opportunities to plough more capital back into their hospital
- They are allowed to treat private patients as well as NHS patients which gives them another source of income.

Disadvantages of trusts

- Professional staff can be involved in a lot of administration which shortens the time available for their specialised work
- The system can lead to duplication of bureaucracy.

Trusts in Northern Ireland

There is a total of 18 NHS trusts in Northern Ireland, as shown in the following table:

Name of trust	Headquarters
Western Board Area	
1. Altnagelvin Group of Hospitals Trust	Londonderry
2. Foyle Community Trust	Londonderry
3. Sperrin Lakeland Trust	Omagh
Northern Board Area	
4. Causeway Trust	Ballymoney
5. Homefirst Community Trust	Antrim
6. United Hospitals Group Trust	Antrim
Southern Board Area	
7. Armagh and Dungannon Trust	Armagh
8. Craigavon Area Hospital Group Trust	Portadown
9. Craigavon and Banbridge Community Trust	Gilford
10. Newry and Mourne Trust	Newry

Table continues on the next page

Table continued

Eastern Board Area	
11. Belfast City Hospital Trust	Belfast
12. Down/Lisburn Trust	Lisburn
13. Green Park Healthcare Trust	Belfast
14. Mater Infirmorum Trust	Belfast
15. North and West Belfast Community Trust	Belfast
16. Royal Group of Hospitals Trust	Belfast
17. South and East Belfast Community Trust	Belfast
18. Ulster Community and Hospitals Trust	Newtownards

ACTIVITY

Look up the 'health' section in the telephone directory to find the answers to the following questions which you should then write in your notebook.

1. Give the name and full address of the trust which serves your home area.
2. Write down the names of the hospitals under the control of that trust.
3. What was the original reason for forming health trusts?
4. State one advantage of trusts.
5. State one disadvantage of trusts.

REVISION

At this stage you should understand:

The differences between public and private sector

Public corporations	Nationalisation	Municipal undertakings
Public private partnerships	Trusts	

As revision, look each one up in the Glossary at the end of the book.

UNIT 1.4

Business Aims

I'm sure you have lots of aims for yourself. In the shorter term you are aiming (I hope!) to get the best possible grades in your GCSEs. In the longer term you possibly are aiming at a certain career. These have become your targets to work towards.

Businesses also have aims which they set out in order to give a focus to their activities. These aims then become their targets and they can judge their progress against their stated aims or objectives.

Having aims is helpful to a business because they provide a:

- guide for the business's activity in the future
- target for the business to achieve
- standard against which the business may compare its progress.

In order to be successful, the business's aims have to be SMART

S	pecific
M	easurable
A	ttainable
R	ealistic
T	imed

Mission Statement

The business's aims and objectives are summarised in a short statement known as a mission statement. The mission statement shows members of the public what the business stands for and what its guiding principles are.

Now study the following selection of mission statements and then do the activities that follow.

McDonald's

McDonald's vision is to be the UK's best quick service restaurant experience. This will be achieved through five strategies:

Development: Lead the Quick Service Restaurant market by a programme of site development and profitable restaurant openings

Our People: Achieve a competitive advantage through people who are high calibre, effective, well motivated and feel part of the McDonald's team in delivering the company's goals

Restaurant Excellence: Focus on consistent delivery of quality, service and cleanliness through excellence in our restaurants

Operating Structure: Optimise restaurant performance through the selection of the most appropriate operating, management and ownership structures

The Brand: Continue to build the relationship between McDonald's and our customers in order to be a genuine part of the fabric of British society

Phoenix Natural Gas

Our aim is to make natural gas the fuel of choice for all energy consumers in Northern Ireland

MISSION STATEMENT

**Through our commitment to excellence,
we will guarantee that every visit to
The Culloden Hotel
will be a special occasion.**

Built for a Bishop . . . . . Fit for a King.

VISION AND VALUES

**Culloden Hotel, the flagship of Hastings Hotels
will be internationally renowned as
the premier hotel in Ireland.**

We will enhance the magnificence and splendour of the Culloden Hotel by:

- *the warmth, friendliness and professionalism of our dedicated team;*
- *continually investing in the quality of our guests' comfort and staff development; and*
- *anticipating and exceeding our guests' expectations.*

ACTIVITY

The Culloden Hotel is situated in Cultra, Co Down in the former residence of a bishop. It is one of the very few five-star hotels in Ireland. In what way does the hotel's Mission Statement convey the quality of the hotel?

ACTIVITY

Answer the following questions in your notebook:

1. What do McDonald's expect of their members of staff?
2. What would you, as a customer, be entitled to expect in a McDonald's restaurant?
3. Suggest one way in which McDonald's could become 'a genuine part of society'.
4. From reading the Phoenix Natural Gas mission statement, what do you think is a very important aim in that company?

ACTIVITY

Find out whether your school has a mission statement.

If it does, you should study it and comment on how it is being implemented.

If your school does not have a mission statement, you should design an appropriate one.

The aims of each business will be different according to the size and type of organisation, although there are usually some general aims and common ideas in most of them.

Business Aims and Objectives

Survival

When a business first opens, it takes some time for it to become established in the market. During the period when it is becoming established it is unlikely to be in a profit-making position, and its basic aim, at the early stage, would simply be to survive.

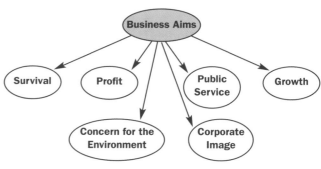

There are other times when established businesses may have difficulty in making sales and even staying in business. This would occur at times when the country's interest rates are high, making it difficult for people to borrow money. The result is that consumers are able to buy fewer and less expensive goods.

At such times the business simply aims to survive and stay afloat until economic conditions improve. In order to do so, the business may reduce prices as low as possible to hold on to their customers or it may reduce other expenditure as far as possible.

Growth

If a business is successful it will aim to grow and expand its market into new areas by opening more branches, by taking over other businesses, or by extending its range of products. A business would have several reasons for wishing to expand in these ways.

By opening new branches the business would have access to a larger market which would normally lead to increased sales and profits. Extension of the range of products, if successful, also would lead to increased profits. Higher profits lead to greater job security for employees and to greater consumer confidence in the business.

Profit improvement

One of the most important aims for a business is to make profit and to improve on the profit levels of previous years. All stakeholders in the business benefit – the owners and shareholders get larger returns on their investment, customers will have an improved variety of goods on offer in the business, while employees have job security and their morale is improved. In addition, making profit is the best way of guaranteeing the business's survival and it also has other benefits for the business since it allows it to expand in the future and to take advantage of economies of scale.

However businesses have to be careful that, in trying to make profit, they do not price their goods so highly that consumers leave and take their custom away. This would cause the profit levels to fall and the custom would go to competitors instead.

The most successful business is one which is able to price and sell good-quality items at prices which are fair. This will retain customers who will return to the business, thereby ensuring that it makes further profit.

Corporate image

For many businesses, the need to have a good corporate image is very important. This means that the business wants to be well thought of by its customers, by other companies and by members of the general public.

In order to enhance and maintain its image, a business may provide a number of customer services such as a restaurant or a crèche. It may also contribute generously to the local community and have a high profile there.

Public service

Businesses in the public sector are set up with the aim of providing a public service rather than making a profit – although they are expected to break even (cover their expenses). The services which the public sector provides – such as electricity, water, and sewerage – would not be economic for the private sector to provide throughout the whole country. Other public organisations such as hospitals, libraries and schools also exist to provide services to members of the public.

Charitable organisations, such as Save the Children Fund or Cancer Research Campaign, are established expressly to render a service. Their aim is to raise funds to help those in need.

Figure 1.25
Phoenix Natural Gas Headquarters

Increasingly, businesses in the private sector are also becoming more aware of their public responsibility. As a result, many private-sector businesses sponsor public and sporting events and play a part in the public life of their communities.

Phoenix Natural Gas makes a presentation

Public service undertaken by Phoenix Natural Gas

Since coming to Northern Ireland, Phoenix Natural Gas has been committed to the development of the local communities where it has been working.

During the year 2001, Phoenix helped over 19 groups in the local community. This involvement was wide ranging, from schools and playgroups to youth clubs and residents' associations.

In addition, the company contributes generously to Northern Ireland charities. Amongst those to benefit in the past were PHAB, the Chest, Heart and Stroke Association and Age Concern.

ACTIVITY

Refer to the Phoenix Natural Gas mission statement on page 47.

In what way, and to what extent, would the charitable work which the company undertakes help it to achieve its mission statement?

Concern for the environment

Some businesses place great emphasis on caring for the environment and enhancing their local area. In order to do this they landscape their grounds attractively and plant trees around their buildings. Sometimes they sponsor competitions and work in the local schools which draws attention to the environment.

Most firms also use recycled paper and packaging materials and are careful that effluent and chemicals from their places of work do not contaminate local rivers and lakes. They also control their noise levels and toxic waste.

ACTIVITY

Copy the following table and match the most appropriate aim to the businesses listed, giving a reason for your choice. The first one is done for you as an example.

Activity continues on the next page

Activity continued

Description of Business	Appropriate Aim	Reason
Small boutique just starting up for the first time	Survival	As the business is just new it will take some time to become established
Large popular supermarket		
Factory situated in an area of natural beauty		
Hospital		
Hotel which is proud of Its reputation for high quality		
Farmer who has been badly affected by poor weather and Foot and Mouth disease		
Hairdresser who is well established and has regular customers		

Class Discussion

The following list gives details of a number of businesses and names one aim which is important to each business. You are asked to say how that aim would affect the activities of that business. You should keep notes of the discussion for your revision later.

Description of Business	Aim of Business
Charity shop	Public service
Large grocery shop	Concern for the environment
Travel agency – during a recession	Survival
International car manufacturer	Growth
Small business which undertakes painting and decorating work	Profit improvement
Upmarket fashion store	Corporate image

How the Aims of a business may be in conflict

On occasions, a business may find that its aims may be in conflict with one another. Keeping one aim can sometimes cause tension between the stakeholders or even with another aim. For example, shareholders are most interested in profit improvement and may be unhappy about some of the profits being given to a worthy cause such as the Third World. On the other hand, the donation to the Third World would improve the business's corporate image, which is another of its aims.

To illustrate this point, let us consider the following business:

A large meat processing factory is situated near a residential area of a major town. The factory is prosperous, profits are good and it provides employment for over 100 local people. However, the local residents are unhappy because heavy traffic to the factory is causing dangers for the children and is damaging the road past their houses. They also complain about a bad smell coming into their houses from the factory.

The factory was due to be extended because it is so successful. The directors also had plans to install new processing machinery which would eliminate the smell. The residents formed a pressure group and have asked their MLA and the local council to help them to ensure that the factory does not get planning permission for the extension.

It seems impossible to satisfy all the stakeholders.

ACTIVITY

Consider each of the following courses of action and complete the spaces to show one group who would be satisfied with the action and a second group who would be unhappy with that action.

ACTION	SATISFIED STAKEHOLDERS	DISSATISFIED STAKEHOLDERS
The factory closes and moves to a different town	....	....
The factory expands on its present site and installs the new processingmachinery	....	....
The factory stays as it is	....	....
The factory spends a large sum of money widening and improving the road	....	....

If you were the Managing Director of this factory, which course of action would you recommend to your Board?

How the Aims of a Business may Change

You should also be aware that a business may change its aims at various stages of its life. Aims are not written at the beginning of the business's life and forgotten about – they are revised on a regular basis.

STAGE 1 When a business is first set up it is likely to be small and owned by a sole trader or perhaps by a partnership. At that stage of its existence, the business would be trying to become established in the market and its main aim would be SURVIVAL

STAGE 2 As the business becomes more established and gains more customers it will start to make profit and its main aim would be PROFIT IMPROVEMENT.

STAGE 3 If the business continues to be successful it will consider opening more branches and expanding its market. Its main aims then would include GROWTH

STAGE 4 Once the business is secure, it can then think of spreading some of its profits by having additional customer services and a higher profile in the wider community. Its aims then would include PUBLIC SERVICE, CONCERN FOR THE ENVIRONMENT and CORPORATE IMAGE.

Distinction between public-sector and private-sector aims

There is also a distinction between the aims of businesses in the private sector and businesses in the public sector. In general, they are as follows:

Type of sector	Aims
PRIVATE SECTOR – Sole trader Partnership Limited companies	To create and improve profit To grow and expand To give customer satisfaction To have a good corporate image
PUBLIC SECTOR	To provide a service To break even
CHARITIES	To be charitable To survive

In this question, where you are asked to 'compare', you must give the aims of the two types of business organisation and then show the similarities and differences between them.

There are 4 marks altogether so you would be expected to give one major aim in each case – for 2 marks. The other 2 marks would be allocated to showing two similarities and differences between them.

EXAMINATION QUESTION

Compare the possible aims of a coffee shop with the aims of a municipal undertaking.

(4 marks)

(CCEA Business Studies, GCSE, Paper 2 Higher Tier, 2001)

Ethical and Moral Issues associated with Business Aims

Obviously, the majority of businesses wish to make profit – that is the basic reason for being in business. However, they also want to deal fairly and honestly with their customers, employees and suppliers. That is their moral duty.

Quite apart from morals, would you ever go back to a business which had treated you dishonestly by giving you shoddy goods and refusing to change them, or by giving you less change than you were entitled to? Of course not, and businesses know that customers will return to them if they are treated fairly and honestly. Businesses do not pursue the aim of 'profit creation' at the expense of these issues and will be willing to reduce their profit a little for that reason.

Most businesses have 'care of the environment' among their aims. We are all responsible for the environment and businesses share that responsibility. For this reason, they landscape their grounds, plant trees, provide litter bins and encourage people to use them.

There are other moral and ethical issues which the majority of businesses see as important even though they may reduce the overall profit slightly:

- Most businesses pay their employees fair wages
- Many businesses refuse to buy goods which have been made in countries where workers are exploited
- Many businesses use recycled paper and packaging and sell biodegradable products in their shops
- The Body Shop has always refused to sell any product which was tested on animals.

R E V I S I O N

At this stage you should understand:

1. What a mission statement is
2. Business aims and objectives
3. Distinction between public-sector and private-sector aims.

Growth of Business

In Unit 1.4 you learned that growth is one of a business's aims and objectives. This unit looks at growth in greater depth.

First of all, what is meant by 'business growth'?

> **Any form of expansion of the business is an example of business growth.**

Growth may be shown in a variety of ways, such as:

- a larger workforce
- opening more branches
- expansion of the business's market share
- increased sales
- adding to the products made by the business.

Why and How Businesses May Grow

Some organisations have expansion and growth as part of their aims. Listen to some of the reasons why business owners wish to achieve growth:

> **Growth would make my business more powerful and influential.**

> **Business growth is likely to achieve increased profits.**

> **If my business were bigger, it would make economies of scale possible.**

> **A larger business would secure a larger share of the market and help my sales.**

If my business grows, it may put some of my competitors out of business.

Businesses may grow either internally or externally.

Internal (Organic) Growth

Internal growth (also referred to as organic growth) takes place inside the business, and without any reference to other businesses. Internal growth is slow to achieve and is a gradual process. The purpose of internal growth – like all growth – is to become better and stronger than other firms in the same type of business.

To achieve internal growth, a business will:

- plough back its profits
- develop new markets for its products
- develop new products.

ACTIVITY

There are probably plenty of examples of internal growth in your town or area. To complete this activity you should do some local research to discover the information required.

1. Give the names of any of the shops in your area which have increased their floor space or opened new branches recently.
2. Find out if any of your local hotels have plans to open, or have opened recently, new facilities such as a leisure centre or conference complex.
3. Ask whether any of the local factories are recruiting extra employees, introducing the latest technology, developing new products or expanding their markets abroad. Give examples.

All of these are examples of internal growth in your local area.

External Growth

External growth is a much faster type of growth and involves the bringing together of a number of organisations to form a single business. External growth may be achieved through amalgamations/mergers/integrations, takeovers or franchising.

Franchising

Franchising is a popular method by which companies expand their operations and open shops in various parts of the country. McDonald's is a good example. There are now 29,500 McDonald restaurants in over 120 countries all over the world. This includes 1,200 restaurants in the United Kingdom. This number grew, through franchising, from the first United Kingdom restaurant opened in 1974, and the company plans to open 100 new restaurants in the United Kingdom every year.

For further details on franchising, you should refer to Unit 1.2 of this book.

Takeover

A takeover takes place when one business buys over the control of another business. To achieve a takeover, a business would have to buy a large number of shares so that it could control the voting in the other business. The business wishing to gain control would offer very high prices to the existing shareholders for their shares in order to secure them.

Takeovers frequently are hostile and not welcomed by the business which is being taken over. In other cases, takeovers are agreed and the business being taken over would advise its shareholders to accept the high offers for their shares. In an agreed takeover, the business being taken over welcomes the opportunity to be part of a larger organisation and gain from its resources.

Merger/Amalgamation

A merger is a voluntary and agreed joining of two businesses in order to form one larger business. It could be seen as a marriage between two businesses.

In the case of a merger, all the capital as well as all resources and assets such as premises, machinery and personnel are joined together in one organisation.

This arrangement has several benefits
- Savings are made because one merged organisation is able to operate with less equipment and other resources than two
- There would be no duplication in running costs
- Fewer administrative staff and directors are required to run a single business
- The business would be operating on a larger scale so would benefit from discounts for bulk purchases of supplies
- The market share would be increased and sales would be improved
- The businesses would be working together rather than as rivals to one another.

Mergers have some drawbacks
- There is a possibility of staff redundancies
- Consumers have less choice.

Integration

To integrate means 'to combine parts into a whole'. In business, integration is achieved through mergers and takeovers. There are three main types of integration:

1. Horizontal integration
2. Vertical integration
3. Lateral integration

Horizontal integration
Horizontal integration takes place between businesses on the same level within the same type of business. For example, if two confectionery shops, 'Sweet Temptations' and 'Sweet Things', decided to merge it would be horizontal integration because they both had previously been selling sweets and chocolate to consumers.

Horizontal Integration

Confectionery Shop 'Sweet Temptations'

Confectionery Shop 'Sweet Things'

Vertical integration
Vertical integration takes place between businesses on different levels within the same type of business. For example, if a chocolate factory decided to merge with a

Vertical
Integration

Confectionery
Shop 'Sweet
Temptations'

Chocolate
Factory

Forward
Vertical
Integration

Confectionery
Shop 'Sweet
Temptations'

confectionery shop it would be vertical integration. This is because, although both organisations were involved in the confectionery business, they were working at different stages of the chain of production – one was manufacturing the chocolate while the other was selling it.

There are two types of vertical integration:

Backward vertical integration

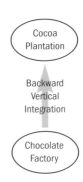

Cocoa
Plantation

Backward
Vertical
Integration

Chocolate
Factory

This is where a business expands by taking over another business which works with the same product but at an earlier stage in its chain of production. In the previous example, if the chocolate factory took over a cocoa plantation, it would be backward vertical integration because the factory actually makes the chocolate bars while the cocoa plantation grows the cocoa plants from which the chocolate is produced.

Forward vertical integration

This is where a business expands by taking over another business which works with the same product but at a later stage in its chain of production. To use the same example again, if the chocolate factory were to take over the confectionery shop, it would be forward vertical integration because it makes the chocolate bars while the shop works with the chocolate at the later stage of selling it to the consumer.

Lateral integration

Lateral integration takes place when a business expands by merging with another business which is in a related but different area. They were not in direct competition before integration took place. Their products may be similar but not identical and the types of skills required to make or handle the products are very alike. For example, if the chocolate factory were to merge with an ice-cream factory, the type of integration would be lateral.

Conglomerate

This is the most usual type of merger and brings together businesses whose products are totally unrelated and dissimilar. The businesses may or may not be working at the same level of production.

This type of merger is also known as diversification, and it takes place mainly because the business is expecting a decline in its market and it is branching out into other lines as a safeguard. An example of a conglomerate would be the merger between the chocolate factory, a jewellery shop and a restaurant.

ACTIVITY

All of the businesses named here are based in one county. A number of them are considering some type of integration. You are asked to study each possibility and to write down in the spaces provided which type of integration each would be.

Activity continues on the next page

Activity continued

Businesses	Type of Integration
A filling station links with another filling station	
A bakery joins with a bread shop	
A filling station joins with a chip shop and the bakery	
A supermarket opens another branch in a different area of town	
A large public house and restaurant takes control of a smaller public house and restaurant	
Two hairdressers agree to join their businesses and work together	
A retailer of furniture links with a furniture factory	
The furniture retailer joins his business with a retailer of bathroom fittings	

A Story of Growth

Balcas is Northern Ireland's largest sawmilling company, with plants in Enniskilllen and Magherafelt as well as in Newtowngore, Co Leitrim in the Republic of Ireland. It also owns a pallet plant in Belfast, a fibreboard plant in Kill, Co Kildare and a sawmill in Estonia.

The Kidney family has been closely associated with sawmilling in Co Fermanagh for four generations, and, from small beginnings almost 100 years ago, Ballycassidy Sawmills Ltd was formed as a private limited company in 1957. Shortly afterwards, the Enniskillen plant was built on its present site, four miles from Enniskillen town. This remains as the site of the Head Office and the company's major plant. The company's new abbreviated name, Balcas, was adopted in 1991.

In Enniskillen, the major activity of Balcas is to work on trees brought in from forests and to process them into planks, ready for building and construction work, fencing and pallet making.

Balcas has grown rapidly, particularly during the 1990s. A look at the profit, turnover and employment figures illustrates the point. In 1990 its situation was:

Number of Employees	200
Annual Turnover	£10 million
Profit	£0.5 million

In 2000 its situation was:

Number of Employees	700
Annual Turnover	£44.2 million
Profit	£2.1 million

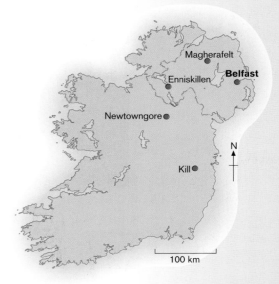

Figure 1.26
Balcas sites

Figure 1.27

How Balcas has achieved growth

Growth in Balcas has been achieved both organically and externally.

Organic growth in Balcas

The company has:

- ploughed back profits in order to expand its operation and update its machinery
- developed new markets for its product
- developed new products.

External growth in Balcas

Other companies have been bought through a series of takeovers and integrations:

- In October 1987 Balcas (then Ballycassidy Sawmills Ltd) began its programme of external growth when it bought an insolvent business in Co Kildare which employed eight people. This firm has now become Balcas Kildare, employs over 70 people, and manufactures architectural pre-primed mouldings such as panelling, dado rails, architraves, door frames and skirting boards.
- In 1993 Balcas purchased the business of Lees Sawmills in Magherafelt – a business which had been placed in administration the previous year. Up to that date it had been a competitor of Balcas and its work had been very similar to that undertaken in Enniskillen. This plant is now known as Balcas Magherafelt and works alongside Balcas Enniskillen.
- In January 1995 Balcas purchased the Pallet Centre in Newtownabbey, Belfast. The Centre was the largest manufacturer of timber pallets in Ireland and Balcas already supplied 80% of its raw materials Since 1995 the Centre's business volume has increased by 20% and its profits have doubled.
- In September 1995 Balcas purchased the firm of AS Richardson in Co Leitrim. That firm had previously been the eighth largest sawmill in Ireland and its work had also been very similar to that undertaken in Enniskillen.

Figure 1.28

Forward
Vertical
Integration

Horizontal
Integration

- In 1996 Balcas expanded into mainland Europe by buying a sawmill in Estonia and creating Balcas Eesti. This new plant gives Balcas easier and more economic access to a vast supply of timber from Eastern Bloc countries. The work undertaken in Estonia is similar to that undertaken in Enniskillen, Magherafelt and Leitrim and broadens the company's range of products.

ACTIVITY

Read the information on Balcas and answer the following questions in your notebook.

1. What do you understand by 'external growth'?
2. What is meant by 'forward vertical integration'?
3. Name two benefits which Balcas gained by buying Lees Sawmills in Magherafelt.
4. If you had been an employee in the sawmills in Magherafelt in 1993, how would you have felt?
5. Why is the purchase of the sawmills in Estonia an example of horizontal integration?
6. Name two benefits which Balcas achieved by buying the sawmills in Estonia.
7. How is the purchase of the business in Kildare an example of forward vertical integration?
8. Name two benefits which Balcas achieved by buying the Kildare plant.
9. What benefits can you see for the business in Kildare by being taken over by Balcas?
10. For what reason would Balcas have wanted to buy the Pallet Centre?
11. How would the Pallet Centre have benefited from being taken over by Balcas?
12. What would Balcas have to do in order to achieve backward vertical integration?
13. If you were a shareholder in Balcas, what advantages would you see in the business's expansion?

Factors which may Limit the Growth of businesses

While the majority of businesses wish to grow and expand, for the reasons stated at the beginning of this unit, others may not have the same ambition.

The very nature of specialised businesses such as dress designers or cabinet makers depends on those businesses being small scale. Their work is done through expensive orders for hand-made articles for which mass production would not be appropriate. To grow into large organisations would take away from their high quality and individuality.

However, other businesses may wish to expand but may be limited in their efforts to do so. This limitation could be caused by a variety of factors which also influence the business's growth or decline:

- Expansion and growth require capital. Capital would be needed to obtain the necessary premises and machinery for the enlarged operation. If the business cannot raise the required capital it would be impossible for it to expand properly.
- Expansion and growth also require resources. If the business is lacking in resources such as stock or raw materials, it would be unable to expand its manufacturing or retailing operation.
- A business could also be hampered by a lack of expertise. If expansion opportunities arise, the business needs to have well-trained staff who are capable of undertaking the more advanced work.
- In order for a business to expand, it is necessary for it to have a good communications network. This would give the business the necessary information about the market and its up-to-date requirements.

- A spirit of entrepreneurship is also needed in a business which would make it possible to see the opportunities and take the risks involved in expansion.
- A business may also be curtailed by very strong rivals who are much bigger and can sell products to consumers at lower prices. This is the case with small shopkeepers who are unable to expand because of the strength of large chain stores which take away their trade.

Implications for a Business of the different Methods of Growth

Internal (organic) growth

Internal growth is very slow and gradual. The main implication of this is that the owners may have little personal gain from the business for many years as they plough back its profits. They will also have to look continuously for new markets and new products in order to gain some competitive advantage over its competitors.

External growth

The main implication of external growth is the loss of control of the business and the introduction of shared management and decision making.

Franchising

A franchised business has to accept that policy is dictated by the franchising company and that there is no opportunity for individuality. The main implication for the business is that it is seen as a branch of a large chain rather than a business in its own right. The owner is seen as a manager rather than as an owner. On the positive side, the implications are that the franchised business enjoys the reputation and ready made market which come with being part of a large enterprise

Takeover

Where a takeover has been hostile, the main implications for the new business are strained relationships at managerial level and enforced control by an outside company. On the other hand, the new business is likely to enjoy greater prosperity as a result of being part of a larger organisation.

Merger

The implications for a newly merged business are the increase in business which comes from a larger operation, resulting in economies of scale and greater profits. As with all joined organisations, methods have to be worked out whereby two workforces and two sets of managers can work as one. A merger has the added implication of shared resources without costly duplication. Another implication is the possibility of staff redundancies.

Horizontal integration

As well as all the implications of a merger, the most important implication in a horizontal integration is the elimination of a competitor in the marketplace.

Backward vertical integration

The principal implication in a backward vertical integration is that the company is assured a supply of raw materials over which it has total control. For example, the chocolate factory discussed earlier is assured supplies of cocoa for its production from its own cocoa plantation. It also has total control over the price of the cocoa.

Forward vertical integration

One of the main implications of forward vertical integration is that the company has an outlet for its products. For example, the chocolate factory, by taking over the confectionery shop, now has its own retail outlet where it can control sales of its own product.

EXAMINATION QUESTION

Hip Hop food retailers is a chain of supermarkets with outlets in Belfast, Bangor, Ballyclare, Enniskillen, Portadown and Coleraine. It hopes to merge its business activities with Alsorts Suppliers Ltd. Alsorts Suppliers Ltd, a large food manufacturer based in Lisburn, supplies and distributes goods to food retailers including Hip Hop.

a **What type of merger is described above?**

(1 mark)

b **Why do you think that Hip Hop food retailers might want to merge with Alsorts Suppliers Ltd?**

(4 marks)

(Adapted from CCEA Business Studies, GCSE, Paper 2 Higher Tier, 2000)

> **Tips for answering this question:**
>
> In Part A, simply name the type of merger, without any explanation. In Part B you are really being asked for the advantages which Hip Hop would gain from being merged with Alsorts. You should state two reasons and give a brief explanation of each reason.

Lateral integration

In lateral integration some economies of scale can take place through joint production. There are also opportunities for joint marketing campaigns for the benefit of both products.

Conglomerate

The main implication for a business involved in a conglomerate is the safeguard given through having a variety of commercial interests. If one aspect of the business should prove to be unprofitable, the other products can compensate.

EXAMINATION QUESTION

Quality Doors Ltd has a factory in Co Fermanagh and is a hi-tech firm manufacturing doors for kitchen and bedroom furniture on a large scale. Quality Doors Ltd is thinking of taking over a competitor in Scotland in order to expand its business.

a **What type of integration is described above?**

(1 mark)

b **Apart from expanding its business, suggest two other reasons why Quality Doors Ltd would want to take over a competitor.**

(4 marks)

(Adapted from CCEA Business Studies, GCSE, Paper 2 Foundation Tier, 2002)

> **Tips for answering this question:**
>
> This question would be treated in the same way as the previous examination question. In Part A, simply name the type of integration, without any explanation. Part B has 4 marks so you need to explain briefly two reasons for taking over a competitor.

Social and Moral Implications of Growth

Figure 1.29
Castle Court Centre, Belfast

The modern tendency in retailing, especially in grocery and light hardware items, is for very large supermarkets to be situated in shopping centres in larger towns or on their outskirts. These large stores are very attractive to shoppers because they offer a wide variety of goods under one roof and at low prices. In addition they offer the convenience of being able to use trolleys and the car parks provided. All of these factors lead to the further success and growth of the large supermarkets.

The growth of the large businesses has taken place at the expense of the traditional small retailers in town centres and villages throughout the country. Those situated in towns have been hardest hit because they are close to the large supermarkets and also have parking problems. Small retailers situated further away in villages have survived because of their convenience to local communities although they too are struggling.

The social implications of this drift to towns could become serious for the rural community in Northern Ireland. It is taking jobs and business away from villages. It is also damaging rural community life and increasing traffic on the roads as people are forced to travel to towns to shop. Perhaps the groups who are most adversely affected are the elderly and non-drivers who are losing the convenience of local shopping.

There is also a moral debate centring on the growth of large shops at the expense of small retailers. It is true that the big get bigger while the small struggle, and everyone has a personal view on the situation. On one hand, it could be argued that the large shops are providing a necessary service because they are supported and people obviously wish to shop there because of their lower prices and convenience. On the other hand, it could be argued that there will always be a role for small shops because of their personal service and local situation.

Current Legislation on Monopolies, Mergers and Restrictive Practices

The government has introduced legislation which is designed to make sure that the growth of businesses is not being achieved against the interests of consumers.

The purpose of such legislation is to ensure that:

- a monopoly situation is prevented; a monopoly exists when any single business controls 25% or more of the market
- there is competition in the market so that businesses cannot become too powerful
- businesses may not charge very high prices, knowing that consumers cannot get the goods anywhere else
- businesses cannot limit the quantity of a product on the market in order to keep its price high.

The principal law which makes sure that the growth of businesses is not achieved against the interests of the public is the Competition Act 1998.

Competition Act 1998

This Act replaces all previous anti-competition legislation such as the Monopolies, Mergers and Restrictive Practices Act and is designed to bring our law on anti-competitive practices into line with European Union law. The Act is enforced by the Office of Fair Trading, and can levy fines of up to 10% of turnover.

The Competition Act 1998 bans any business arrangement which:

- prevents competition
- agrees to fix buying or selling prices or other trading conditions
- agrees to limit or control production
- agrees to share markets
- applies different trading conditions which would place some parties at a disadvantage.

There are some situations which can be excluded from the terms of the Act. These are:

- where it is necessary to avoid conflict with international obligations
- where there are overriding policy considerations.

In this country, mergers and monopolies are not illegal but the government has established the Competition Commission to investigate such situations and make sure that mergers between businesses are fair to consumers.

Competition Commission

The Competition Commission (CC) was set up in 1999 through the terms of the Competition Act. It is an independent body which has been established for the purpose of investigating mergers and monopolies.

The Competition Commission replaces the former Monopolies and Mergers Commission and carries out its responsibilities.

The aim of the Competition Commission is to make markets work well for consumers by increasing the level of competition.

The Commission has two functions:

1. It carries out inquiries into monopolies and mergers.
2. It hears appeals against decisions made on monopolies and mergers and on the abuse of market power.

The Competition Commission publishes the results of its investigations and its decisions on mergers and monopolies are made on the basis of the public interest.

ACTIVITY

Answer the following questions in your notebook

1. What is the name of the main law which prevents anti-competitive practices?
2. What is the name of the Office which sees that this particular law is not broken?
3. Who is that particular law designed to protect?
4. Why might this protection be necessary?

ACTIVITY

A GCSE candidate has written the following piece about business growth. Unfortunately, this candidate has made many mistakes and will not pass unless a lot of serious revision is done before the examination. Use a computer to rewrite the candidate's work, correcting all mistakes.

Some organisations want to expand although I do not think that there are any advantages for them in doing so. Businesses may grow either internally or externally and external growth is also called organic growth. Internal growth takes place inside the business, and is a very fast way to grow. To grow internally the business has to plough in money it borrows from the bank and try to sell more goods. External growth is a much slower type of growth and happens in different ways. One of these ways is franchising which is used by McDonald's. McDonald's allows you to be its manager if you pay money. Another method is the takeover. This is not always friendly and is called a warring takeover if it is not welcomed. Another firm buys a large number of shares so that it can control the voting in the other firm but does not pay much for the shares. A merger is a friendly way of joining two firms. Two advantages of a merger are (I've forgotten what they are). I do remember that mergers often make people redundant.

Horizontal integration takes place between firms on different levels and they do not have to be in the same type of business. Vertical integration takes place between firms on the same level and they might be in the same type of business. There are two types of vertical integration. One is called backward vertical integration and this is where a firm expands by taking over another firm which is behind it. The other type is forward vertical integration, and this is where a firm expands by taking over another firm which is in front of it. Lateral integration takes place when a firm expands by merging with another firm which is in a related but different area. They were in competition so the merger takes away a competitor Finally there is a conglomerate but it is very rare. It is between firms who have no connection with each other whatsoever. It takes place because the firm is fed up with its work and wants a change.

The government has introduced legislation which helps firms to grow and become monopolies. The main law is the Competition Act 1998. It is enforced by the Citizens Advice Bureau and has also set up the Competition Mission.

REVISION

At this stage you should understand:

Business growth	Organic growth	External growth
Merger	Horizontal integration	Vertical integration
Lateral integration	Conglomerate	Monopoly
Competition		

As revision, look each one up in the Glossary at the end of the book.

Resources

The Factors of Production

A country's resources are used to meet the needs of the people living in that country. Four of those resources are known as the 'factors of production' and they are essential to every business before production can take place.

Those factors of production are: **land**, **labour**, **capital** and **enterprise**.

Land

A basic need in business is the land on which to place the business premises, houses, roads and farms. However, 'land' is used more widely in this economic sense and includes not only the surface of the land but also the oceans and all natural resources and raw materials which are contained either on, above or in the earth. Such resources and raw materials would include oil, gas, trees, water, fish, coal and minerals.

Supplies of land are limited which makes it a very valuable resource.

Figure 1.30

Labour

The term 'labour' refers to the human resource in the business – the workers who are employed to manufacture the product or provide the service for which the business has been set up. The labour used in the business may be physical labour or mental labour, depending on the nature of the business's final product.

Supplies of labour with the appropriate skills are also limited.

Capital

Capital is defined as 'wealth which is employed in the creation of further wealth'. It is the element contributed by capitalists – the owners – to set up and maintain the business. Capital includes the money which the owners invested in the business at the beginning, but also includes the items which were bought with that original investment – items such as premises and machinery.

Capital is always in short supply and capitalists will risk investing it only in safe business projects.

Enterprise

Enterprise is contributed to a business by people known as entrepreneurs.

Entrepreneurs are the managers and they play a most essential role in business. They are people with successful business ideas plus enough drive and vision to make their ideas work. Entrepreneurs are essential if the business is to be profitable.

It is the role of the entrepreneur to organise the capital, the land and the labour in the correct proportions to run the business successfully. For example, some businesses, such as large factories require vast amounts of capital and land but, because they are heavily mechanised, they may require proportionately less labour. Other businesses, such as large department stores, may be very labour intensive. For this reason, they would use a large amount of labour but proportionately less land.

In addition, entrepreneurs must be able to estimate future demand and to have production at the correct level to meet that demand.

A business would not be successful unless it had all four factors of production.

A person might have adequate amounts of capital but unless that person has enterprise he/she would not be able to start a business.

Equally, an entrepreneur may have great ideas for a successful business but unless he/she has land on which to start the business and labour to operate it, there would be no business.

On the other hand, a landowner may own large areas of land but without the ideas contributed by enterprise or sufficient amounts of capital, he/she would not have a business.

Each of the people who contribute the factors of production have to be rewarded. The following table shows how.

Factor of Production	Contributed by	Rewarded by
Land	Landlords	Rent
Labour	Employees	Wages and salaries
Capital	Capitalists	Interest
Enterprise	Entrepreneurs	Profit

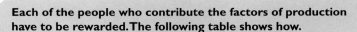

ACTIVITY

Robert has come up with a good idea for a new business. He knows that the business would be successful but his difficulty is that he would need finance and premises. Some friends agree to

Activity continues on the next page

Activity continued

join the business. Fred will provide the necessary finance, Eric has premises which he will allow the business to use and Roy will work in the business.

Using the spaces provided, show the role of each person and the rewards which he can expect.

Name	Role	Reward
Robert		
Fred		
Eric		
Roy		

EXAMINATION QUESTION

Cable Electrics is a large manufacturing firm producing televisions and other electrical goods. Increased specialisation has resulted in a rise in output. Productivity has been improved by using new technology.

Explain how Cable Electrics has used two resources (factors of production).

(4 marks)

(CCEA Business Studies, GCSE, Paper 2 Higher Tier, 2000)

Tips for answering this question:

Here you can name any two of the factors of production. When explaining their use, make sure that you relate your answer to this particular business.

What it means to be Enterprising

The government is keen to encourage enterprise and to develop an 'enterprise culture' in this country. For these reasons it has set up various schemes to help entrepreneurs to succeed. People are encouraged to try their ideas in business and to establish their own businesses rather than be unemployed.

There are several reasons why the government encourages enterprise:

- it reduces unemployment
- new ideas may succeed and provide fresh opportunities
- people feel motivated
- competition ensures a healthier business environment.

What Makes an Entrepreneur?

A successful entrepreneur is the real key to a business's success. This is the person who brings all the other factors together successfully. An entrepreneur's qualities would include the following characteristics:

- An entrepreneur contributes original ideas which give the business an edge on its competitors

- An entrepreneur has vision of what the business could become and works single-mindedly towards that goal
- An entrepreneur has the energy to work hard and make sure that the business achieves its full potential
- An entrepreneur is willing to take business risks and to encourage other financiers such as banks to lend money to the enterprise
- An entrepreneur can motivate others in the work team and inspire them with enthusiasm.

A Story of Enterprise on the Farm

Alpacas on a Fermanagh Farm

The farming industry has been badly affected in recent years by poor weather conditions and by the outbreak of Foot and Mouth disease.

Patrick has a farm in Fermanagh and decided to try something completely different by importing a small herd of alpacas. An alpaca is a native of Chile and Peru and is related to the larger llama and camel. The animals can be shorn twice a year, need little space, do not damage the ground, and are economical to feed.

Patrick knew that alpacas were farmed successfully in other parts of the world for the high-quality fibre they produce. This fibre is in short supply which makes it even more sought after than the high-quality cashmere. As a result, it sells very well to the clothing industry where it is used for the most expensive range of garments.

This enterprising farmer also runs open days on his farm so that people can visit his unusual animals.

ACTIVITY

Have you got what it takes to be an entrepreneur? Answer the following questions truthfully to find out! The good entrepreneur's answers are given at the end.

1. What do you do if you find a task difficult?
   a   Keep trying until you get it right
   b   Give up
   c   Ask for help
2. Can you make decisions?
   a   Always
   b   Never
   c   Depends on the circumstances
3. If you won the lottery which of the following would you do?
   a   Tour the world
   b   Treat all your friends to the greatest party ever
   c   Invest it

4. How single minded are you? When you are working, are you
   a   Easily distracted?
   b   Oblivious to everything around you?
   c   Able to concentrate – but only if you like the work?
5. How energetic do you think you are?
   a   Very energetic at everything
   b   Energetic at the things I enjoy
   c   There are lots of things I can't be bothered with
6. How well do you work with people?
   a   I'd rather work on my own
   b   I love being in a team
   c   I must be the team leader

Answers: 1a, 2a, 3c, 4b, 5a, 6c

Essential qualities and skills required by today's workforce

In Section 2 you will study the features of modern employment which will illustrate the qualities and skills required by today's workforce and how employees have to be able to adapt to changing conditions.

It is now accepted that the nature of the work which workers are employed to do changes regularly. Most employees can expect to have several career changes in their working lives. This means that they have to be able to accept change and be ready to re-train if necessary. Today's employees, therefore, have to be adaptable to changing conditions and they must be flexible if they are to succeed in a variety of roles.

To summarise the essential qualities required by today's workforce:

- Employees have to be able to accept change
- Employees must be willing to retrain throughout their working lives
- Employees have to be adaptable
- Employees have to be flexible
- Employees have to be able to work in teams.

ACTIVITY

Arrange an interview with any employee who has been working in industry for more than 10 years.

a   Find out how that employee's work has changed over the 10-year period
b   From talking to the employee, can you add any other qualities to the above list?

REVISION

At this stage you should understand:

Land	Labour	Capital
Enterprise	Entrepreneur	

As revision, look each one up in the Glossary at the end of the book.

UNIT 1.7

Management

Every business has to have an organisational structure which will have been designed to meet the individual needs of that particular business. The type of structure in a business depends on its size and on a variety of other factors such as whether the business is all on one site or situated in a number of countries.

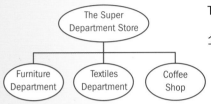

The three most common organisational structures are:

1 **Organisation by product or process**
Sometimes a business will be organised according to the goods it makes or sells. For example, a department store which sells furniture and textiles and also has a coffee shop would probably be organised in three sections – one for each of its main operations. Teams of employees work in each department.

2 **Geographical organisation**
A geographical structure is usual for a multinational business which has branches in a number of countries. This type of organisation divides the company into the regions or countries in which it operates. For example, a chemical business which is based in England but has plants in Northern Ireland, France and Italy would be organised in four sections to cover the four countries in which it works.

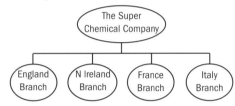

3 **Organisation by function**
It is very common for a business to be organised according to the work – or function – which the people do in that business. The business would be divided into departments and each department would have a specific role. In a functional organisation each department is managed by one person who has responsibility and authority in that area.

Functional areas of a business

Each business organises its departments to suit its individual needs but the following are usual in a manufacturing business.

Figure 1.31

Human Resources

The Human Resources Department is responsible for:

- manpower planning
- advertising vacancies
- processing internal promotions and staff transfers
- the recruitment and selection of new staff
- all induction and staff training
- the business's appraisal system
- keeping all staff records
- the welfare of the people who work in the organisation
- organising social facilities in the business
- linking with trade unions

- negotiating pay and conditions of service for employees
- applying the business's disciplinary procedures
- dismissing members of staff if necessary
- overseeing staff redundancies and retirements.

Purchasing

The Purchasing Department is responsible for:

- negotiating with suppliers
- buying raw materials or other component parts needed to manufacture the business's products
- record-keeping relating to purchases.

Production

The Production Department is responsible for:

- research and development of new products
- ordering and maintaining stocks of raw materials
- the actual manufacture or construction of the goods produced by that business
- undertaking quality control of the finished goods
- undertaking stock control in order to make efficient use of resources
- maintaining the machinery to ensure efficient production and the safety of employees.

Marketing

The Marketing Department is responsible for:

- market research to see what consumers need
- developing and planning new products
- extending the market opportunities for the business
- the promotion and advertising of the business's products
- the placement and distribution of the products.

Some businesses have a separate Sales Department. Where this does not exist, the functions of the Sales Department would be undertaken by the Marketing Department.

Sales

The Sales Department is responsible for:

- finding customers and staying in communication with them
- customer care
- answering enquiries
- making the final sale of the product
- completing all sales documentation such as invoices and delivery notes
- monitoring sales levels.

Finance

The Finance Department is responsible for:

- the financial transactions and keeping records of all the money coming in and going out
- dealing with debtors and creditors
- paying the wages and salaries
- dealing with taxation

- paying for all raw materials, goods and services bought by the business
- receiving the payment for all goods sold by the business
- generating accounts and sending out bills
- overseeing the preparation of the final accounts
- calculating the profit or loss for the year's trading
- preparing budgets and forecasts
- maintaining cash flow levels.

Dividing an organisation in the ways described above has advantages for the business:

- Employees have the opportunity to specialise in one area of work
- Employees are better motivated because there are more opportunities for promotion
- A team spirit builds up within each smaller group.

But there are also disadvantages:

- Communication is more difficult across the organisation as a whole
- Employees may not feel part of the larger organisation and may not know workers in other areas of the business
- The directors at the very top of the organisation have less control of the day-to-day work.

ACTIVITY

It is very likely that your school is divided into functional areas or departments, for example the Business Department.

1. Use a computer to make a list of the functional areas within your school.
2. Write a brief description of the responsibilities of each area or department.
3. Give your list a suitable title.
4. Save your work – you will need it later.

Organisation Chart for Prime Products plc

Functional Organisation Chart for a Business

The organisation of a business can best be illustrated in an organisation chart. It shows:

a the relationship between all the people working in that business

b how the responsibilities in the business are divided

c the level of authority and responsibility which each person has in the business

d who should report to whom

e the composition of all the departments in the business

f the lines of communication within the organisation

g lines of possible promotion.

The chart opposite is typical for a manufacturing company which has a functional organisational structure.

ACTIVITY

You are now asked to draw an organisation chart for your school. This activity needs to be divided into stages and the following are suggested:

1. Call up the list of the school's functional areas which you prepared in the last activity.
2. Make a list of all the teachers who work in each department, showing the name of the Head of Department at the top of each department's list. Some teachers may work in a number of departments, so place each one in the department where he/she is most frequently employed.
3. List all the other members of staff who do not fit easily into departments – not forgetting the Principal and Vice Principals!
4. Design your organisation chart on the computer, starting with the Principal and working your way downwards.
5. Give your chart a suitable title.

Types of Management Structure and their Implications

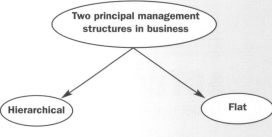

Hierarchical structure

A hierarchical structure is illustrated as a pyramid with one person at the top and a large number of employees at the bottom forming a broad base to the pyramid. There are several layers in between the top and bottom. The further up the pyramid you go, the fewer people there are on each level.

In a hierarchical structure, the person at the top of the pyramid is the most powerful and authority comes from the top of the organisation. Decisions are made at that level while the workers on the bottom layer have little responsibility. Employees on each level are accountable to the level above them and are controlled by the people working at that level.

A hierarchical structure is very traditional and is commonly found in government departments, for example.

Advantages of a hierarchical structure
a There is a clear structure and everyone understands where he/she fits into it
b Areas of responsibility are clearly defined
c Every employee knows who his/her boss is and reports to that person
d There are more opportunities for promotion so employees are motivated.

Disadvantages of a hierarchical structure
a There are too many layers between top and bottom, and people at each of these levels often do not know each other
b Communication can be poor between the various levels
c Employees at the lower levels have little opportunity to use their initiative as they have no links with the decision-makers.

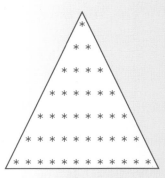

A tall hierarchical structure

A flat organisational structure

Flat structure

A flat structure is the opposite of the hierarchical structure, is more modern and works in smaller, less complicated organisations. A flat structure has fewer levels but has a large number of people working at each level.

Generally, the atmosphere in a flat structure type of organisation is less formal and all employees are encouraged to contribute to decision making and to put forward their ideas for the benefit of the organisation.

Advantages of a flat structure
a There are few levels of management and employees feel part of a team
b Communication is more efficient from management to employees
c Every employee has responsibility as part of the overall team
d Motivation is high amongst all employees and they are encouraged to use their initiative.

Disadvantages of a flat structure
a There is no clearly defined boss
b This structure works only in a small organisation.

ACTIVITY

Refer to the organisation chart for your school which you drew in the last activity.

1. Use it to help you to name the type of management structure which is used in your school
2. Write down your reasons for your choice of structure.

ACTIVITY

Copy and complete the following sentences in your notebook.

The two types of management structure are .... and ....

a A .... structure has one person at the top and can be illustrated as a ....
b A .... structure has ..... levels but has a ..... number of people working at each level.
c There are few levels of management in a .... structure and employees feel part of a ....
d In a .... structure, authority comes from the ... of the organisation.
e In a .... structure all .... are encouraged to contribute to decision making
f Workers on the bottom layer in a .... have little responsibility.
g A hierarchical structure is often found in ....
h A .... structure is more modern and works in .... organisations.
i In a hierarchical structure .... can be poor between the various levels
j Communication is more efficient in a .... structure between .... and ....
k Some employees do not like a flat structure because there is no clearly defined ....
l Areas of responsibility are clearly defined in a .... structure

Span of control

There are a few other terms you should be aware of when learning about organisational structures: terms such as 'span of control', 'chain of command' and 'delayering'.

The span of control refers to the number of people over whom a manager or supervisor has direct control. A wide span of control gives more freedom to the workers while a narrow span of control allows managers and supervisors to maintain tighter control.

It is important to note that the span of control refers only to those people in the direct line of control and does not necessarily refer to everyone working on levels below the manager or supervisor. However, the manager would have responsibility for all those workers.

To illustrate this point, study the extract opposite from Prime Products' organisation chart shown earlier in this unit.

In that business, the Production Manager has a span of control of three although s/he has responsibility for a total of 38 people.

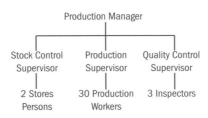

Production Manager

Stock Control Supervisor — Production Supervisor — Quality Control Supervisor

2 Stores Persons — 30 Production Workers — 3 Inspectors

ACTIVITY

Study the above extract from the organisation chart and answer the following questions.

1. How many people are in the span of control of the Stock Control Supervisor?
2. How many people are in the span of control of the Production Supervisor?
3. How many people are in the span of control of the Quality Control Supervisor?

Chain of command

The chain of command is the route by which orders and decisions are passed downwards through the organisation.

In a tall, hierarchical structure the chain of command is long and has to pass through many levels of management. This is because all decisions are made at the top level in a hierarchy and it takes time for those decisions to reach the lower levels. By contrast, in small organisations with flat structures, the chain of command is short.

To illustrate this point, study the extract opposite from the organisation chart for Prime Products plc. The chain of command has been highlighted in red.

Prime Products plc

Board of Directors

Managing Director

Production Manager

Production Supervisor

30 Production Workers

ACTIVITY

1. In Prime Products Ltd, how many layers does a decision made by the Board of Directors pass through before it reaches the production workers?
2. Make a list of the disadvantages you can think of in this system.

Delayering

The modern trend in business is for delayering. This simply means that modern businesses try to reduce the number of levels in the organisation and aim to give all employees a greater say in the business's decision making.

Advantages of delayering

a Communication is simplified and more direct so it becomes more accurate

b Management and workers are less separated from each other

c Workers feel more motivated and trusted

d There is a better team spirit in the business.

ACTIVITY

Anne is employed as a sales assistant in the Super Sports Store. All employees in the store are encouraged to have a say in the running of the business.

1. Name one advantage which delayering in the store has for Anne.
2. Name one advantage which delayering has for the Super Sports Store.
3. Give details of any disadvantage which delayering would have for the Store.

REVISION

At this stage you should understand:

a The different methods of organisational structure – by product, geographical organisation and organisation by function

b The work of each functional area of a business

c An organisation chart for a business

d Hierarchical and flat structures

e Span of control

f Chain of command

g Delayering.

Communication

> **Communication is the giving and receiving of information from one person (the sender) to another person (the receiver).**

Communication is natural to us all. Think of your day so far – you have already communicated with members of your family, with people on the transport system which brought you to school, with your teachers, with your friends in class and perhaps with people working in shops or in the school canteen. In each case it was important that you understood each other clearly.

Communication is equally important in business. People in business have to communicate with one another in order to:

- share ideas and get feedback
- give information or instructions
- aid understanding
- keep people up to date
- improve and maintain the business's image
- persuade other people to accept their products or services
- negotiate and finalise deals.

It is of vital importance, therefore, that communication is effective and clear so that misunderstandings do not arise.

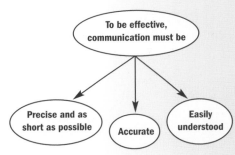

ACTIVITY

Have you ever played Chinese Whispers? Try this in class.

a The teacher should whisper a message to the first person in the group. The first person whispers it to the second and so on round the entire group. The last person tells the message back to the teacher and everyone is able to compare the final message with the message received at the beginning.

b As a group, discuss what went wrong with the communication.

c You should then write down six reasons why you think the message was distorted.

d Finally, check your list with the reasons listed in the next section.

Reasons why communication may go wrong

- **Jargon** — Using language or abbreviations which are unfamiliar to the other person means that s/he does not fully understand the information

- **Noise** — Loud background distractions make the message difficult to hear and understand

- **Wrong channel** — Complicated instructions would be better written down. If detailed instructions are given over the telephone for example, they may not be understood fully

- **Timing** — Information may be received about available goods or available services at a time when the receiver is not interested. Receiving information about summer clothes in November would be an example of poor timing

- **Attitude** — If the receiver of the information does not like or trust the sender, the message is less likely to be heeded properly

- **Feedback** — If the receiver gives some feedback, it acts as proof that the message has been understood. For example, if you telephone someone and leave your number for a return call, the other person should read the number back to you to prove that it has been taken down correctly

- **Poor technology** — Information may be lost or misunderstood if the quality of the reproduced message is poor. This may occur, for example, if a fax machine needs to have its cartridge replaced

- **Inefficient use of equipment** — Electronic mail is an excellent means of communication but its benefits are lost if, for example, the receiver does not open the mailbox regularly

- **Imprecise message** — The message must be given clearly, using as few words as possible so that the receiver does not become confused

- **Too many people** — To achieve accuracy, communication needs to be given directly from the sender to the receiver. Passing a message through a number of other people is very likely to alter it

- **Delays** — Communication should be as immediate as is practicable. If the sender delays, the receiver is going to see him/her as inefficient, and the point of the communication may be lost

To avoid problems in communicating you should:
i.   gather your thoughts beforehand and be clear about the information you wish to give
ii. present your information clearly and use simple sentences
iii. ask for feedback
iv. use the most appropriate method of communication.

You definitely should not:
use technical jargon or slang or be offensive. This will only annoy the other person who will not then be able to listen properly to your message.

Communication may be one-way, two-way or multi-directional

One-way communication exists where instruction is being given and no feedback is required.

Two-way communication exists where two people are taking part in a discussion. Immediate feedback is received.

Multi-directional communication takes place between a number of different people who are all both giving and receiving information.

Communication may be either external or internal

External communication is between someone who works for the business and someone outside it. One example of external communication would be between the business's financial director and the bank manager.

Internal communication is between people who work for the same business. However, these people need not necessarily work in the same building or the same branch of the business. An example of internal communication would be between the business's financial director and an accounts clerk.

Internal communication may be horizontal or it may be vertical

Horizontal communication takes place between people who are working at the same level in the business, for example between the financial director and the sales director.

Vertical communication takes place between people who are working at different levels in the business, for example between the business's financial director and an accounts clerk or between a manager and shop floor workers.

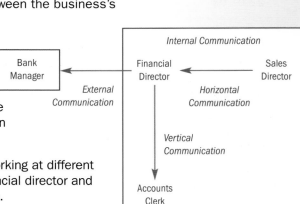

Methods of Communication

There are many methods of communication and it is important that the most effective method is chosen for each particular situation. The choice of method of communication depends on:

- Whether or not the information is confidential
- The urgency of the message
- How far away the receiver is from the sender
- Whether or not a record is required
- The cost involved
- Which methods are available
- Whether or not an answer is needed
- How many people have to receive the same message.

Communication may be:

WRITTEN	ORAL
VISUAL	ELECTRONIC

Written communication

- **Letter**   A letter is used as a formal, external means of communication. It provides a written record which may be referred to at a later date.

   A letter may also be copied to other interested parties

- **Memo**   A memo is used as a less formal, internal means of communication. Like a letter, it provides a written record for later reference

- **Report**   Reports may be written or may be delivered orally perhaps at a meeting or conference. Such reports would be on subjects of interest to the business – on topics of research or new methods, for example. An annual report is written and published by a company to provide details of the year's activities and financial affairs. This provides a record for later reference.

- **Notice**   A notice board carries general information which applies to a large number of people. The notice must be eye-catching to attract attention and the difficulty is that it is impossible to make sure that the notice has been read by everyone.

- **Minutes**   Minutes are a written record of a meeting and present a full record of all the decisions made at the meeting as well as other details such as the names of all those who attended. Minutes may be referred to later if necessary.

- **Agenda**   An agenda is a list of the discussions to take place at a meeting. The agenda also gives details about the time, date and place of the meeting.

> Welcome to
> Sarah Jones
> who has joined the
> Marketing
> Department.
> 22.01.03

ACTIVITY

a   Use a computer to write a letter to the Reservations Manager in the Ballygally Castle Hotel, Coast Road, Ballygally, Larne, Co Antrim, BT40 2QZ, reserving a single room for the night of 14 September this year. You will require breakfast in the hotel. Use your own name and home address and sign the letter.

b   Re-read your letter to make sure that all the details are correct.

c   Address an envelope to the Reservations Manager.

Figure 1.32
Ballygally Castle Hotel, Co Antrim

Oral communication

- Telephone   This is a very fast way of communicating by which the sender can get instant feedback. There is a possibility of information being misheard or misinterpreted and there is no written record. For this reason, agreements reached via the telephone are always backed up later by a letter. To overcome this disadvantage, some firms record their telephone conversations. The telephone is probably the most accessible method of communication there is in modern business as almost everyone has a telephone and, nowadays, mobile phones make contact possible at all times.

- Voice mail   This method allows communication to take place between two people via the telephone and stores a message until the receiver is available to take the call. There is no permanent record of the call.

- Face-to-face   Interviews, meetings and conferences are all face-to-face and are very effective methods of communication since body language can be interpreted as well as what is actually said. Meetings and conferences permit the interchange of ideas among many people and disseminate information over a large audience. Records of meetings are kept as Minutes which must be ratified by all present. Increasingly, a taped record is kept of meetings but the tapes are generally erased after the official minutes have been agreed.

ACTIVITY

a   Name two advantages which the telephone has over a letter as a means of communication.
b   Name the major disadvantage of the telephone as a means of communication.
c   State the main advantage of communicating by letter.
d   Describe the main purpose of minutes.
e   What is the function of an agenda?

Visual communication

- **Charts, tables, diagrams and graphs**
  These are clear methods of giving numerical information, in particular. They have immediate impact and can illustrate their points quickly and have the ability to put across a lot of information using one diagram or a series of related diagrams.

- **Demonstrations**
  Live demonstrations are very useful in showing correct processes and methods. Cookery demonstrations, for example, are very successful. Sales representatives also sometimes set up demonstrations to show the use of machines such as vacuum cleaners, and fashion shows are really demonstrations of how clothes can look. In some cases, demonstrations are given through the medium of video or television.

- **Pictures and films**
  These are pictorial methods of transmitting information. They are attractive ways of presenting information and immediately focus attention. It is said that 'a picture is worth a thousand words, which illustrates their usefulness in making a point clearly.

ACTIVITY

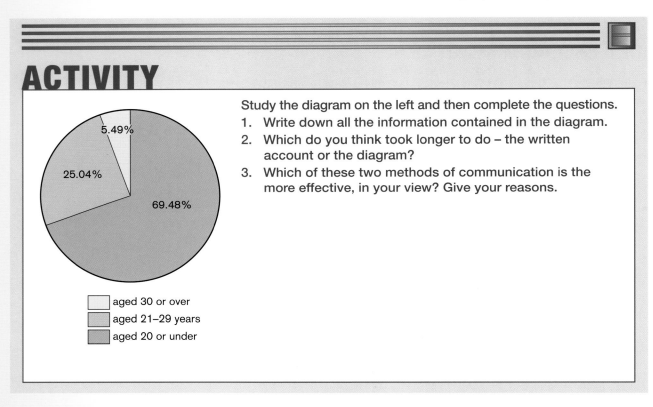

Study the diagram on the left and then complete the questions.
1. Write down all the information contained in the diagram.
2. Which do you think took longer to do – the written account or the diagram?
3. Which of these two methods of communication is the more effective, in your view? Give your reasons.

aged 30 or over
aged 21–29 years
aged 20 or under

Electronic communication

- **Facsimile**
  The fax gives almost instant access to the receiver. It allows one person to send a written document to another person using the telephone. This method has all the advantages of a letter, in addition to its speed of transmission.

- **Computers**
  Computers may be networked via a modem. This permits all users of the network to have access to any data stored on the system.

- **Electronic mail**
  E-mail links computer terminals to one another, allowing the sender to communicate with people nationally and internationally. The advantages of electronic mail are that it is very fast, is available to everyone who has the necessary electronic equipment and can be

stored as a written record for later reference. The system also has the advantage of being accessible at any time of the day or night. Lengthy documents may be transmitted by e-mail as well as shorter messages.

Figure 1.33

- Electronic Data Interchange

The Interchange networks a number of businesses electronically. Records of stock, orders and payments are kept by them all. In this way the supplier knows when stocks are low and can replace them without an order form being processed. Payments can also be made through the system without the use of cheques.

- Internet

Provided users have the appropriate equipment, they may access the Internet, giving immediate entry to a world-wide communications network through the telephone and a modem. Businesses use the Internet to advertise their products and services and to give information likely to be of use to potential customers.

- Intranet

This is a system which stores internally all the records of that particular organisation. In this way, information is shared among all users of the system inside the business.

- Video conferencing

This method allows people to meet via cameras and provides all the advantages of a meeting or conference. In addition, video conferencing can be conducted between people who are in different locations. This saves the expense involved in bringing a number of people together in one place.

ACTIVITY

What method of communication would you use in each of the following situations?

1. The Manager wishes to inform all employees that the company dinner is being held in the Ramada Hotel, Belfast, on 16 April.
2. The Finance Director wishes to give shareholders information about the business.
3. The Production Manager wishes to inform all production workers about new methods being introduced in the factory.
4. The Sales Manager wishes to let a customer know that his goods are ready for collection.
5. The Office Manager has to inform one of the clerks that he is being dismissed because he has not responded to warnings about his poor time keeping.

Impact of Information and Communications Technology (ICT) on Communications

ICT has caused the greatest change of all time in communications and general methodology in business. The use of word-processing, databases, spreadsheets, e-mails, presentation software such as Powerpoint, desk-top publishing, accounts packages, the Internet and intranet is now commonplace.

Figure 1.34
ICT being used in the offices of Phoenix Natural Gas

The impact on business has been huge – mostly beneficial but there are draw-backs too!

Benefits of ICT for communications

- Faster production   Word processors produce a greater quantity of material in a shorter period of time.
- Use of resources   Material can be altered and improved without having to start again or reprint. This results in less wastage of paper.
- Improved quality   The finished work has a more professional appearance.
- Improved circulation   Information can be circulated easily to all those involved so everyone is up to date.
- Data source   The business has access to a vast range of material. This keeps the business well informed.
- Informed decisions   The greater use of up-to-date material results in more enlightened decision making and keeps it at least level with the competition.
- Efficient image   The public image of the organisation is enhanced.

Disadvantages of ICT for communications

- Capital investment   There is a vast outlay of capital in installing the new technology and in keeping it up to date.

- Training costs   All employees need training in the correct use of the technology and re-training as the technology is updated.
- Technological breakdown   Computers occasionally go down, causing a break in work and perhaps lost material.
- Health and safety   Computer operators may suffer from eye-strain, headaches or wrist strain.

EXAMINATION QUESTION

Cable Electrics is a large manufacturing firm producing televisions and other electrical goods. Increased specialisation has resulted in a rise in output. Productivity has been improved by using new technology.

Explain the possible effects of the new technology on Cable Electrics.

(4 marks)

(CCEA Business Studies, GCSE, Paper 2 Foundation Tier, 2000)

Tips for answering this question:

When you are asked to 'explain' something, the examiner wants to see if you understand the topic. In this question, you should think of two effects of technology on the business. These effects may be either advantages or disadvantages for Cable Electrics. Name the two effects and then say how each one would be either helpful or not to the business.

REVISION

At this stage you should understand:

a Characteristics of, and need for, good communication.
b Reasons why communication may go wrong.
c Types of communication.
d Impact of ICT on communications.

Assistance for Business

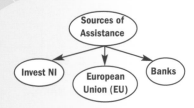

Figure 1.35

● existing offices
○ planned offices

Businesses in Northern Ireland have various sources of assistance. Three of the main ones are shown in the diagram on the left.

Invest Northern Ireland

Invest Northern Ireland (Invest NI) is Northern Ireland's new economic development agency. It is a public body and was established in April 2002 to take over the functions previously carried out separately by the Industrial Development Board (IDB), the Local Enterprise Development Unit (LEDU), the Industrial Research and Technology Unit (IRTU), the Business Support Division of the Department of Enterprise Trade and Investment (DETI) and the business support functions of the Northern Ireland Tourist Board (NITB).

Invest Northern Ireland has local offices throughout Northern Ireland and these are based in Belfast, Ballymena, Londonderry, Newry and Omagh. Extension offices are to be formed in Craigavon, Coleraine and Enniskillen.

Invest NI is working to:

- encourage economic development in Northern Ireland
- create a base of world-class companies in Northern Ireland
- develop a more entrepreneurial culture in Northern Ireland
- encourage a greater number of new businesses to start up
- encourage business innovation
- develop existing businesses, helping them to be more competitive
- promote e-commerce in order to improve competitiveness
- help businesses to establish a greater presence overseas
- attract more foreign businesses to invest in Northern Ireland
- assist the business development element of tourism.

The organisation's formal objectives can be seen in its mission statement which is published in its corporate plan:

To accelerate economic development in Northern Ireland, applying expertise and resources to encourage innovation and to achieve business success, increasing opportunity for all within a renewed culture of enterprise.

Invest Northern Ireland's assistance targets three main groups:

- entrepreneurs wishing to start their own businesses
- established businesses needing support and assistance
- foreign business organisations considering setting up in Northern Ireland.

These groups are helped through the following INI major programmes.

Business Start Programme

This programme assists people to start their own businesses and provides a comprehensive package of support. A business counsellor is assigned to each new project to offer advice on planning and getting the business started.

It also provides a training course which covers sales, marketing, financial management and legal issues as well as practical computer experience and help on the use of the Internet.

In addition, the Business Start Programme offers a financial planning service giving advice on the amount of funding required for the business and on possible sources of funding.

Be what you want   Be positive   Believe

The Business Start Programme's encouraging message

Programmes for Established Businesses

Invest NI has developed a number of programmes designed to help businesses be more competitive, particularly in the export market:

- **Marketing Awareness Programme** — This programme focuses on marketing and helps business people to develop a marketing plan and a successful marketing strategy.

- **Export Development Programme** — The Export Development Programme aims to assist in extending the Northern Irish market abroad and to remove the difficulties which businesses may experience in developing an export market.

- **Company Development Programme** — This programme gives assistance to businesses to improve their competitiveness by encouraging them to invest in people development, and by helping them in staff training.

- **Technology Transfer Programme** — The Technology Transfer Programme promotes the use of modern technology and best practice in management techniques in order to make Northern Ireland businesses more competitive on the global market.

- **Research and Development Programmes** — There are several programmes designed to draw attention to the importance of research and development if businesses are to be successful. The Research and Development Programmes provide practical advice and assistance in this area.

Figure 1.36
One of Northern Ireland's oldest businesses

Programmes for Foreign Businesses Setting up in Northern Ireland

Inward investment is a major part of Invest NI's work as the organisation seeks to encourage foreign businesses to establish in Northern Ireland.

To do this, Invest NI:

- provides a range of practical and financial support to help them get started quickly
- offers leases on a number of sites in business and industrial parks throughout Northern Ireland
- works closely with each company during the set-up period of their business
- organises visits to Northern Ireland for prospective new foreign investors
- arranges contacts for them with local professional services
- gives financial incentives to new companies.

European Union (EU)

Northern Ireland, as a part of the United Kingdom, has been a member of the European Union since 1973.

Northern Ireland was originally classified by the European Union as 'a region whose development was lagging behind'. For that reason, extra funding was directed to the province. For example, £750 million came to Northern Ireland from the European Union over the period 1989–1993.

Northern Ireland no longer qualifies for that degree of assistance because its level of prosperity has risen above the criterion for funding. That new level of prosperity is largely due to the EU's intervention. The European Union has, therefore, had a very positive influence on businesses in Northern Ireland by targeting money from its Structural Funds to make companies more competitive and by helping to create a larger market for their products.

One of the principal points about European Union membership is that there is a Single Market which means that no tariffs (taxes) on trade are imposed between countries in the EU. In addition, there are few formalities for goods moving from one EU country to another. This assists businesses since it cuts out the red tape and also protects industries operating in EU member states.

Figure 1.37
Improvements made at Belfast City Airport

Northern Ireland is physically situated on the edge of Europe which makes transportation of people and goods more difficult than it would be in countries situated in mainland Europe. The European Union has helped Northern Irish businesses to overcome the problems of distance through the Trans-European Networks Scheme aimed at creating a better infrastructure by improving roads, ports and airports.

Two industries in Northern Ireland have been given special attention by the European Union – tourism and agriculture.

Figure 1.38
Northern Ireland's agriculture and tourism are helped by the European Union

The tourist industry has been assisted notably by marketing the province abroad to attract increased numbers of visitors, and by extending the range of amenities and accommodation available. As a result, over 350 jobs have been created in the tourist industry in Northern Ireland.

Several projects have been run to improve the agri-food industry, to modernise farming, and to regenerate the rural economy.

European Union funding has been used for Northern Ireland's businesses to:

- promote economic development and competitiveness
- support modernisation of industry and improvements in quality of products
- organise trade fairs abroad in order to promote products
- assist with promotional materials, translation costs, advertising and distribution
- provide interest-free loans for small- and medium-sized businesses
- offer interest rate relief and support for small- and medium-sized firms
- encourage research and development
- help employees keep up to date by training in new industrial skills and techniques
- improve technological skills and equipment
- improve managerial skills
- lower unemployment levels.

Banks

There are four main commercial banks in Northern Ireland and they all provide assistance for businesses. The four banks are:

- Northern Bank
- Ulster Bank

Figure 1.39
Northern Bank – Omagh Branch

Figure 1.40
Bank of Ireland – Newry Branch

Figure 1.41
First Trust Bank – Lurgan Branch

- Bank of Ireland
- First Trust Bank.

In addition, HSBC has two branches in Northern Ireland – in Belfast and Omagh.

Banks help businesses which are just setting up as well as established businesses in the following ways:

- discuss the viability of their business idea and the most suitable structure for it
- assist in the preparation of the business plan
- advise on the use of premises and equipment
- explain legal and tax considerations
- advise on insurances
- provide day-to-day banking services
- offer business borrowing facilities.

ACTIVITY

Each bank named above has its own programme of assistance for business. There are slight differences in the way the banks provide this help.

Your class should divide now into four groups and each group should contact one of your local banks to ask for details of the help it offers either to new or established businesses. Make sure that your research covers the Northern, Ulster, the Bank of Ireland and First Trust.

You should share the information by reporting back to the whole class in a discussion session.

ACTIVITY

Here are the names of five other possible sources of help for businesses:

1. British Chamber of Commerce
2. Confederation of British Industry
3. Institute of Directors
4. Information Age Initiative for Northern Ireland
5. Northern Ireland Growth Challenge.

You could extend your study by searching the Internet for the type of assistance each one gives.

Cable Electrics is a large manufacturing firm producing televisions and other electrical goods.

Outline two sources of advice and assistance available to Cable Electrics, giving examples of the help these sources can offer.

(4 marks)

(Adapted from CCEA Business Studies, GCSE, Paper 2 Higher/Foundation Tiers, 2000)

Tips for answering this question:

When you are asked to 'outline' it means that you have to give a short description. Here, you should name two sources of advice and assistance and describe what each one does. One mark would be given for naming each part and one for the brief description of each so do not spend too long on the description.

REVISION

At this stage you should understand:

- The main sources of assistance for business
- The work of Invest Northern Ireland
- The type of help given by the European Union
- How the banks assist businesses.

UNIT 1.10

Business Planning

A business plan is a detailed description of what a business hopes to do over a period of usually one to five years.

The business plan shows the business's:

- costs during that period
- expected level of sales and income
- timescale for starting to make a profit
- expectation of when it would be able to repay loans.

Figure 1.42

If you were travelling by car from your home to Cork, you would consult a map before you started out and that would act as a guide for your route. On the actual journey you would refer frequently to the map or to the signs along the road to make sure that you were going in the right direction.

A business plan is just like a map because it acts as a guide for the business and can be referred to frequently to make sure the business is meeting its targets.

The name 'plan' indicates that a business plan is for the future, but it has to cover quite a short period of time because it is not possible in business to predict what will happen in the longer term with any degree of certainty.

The importance of planning in business cannot be overemphasised. According to a study carried out in 1993 by the Federation of Small Businesses, 400,000 small businesses were set up that year, 55,000 of which failed. The major factor for failure was given as inadequate planning. Another study in 1996 found that companies which had planned properly had 50% more income and profit growth than businesses which did not have clear plans.

Going into business without a business plan is like trying to drive a car without a steering wheel – there is no way of directing it!

A business plan would be worked either by a new business or by a business wishing to expand – perhaps by bringing out new products or by selling in new markets.

So, why work a Business Plan?

- A new business, or one which is hoping to expand, is likely to need to borrow money from the bank or other source. The bank manager would be unwilling to lend money unless he/she was reasonably sure that the business would be able to repay both the loan and the interest on the loan. The purpose of a business plan is to work out accurately the amount of money which is required, and then to convince the bank manager that the business idea is viable and that the loan is a safe investment from the bank's point of view.

- The business would probably have shareholders who will have invested finance in the business. They will use the business plan to gauge the strength of the business, and to decide whether or not they wish to remain as shareholders.
- The business may hope to encourage other investors to put money into the business. These potential investors would also study the business plan to see if they would receive a worthwhile return on their investment.
- The actual process of compiling the business plan is a valuable one because it forces the business owners and managers to think about every tiny detail of the business. This makes sure that nothing is left out and that there are no forgotten costs to be discovered later. This fact also adds to the confidence of the bank manager and other investors who can see that the business idea has been carefully thought out.
- The business plan is also very useful to the managers in the business who can monitor the actual progress of the business against the plan. The business's managers will be constantly comparing its performance with how it expected to perform, and they will also compare their performance against that of their competitors.
- The accounts produced as part of the business plan will be used to check the monthly figures and any differences can be investigated before they become too great.
- The business owners and managers would also use the business plan to monitor whether and how the stated aims and objectives are being met in the running of the business.

Style of the Business Plan

Most businesses go to great trouble to make their business plans very professional. Some are bound, but all are presented in covers with the business name and logo. This is to present an image to potential financiers and to make them interested in the business.

Business plans are usually written in the third person, and should be word-processed.

The best way to learn about a business plan is to work one. However, that would be a very long activity so this one has been broken down into sections. By the end of this unit, you should have a complete business plan if you proceed through the unit step by step.

You should be warned that you are not ready to do this activity unless you have previously studied the different forms of private-sector business ownership, business aims, market research, the marketing mix, forecasting, final accounts and the balance sheet.

You and your teacher may consider using this activity to form the basis of your coursework.

Alternatively, you may work the activity on your own or in pairs.

ACTIVITY

This is your chance to put your big ideas into practice! You can now plan to open that business you have always dreamed of and which you just know would be a success.

Activity continues on the next page

For those of you who can't think what type of business you might like to run, the following ideas may be helpful. Choose one which would suit your talents and interests, and one which would be likely to be successful where you live.

It is useful if you know some people in that type of business because they could act as your consultants and give you the benefit of their experience.

Some ideas to get you going: Garden centre and landscape gardening

Music shop	Leisure centre
Day crèche	Artist
Printer	Restaurant or café
Hairdresser	Any type of shop
Fun fair	

a   When you have chosen, you should start by thinking of a name for your business and designing a logo for it.

b   You should also carry out some market research at this stage to help you to estimate the demand for your product, your niche market, and the price at which the product will sell.

Figure 1.43
You may wish to open a fun fair!

Components of a Business Plan

Business plans differ in design and layout but the following information is common to them all. The sub-headings, and their order, may vary according to the type of business being planned for. For example, many business plans have 10 to 12 headings, so the following are suggested only as a framework.

- Introduction to proposed business
- The business and its objectives
- Resources plan
- Marketing and Marketing Mix
- Production plan
- Financial plan
- Appendices.

Introduction to proposed business

- This is where the business makes its first impression and therefore it is very important to get the introduction right. The impact of this page should make people reading the business plan want to invest in the business. The introduction should be short and attention-grabbing.
- Include the business name and address in the introduction.
- The introduction should give a description of the business idea. Describe very clearly what goods or services are to be produced.
- Briefly state why that product is marketable and its benefits – for example, it may be especially easy to use.

Classic Computers is the name of a proposed business in Armagh. The business is being planned by Derek Brennan and he is preparing his business plan which he hopes to submit to his bank manager.

Derek has previously carried out market research and he has discovered that there is little competition in the area. He has also found out that there is a demand for high quality computers and for all types of computer software. His research has informed him that his niche market is mainly from the local business community which would like to be able to buy computer supplies locally and quickly. There are large numbers of students in Armagh who would also be an important part of his market.

Opposite is the 'Introduction' that Derek has prepared.

CLASSIC COMPUTERS
ARMAGH

Business Plan
for a new retailing outlet
selling high-quality computer hardware
and associated software products

by Derek Brennan

*The computer products for sale
will be sophisticated models
offering the best technology at keen prices*

ACTIVITY

You are now ready to design and write your introduction.

Using the guidelines provided in this unit, prepare the 'Introduction to your Proposed Business' and file it.

The business and its objectives

- This section gives details of the business and explains its work.
- The strengths of the business should be shown clearly and its past achievements should be included.
- A brief summary of the value of the business and how it has been funded are needed.
- This section must show the legal status of the business – is it run and owned by a sole trader, partnership or company?
- Has the business been given any service awards in the past? If so, they should be detailed here.
- The goals or objectives of the business should also be described. These are likely to include levels of profit, sales expectations, future product development etc.
- A mission statement would be appropriate in this section.
- The personal details of the owner should be included in this section.

Derek Brennan's proposed business in Armagh is a completely new one so it has not got any past achievements or awards to show.

This is the 'Business and its Objectives' section that Derek has prepared:

Classic Computers – the business and its objectives

Ownership	Derek Brennan and Anne Brennan
Rented business premises	32 High Street ARMAGH
Private address	Deanne House 88 Church Spires ARMAGH
Legal status	Partnership with two equal partners
Purpose of the business	Classic Computers is being established for the retail sale of: ■ high-quality computers ■ other hardware components ■ high-quality software products such as floppy disks and ink cartridges ■ high-quality stationery for computer use.
Strengths of the business	Derek Brennan has an established good reputation in this trade and a firm knowledge of this type of business
Value of the business	Derek and Anne Brennan have joint savings of £20,000 for investment in Classic Computers. Additional funding of £20,000 is being applied for from their bank.
Business objectives	Projected turnover: £75,000 per annum Projected gross profit: £40,000 per annum
Mission statement	We aim to match the highest quality products with the highest quality service

ACTIVITY

You are now ready to write the next section of your business plan.

Using the guidelines provided in this unit, prepare the 'Business and its objectives' section and file it with your introduction.

Resources plan

- This section describes the people involved in the business together with details of their special contributions to the business.
- It also includes a description of the premises – its size, location and special features.
- Details of the equipment available would be appropriate here.
- Description of raw materials required – if the business is a manufacturing one.
- Required levels of working capital should be estimated.

Derek Brennan's proposed business is a retailing business so it will not have raw materials.

Here is the Resources Plan that Derek has prepared:

Classic Computers – the resources plan

Management	Derek Brennan. In Year 1 he will take only £1000 per month from the business for living expenses
Managerial experience	Derek Brennan has been the manager for 10 years with the business of 'Technology Supplies' in Craigavon. He has established contacts with suppliers in this trade.
Clerical assistant	Anne Brennan, working on a part-time, voluntary basis, will assist in the preparation of accounts while retaining her part-time job in the offices of a local accountancy firm
Employees	No other people will be employed at the beginning. Later, it is planned to employ one assistant
Premises	Situated at 32 High Street, Armagh. Premises rented for £300 per month comprising one shop area (40m x 30m), one store (50m x 25m) with street access.
Equipment	Shelving and display stands for small items Six desks for computer display with six chairs New delivery van (on credit until July)
Working capital	£15,000 in Year 1, rising to £20,000 in Year 3.

ACTIVITY

It is your turn now to write the next section of your business plan.

Using the guidelines provided in this unit, prepare the Resources Plan and file it with the remainder of your work.

Marketing and Marketing Mix

- This section gives details of the likely types of customers for the new product.
- Details of the competition should also be shown.
- Estimations of the overall demand for the product, projected as far as possible into the future, are included here.
- Information received from previous market research about the demand for the new product should be given.
- Include a description of where you propose to market the product and how you will distribute it – the *place* part of the Marketing Mix.
- Give details of any expected future developments to the product – the *product* part of the Marketing Mix.
- Details of the price at which the product is to be sold need to be given – the *price* part of the Marketing Mix.
- This section should include details of how the product is to be promoted and advertised – the *promotion* part of the Marketing Mix.

Have a look at the following marketing plan that Derek has prepared.

Classic Computers – the Marketing Plan and Marketing Mix

Customers	The main customers are the many business organisations in Armagh and the surrounding area which have indicated that they would value a local supplier. A large number of schools and their students as well as university students living in the area would be part of the market.
Competition	There is one other computer retailer in Armagh. The market is too large for one supplier.
Demand	In the first year, the demand is estimated at 50 computers. Demand for supplies of software is estimated at £15,000 per year and £5,000 for stationery. With increased lines these figures could be doubled within five years.
Suppliers	Main supplier will be 'Ever Ready Technology' who will supply on one month's credit. A second supplier will deliver extra goods in December for cash.
Market place	Sales will be conducted at the premises in Armagh.
Distribution	All computers sold will be delivered and installed. A personal back-up service would be guaranteed.
Future development	Product lines would be extended in later years to include a range of popular computer games and educational packages.
Price	The average prices are: ■ Computer – £1,100 including printer ■ Ink cartridges – £25

	■ Floppy disks – £6
	■ High-quality – 100g computer paper – £10 per ream
Promotion	Weekly advertising during the first six months in each of the local papers. An opening launch of the business to include viewing and demonstrations of computers. Free mouse mat with every computer sold.

ACTIVITY

You can now go ahead with writing your marketing plan. Use the guidelines provided in this unit to help you, and then file it with the remainder of your work.

Production plan

- (This section is required only in a manufacturing business.)
- A full description of the production process is included in this section.
- Details of how the premises will be used in the production process are given.
- Details are needed of the layout of the equipment and the design of the work area.
- Evidence should be provided that features such as health and safety requirements and ergonomics have been catered for.

Classic Computers is a retailing business and none of the details normally shown in a production plan, apply to it. Derek Brennan, therefore, did not write a production plan.

ACTIVITY

If a production plan applies to the business you are setting up, you should prepare it now. When you have it completed, check it against the details on a production plan provided in this unit, and then file it with the remainder of your work.

Financial plan

- A break-even analysis is required here – in order to show the point at which profit can be expected. This will also show sales estimates.
- A cash flow statement is included to explain the likely timing of the business's income and payments.
- A statement of the capital invested by the owners to show the funding of the business.
- Details of other loans already given to the business must be shown together with details of the terms of those loans.
- Details of mortgages on the premises.

- Most recent trading accounts, profit and loss accounts and balance sheet would be included to show the financial history of the business.

Derek Brennan's business is a new one so he has to present forecasted final accounts and balance sheet rather than actual ones. The premises for Classic Computers are rented so Derek does not have a mortgage. He does not have any loans other than the one he is hoping to get from the bank.

The following accounts have been prepared by Derek as his financial plan.

Statement of Capital Invested on 1 January 20..

	£3
Derek Brennan	10,000
Anne Brennan	10,000
	£20,000

Cash Flow Forecast for Derek Brennan for Year 1

	Jan	Feb	Mar	Apr	May	June	July	Aug	Sept	Oct	Nov	Dec	Total
Receipts													
Capital	20000												20000
Loan	20000												20000
Sales	2648	2900	3885	4298	5888	6915	7850	5300	6250	7541	11990	9535	75000
Total Receipts	**42648**	**2900**	**3885**	**4298**	**5888**	**6915**	**7850**	**5300**	**6250**	**7541**	**11990**	**9535**	**115000**
Payments													
Rent	300	300	300	300	300	300	300	300	300	300	300	300	3600
Purchases	3125	4150	5000	2500	3700	1000	1000	1500	8500	775	23125	54375	
Rates	100	100	100	100	100	100	100	100	100	100	100	100	1200
Electricity			200			200			200			200	800
Shelves	750												750
Desks	720												720
Chairs	300												300
Décor	1500												1500
Wages	1000	1000	1000	1000	1000	1000	1000	1000	1000	1000	1000	1000	12000
Advert	200	200	200	200	200	200							1200
Van	40000												40000
Telephone			120			120			120			120	480
Insurance	500										1000		1500
Office	50												50
Stationery													
Loan Interest	80	80	80	80	80	80	80	80	80	80	80	80	960
Total Payments	**5500**	**4805**	**6150**	**6680**	**4180**	**5700**	**42480**	**2480**	**3300**	**9980**	**3255**	**24925**	**119435**
Opening Balance	0	37148	35243	32978	30596	32304	33519	-1111	1709	4659	2220	10955	220220
Add Receipts	42648 42648	2900 40048	3885 39128	4298 37276	5888 36484	6915 39219	7850 41369	5300 4189	6250 7959	7541 12200	11990 14210	9535 20490	115000 335220
Less Payments	5500	4805	6150	6680	4180	5700	42480	2480	3300	9980	3255	24925	119435
Closing Balance	37148	35243	32978	30596	32304	33519	-1111	1709	4659	2220	10955	-4435	215785

Forecasted Trading Account of Classic Computers
for the year ended 31 December 20..

	£	£
Sales		75,000
Less: Cost of Sales:		
Purchases	54,375	
Less: Closing Stock	20,000	
Cost of Sales		34,375
GROSS PROFIT		£40,625

Forecasted Profit and Loss Account of Classic Computers
for the year ended 31 December 20..

	£	£
Gross Profit		40,625
Less: Electricity	800	
Stationery	50	
Rates	1,200	
Rent	3,600	
Interest on Loan	960	
Wages	12,000	
Insurance	1,500	
Decoration	1,500	
Advertising	1,200	
Telephone	480	23,290
NET PROFIT		£17,335

Forecasted Balance Sheet of Classic Computers
as at 31 December 20..

	£	£	£
FIXED ASSETS			
Fixtures and Fittings		750	
Furniture		1,020	
Motor Van		40,000	41,770
CURRENT ASSETS			
Debtors	3,125		
Stock at close	20,000	23,125	
CURRENT LIABILITIES			
Bank Overdraft	4,435		
Creditors	3,125	7,560	
c.f Working Capital			15,565
			£57,335

	£	£	£
b.f. Working Capital			15,565
			£57,335
LONG TERM LIABILITIES			
Capital		20,000	
Add: Net Profit		17,335	37,335
Bank Loan			20,000
			£57,335

ACTIVITY

You should now prepare the accounts needed for your financial plan. Go ahead and prepare:

a a statement of capital
b a cash flow statement
c details of loans and mortgages
d most recent (or forecast) trading accounts
e most recent (or forecast) profit and loss accounts
f most recent (or forecast) balance sheet.

When you have the accounts finished, file them with the rest of your business plan. Be warned that the financial plan is the slowest part of the business plan!

Appendices

An appendix is usually added and acts as a place to show any additional background material. This material might include:

- any technical information on the product which has not been included previously
- any additional material from market research
- CVs for the staff
- photographs and drawings
- copies of legal documents such as partnership agreements or loan agreements.

Derek Brennan decided to include the following in his business plan:

a his own CV
b a copy of his partnership agreement with his wife and business partner, Anne
c a photograph of the premises he was planning to rent.

ACTIVITY

If there any documents which you can attach as an appendix, you should do so now to complete your business plan.

Evaluation of a business plan

ACTIVITY

The GCSE specifications require you to be able to evaluate a business plan. It is extremely unlikely that you would have access to a real business plan, but that doesn't really matter.

Instead you should now swap the business plan you have just prepared with another student in your class. Evaluate each other's work constructively – that means that you look for its positive points but also should point out any omissions or details which are unclear.

As you study the business plan you are evaluating, ask yourself:
- Would I lend money to the proposed business?
- Does this business sound profitable?
- Would I want to buy from or sell to the proposed business?
- Do I need any additional information about it?

EXAMINATION QUESTION

Henry Smith runs JP Ltd which specialises in designing and making soft toys. He wants to expand the business into another area of the toy market and has decided to produce a business plan.

a Outline two essential components that Henry should include in his business plan.

(4 marks)

b Explain the benefits which Henry will get from producing a business plan.

(4 marks)

(CCEA Business Studies, GCSE, Paper 2 Higher/Foundation Tiers, 2001)

Tips for answering this question:

a When you are asked to 'outline' it means that you have to give a short description. In this question it would be appropriate to name two of the parts of a business plan and briefly describe what would be included in those parts. One mark would be given for naming each part and one for the brief description of each – another clue that you should not spend too long on the description.

b When you are asked to 'explain' something, the examiner wants to see if you understand the topic. In this question, you should think of two benefits of producing a business plan and say why a business plan would be useful to Henry in these ways.

REVISION

At this stage you should understand:

a the purpose of a business plan
b components of a business plan
c how to evaluate a business plan.

SECTION TWO

Human Resources

Learning Objectives

To develop a knowledge and critical understanding of

- the importance of people to business
- the roles, relationships and management of people in business
- the controls and procedures governing recruitment, selection and training
- the importance and methods of motivation and appraisal of employees
- employer/employee relationships in modern business.

To develop an appreciation of

- modern work patterns
- moral and ethical issues underlying recruitment and relationships in business.

UNIT 2.1 Roles and Contemporary Work Patterns

Inter-relationship of Roles Within Business

> In modern business there is a much greater emphasis on co-operation and teamwork than there once was.

People at all levels in a business organisation are encouraged to see themselves as part of a team and to contribute ideas for the improvement of the business. Roles are less clearly defined now than they used to be and can overlap. This working together and overlapping is known as the inter-relationship of roles.

It is commonplace now to find owners and managers and employees all on first name terms with each other – that would have been unheard of some years ago. It is also quite usual to find various types of employees from different levels of the firm working together with management, in quality circles for example. (See Unit 2.6 for more on quality circles.)

Figure 2.1
How it used to be!

ACTIVITY

Rosemary works in a modern industry and is aware that being part of a team there increases her opportunities as well as her responsibilities.

a   Name two opportunities which Rosemary could have because she is part of a team.
b   Name two qualities which Rosemary must have if she is to succeed in this situation.

Even though roles are inter-related, employees are employed to do certain jobs and to take on a given set of responsibilities. The usual roles in a manufacturing company are shown in the following diagram with authority coming from the top in a downward direction:

Director
↓
Manager
↓
Supervisor
↓
Operative

Director

Directors are appointed to set the policy of the business and to take responsibility for management decisions. Overall responsibility for the day-to-day running of the business is taken by a Managing Director. It is usual in larger businesses to have a director to take responsibility for each functional area in the business (see Unit 1.7).

There are two types of director – executive director and non-executive director. Executive directors, such as the Finance Director or Sales Director, actually work in the business full time. Non-executive directors do not work full time in the business but give some of their time to it by attending board meetings for example.

All directors have places on the Board of Directors and the Board is run by the Chairman (who is often a non-executive director).

Manager

Managers are appointed to carry out the policy of the directors and to make sure that the business runs efficiently.

Each department in the business has its own manager who will supervise the running of that department and the work of all the employees in it.

Some larger organisations may have several managers in each department – often known as senior and junior managers.

Supervisor

The supervisor is on the lowest level of management and often will have been promoted from an operative's position because s/he was a very good worker and showed leadership qualities.

The supervisor is a person who really understands how the tasks in that department should be done and can deal with problems as they arise. This is the person who is closest to the workforce and has the most contact with them.

Operative

An operative is a shop floor worker and is responsible for the making of the business's product.

In some businesses the operative's role may be very limited – joining two parts of a toy together on a toy factory production line, for example. In this case the operative would have to follow precise instructions and work within a set time limit so that the toy passes on to the next stage in its production and the quality of the finished toy is perfect.

ACTIVITY

You are the manager of a restaurant which employs one supervisor and eight full-time operatives.

a   Write down the responsibilities you would give each one of the eight operatives.
b   Describe how the roles of these eight people would be inter-related.

ACTIVITY

Answer the following questions in your notebook.

a   Why are co-operation and teamwork very important between all types of workers?
b   What is meant by 'the inter-relationship of roles'?
c   What is the main difference between an executive director and a non-executive director?
d   Which role in the business has overall responsibility?
e   To whom does a manager have to report?
f   What is an operative responsible for?
g   Which person in the business do you think would be paid most?
h   Why, in your view, is that person paid the most?

The tradition of getting a full-time job on leaving school and staying in that position until retirement is now very rare. Most of you can expect to have several career changes in your lifetime and to have to retrain, perhaps several times, to meet changing work patterns and conditions. So, as a modern employee, you will have to be adaptable to changing conditions and be flexible in order to cope with those changes.

The Labour Government has brought in a series of measures which are aimed at creating a better work/life balance for employees. The Government's Work and Parents Taskforce has set out new rules which come into effect in April 2003, and which permit any employee to make a written request to work flexible hours. The employer is bound to consider the request and to give a written explanation if, and why, the request cannot be accommodated.

Some of the features of modern employment are:

- there may be both part-time and full-time employees in a business
- there are both permanent and temporary employees
- many people are now self-employed
- some employees may work flexitime
- job sharing is growing in popularity
- an increasing number of people work from home
- more people are employed on short-term contracts
- more employees are on the Annualised Working Hours system.

Let us look at some of these trends in more detail.

Part-Time and Full-Time Employment

These simple terms explain themselves. A part-time employee works less than a full week – perhaps three days per week or every morning, for example. Part-time employees are usually paid on an hourly basis. Many of you probably have jobs after school and at weekends – these obviously are part time.

A full-time employee is one who is employed to work the full number of hours the business is open.

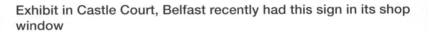

ACTIVITY

Positions Vacant

Part Time Sales Assistant

Please Apply In Store

Exhibit in Castle Court, Belfast recently had this sign in its shop window

Answer the following questions in your notebook:

a What is the person required to do?
b How is the person likely to be paid?
c Describe one type of person who may be interested in the position
d How would you apply for this job?
e Name one advantage for the shop of this form of application.

Permanent and Temporary Employment

A person in permanent employment is one who is contracted to work for that business until he/she leaves because of resignation, retirement, redundancy or dismissal.

A temporary employee is engaged to work only for a specified period of time – often one year. If the job is still available at the end of the period, the temporary contract may be renewed.

ACTIVITY

It is possible to have employment which is either permanent or temporary as well as full or part time.

In each of the following work situations, tick the boxes which are relevant.

Activity continues on the next page

Employment Description	Permanent	Temporary	Part Time	Full Time
Mary works from 0900 hrs to 1300 hrs for as long as she wants the job				
Monica works a full day but only for this year				
Richard works from 0800 hrs to 1800 hrs all the time				
Sean works from 1800 hrs to 2200 hrs for the summer months				

Self-Employment

As the name suggests, a self-employed person is one who has set up his/her own business and works for him/herself. A self-employed person takes all the responsibility for the business, raises all the capital, keeps any profit which is made or bears the loss if the business is less successful.

More and more people have had to set up as self-employed because of the difficulty of finding suitable work while others like the idea of being their own bosses.

Short Contracts

Today it is becoming more common for employees to accept short-term contracts for fixed periods of time. This work is temporary.

An example would be where hotels employ extra staff to cover the summer months when they are busiest. In this way labour is hired for the period when work is plentiful but can be reduced when work is scarce in the winter months. This method also saves having to make workers redundant.

Study the following report from the *Belfast Telegraph* which shows how supermarkets employ temporary staff to cater for the Christmas rush.

Tesco recruits for Christmas

SUPERMARKET chain Tesco is aiming to recruit new staff, the bulk of which will be seasonal workers over the Christmas period, it said today.

The group said it aimed to take on 12,000 staff to work in its 730 stores over Christmas, and is targeting parents, the over 50s and students.

Tesco retail director David Potts said: "Our stores are busier than ever before and we want to make sure that our customers get the best possible service."

The supermarket chain will be competing against other high street names to recruit the staff.

The following firms have recently announced major recruitment programmes:

- Health and beauty chain Boots is planned to recruit 7,000 new staff for Christmas. The Nottingham-based retailer employs 55,000 people at 1,400 stores.
- Marks & Spencer is aiming to recruit 18,000 staff in the run up to and during

Christmas. The staff, who will be recruitied on a temporary basis, will be employed across the group's 318 UK stores. M&S employs 60,000 staff in total in the UK.

- Asda is aiming to take on 10,000 staff over Christmas to help out as car park hosts, bag packers and store greeters.
- High street chain Woolworths plans to recruit an extra 6,000 and add 800 tills to cope with the rush.

Flexitime

A flexible working hours system allows the employee to have some choice about when to start work and when to finish during the working day, as long as the total number of hours are worked per week. Most businesses require their employees to be present during a set period each day (known as the core time).

This system has the advantage of giving the employee some flexibility and also usually means that the business will have workers present for a longer period each day since some will start early and others will finish later.

The disadvantage of this for the business is the increase in lighting and heating costs. Flexitime works successfully in offices but would be less successful in factories or shops, for example.

Working from Home

Home working is becoming more commonplace and falls into two types

The first category, found most commonly in the service industries, is known as teleworking and is possible because of advances in technology. This is where people who would otherwise have to go to the office are now able to keep in touch with their business by computer and other technological links.

Figure 2.2

The second category of home working is where work is done by a person in his/her own home for another person's business. Examples are knitting sweaters for shops, completing manufacturing processes such as jewellery making or toy painting, gift card packaging or addressing envelopes for offices.

Job Sharing

Job sharing is another popular trend in modern employment. It appeals to people who have other commitments and do not have the time to undertake full-time employment. Under this system, two people undertake one job and share its duties between them. For example, two teachers might job share. One might undertake teaching duties on Monday, Tuesday and Wednesday mornings. The second teacher would cover the remainder of the week. In addition, both would have to be available for scheduled meetings and training sessions. (See also Unit 6.2.)

ACTIVITY

Answer the following questions in your notebook

a   Give details of one disadvantage of job sharing, from the employer's point of view.
b   State one advantage of job sharing, from the employer's point of view.
c   Name the major advantage of job sharing for the employee.

Annualised Working Hours

Another modern feature is a system known as the Annualised Hours System. Under this system workers are contracted to work a given number of hours in a year rather than a given number of hours in a week.

This means that the business can vary the number of hours per day or per week to meet its needs. This would be especially useful to a shop during the Christmas rush, for example.

Research has shown that contemporary work patterns have improved staff commitment and reduced absenteeism because employees are better able to balance their home and work responsibilities.

For example, Xerox (UK) Ltd has saved over £1 million during the last five years by introducing flexible working schemes. The AA found that working from home has boosted productivity by 30%. BT showed that absenteeism was reduced by 20% to 40% and productivity boosted by the same percentage.

ACTIVITY

Make a list of at least five reasons why employers are introducing the more employee-friendly working practices and arrangements which are described in this unit.

R E V I S I O N

At this stage you should understand:

Director	Manager	Supervisor
Operative	Part-time employment	Full-time employment
Permanent employment	Temporary employment	Self employment
Flexitime	Job sharing	Short-term contract
Annualised Working Hours		

As revision, look each one up in the Glossary at the end of the book.

UNIT 2.2

Recruitment

> **Recruitment is the employment of new workers.**

Good employers realise that the most important resource in any business is the people who work there. It is possible for a business to have very modern technology and state-of-the-art premises but unless it employs the best possible work force, it will never achieve its best results.

For this reason, employers put great emphasis on their recruitment procedures and on getting the best employees to suit their requirements.

Businesses need to recruit new employees for several reasons. They may need to:

- employ extra workers because the business has grown
- bring in people who have skills they need, but do not have, in the business
- replace employees who have left because of – retirement
  resignation
  promotion
  dismissal.

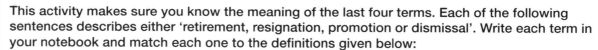

ACTIVITY

This activity makes sure you know the meaning of the last four terms. Each of the following sentences describes either 'retirement, resignation, promotion or dismissal'. Write each term in your notebook and match each one to the definitions given below:

a This is when a person leaves because he has reached the end of his working life.
b This is when a person has lost his job because of poor work or behaviour.
c This is when a person leaves the post to move to a more senior post.
d This is when a person leaves to go to another job.

The best way to understand the documents used in the recruitment procedure is to work a set of documents through from beginning to end in a practical activity.

That would be a long activity to do all at once, so it has been broken down for you into stages. Since the information in the job analysis and the information in the job description overlaps, you are not asked to work both of those documents.

You should proceed now through the activities in this unit step by step.

ACTIVITY

Start by looking in the Job Finder section of either your local newspaper or one of the national newspapers – there may be more variety in the nationals. Choose any job advertisement which interests you, cut it out and put it into your notebook.

Recruitment Procedure

The stages in the procedure may vary from business to business, but the list below is typical.

Documents Required in the Recruitment Procedure

Needs analysis

The first thing the employer must do is to decide exactly what the business needs. Decisions are needed on:

- which skills and qualifications are required in the business?
- how many new employees are needed?
- are the new employees required full time or part time?
- will they be permanent or temporary?
- how soon will the new employee(s) need to start work?

Carry out a needs analysis
↓
Carry out a job analysis
↓
Draw up a job description
↓
Design a person specification
↓
Advertise the post and invite applications
↓
Sort applications and draw up shortlist
↓
Interview applicants who meet
the criteria stated in the advertisement
↓
Select successful applicant and offer the job
↓
Complete the contract

Dungannon and South Tyrone Borough Council needs a person to work as a Tourist Information Receptionist in Killymaddy Tourist Information Centre, Ballygawley Road, Dungannon. The Human Resources Manager has drawn up this needs analysis.

DUNGANNON
& SOUTH TYRONE

Borough Council

- Duties required · · · · · · · · · · · · · To carry out all receptionist duties
- Skills and qualifications required · · · · · 6 GCSEs at minimum Grade C (must include English Language)
- Number of employees required · · · · · · One
- Terms of employment · · · · · · · · · · · Full time
  Permanent
- Required date of employment · · · · · · · 1 March 20..

ACTIVITY

You are now ready to carry out your needs analysis.

Assume you are the Human Resources Manager in the business named in your advertisement. Use the details on the advertisement to help you to work a needs analysis for that business. File your needs analysis with the advertisement.

Figure 2.3

Job analysis

Job analysis is a process to identify the particular duties and needs of a given post. Information might be collected on the tasks and duties of the post, the equipment needed, and the knowledge, skills and abilities required for the work.

The analysis is conducted of the job – not the person. While it is possible that information about the job may be obtained from the employee, the reason for doing this is to find an analysis or description of the job – not the worker in the job.

The information gathered during job analysis is used in planning future training programmes, in setting wage and salary levels, as well as in recruitment and selection.

Several methods are used in job analysis. The most usual are interview, observation and questionnaires.

Job description

Purpose of a job description
The most important purpose of the job description is to define the main duties and responsibilities of the post. This is essential so that both the employee and the line manager are clear about what the employee might be expected to do

A copy of the job description is sent to each applicant for the job so that he/she is clear what is required in the job.

Content of a job description
The job description should show:

- the title of the job
- the place where the job will be done
- a list of the main duties required in the job
- the person to whom the job holder reports (the line manager)
- names of any people who report to the job holder
- details of any equipment or parts of premises for which the job holder is responsible
- date of first issue of the job description and dates of any update.

Figure 2.4
Killymaddy Tourist Information Centre

Here is the job description for the receptionist's post with Dungannon and South Tyrone Borough Council:

DUNGANNON AND SOUTH TYRONE BOROUGH COUNCIL

Receptionist Job Description

Post	Tourist Information Receptionist
Place	Killymaddy Tourist Information Centre Ballygawley Road, Dungannon
Job purpose	To provide tourist information to members of the public visiting the Killymaddy Tourist Information Centre
Main duties	To meet the public in the Centre To answer questions and provide tourist information in person To answer telephone enquiries To handle sales in the tourist shop in the Centre To be responsible for cash and its safe deposit in the bank To provide monthly reports on the Centre's activities
Reports to	Information Officer
Date of issue	30 November 20..

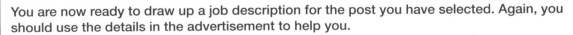

ACTIVITY

You are now ready to draw up a job description for the post you have selected. Again, you should use the details in the advertisement to help you.

File your job description with your other work.

Person specification

A person specification is drawn up after the job description has been prepared. Its purpose is to identify what an ideal applicant for the post should have in terms of:

- personal qualities
- knowledge
- qualifications
- skills
- previous work experience.

Usually the characteristics, achievements, qualifications, skills and previous work experience are listed, under three sub-headings, as Essential, Helpful or Optional.

The person specification for the Receptionist's post with Dungannon and South Tyrone Borough Council would look like this:

DUNGANNON AND SOUTH TYRONE BOROUGH COUNCIL

Receptionist Person Specification

	Essential	Helpful	Optional
PERSONAL QUALITIES:			
Good interpersonal skills	x		
Well groomed, tidy appearance	x		
Clear speaking voice	x		
KNOWLEDGE/SKILLS:			
Another European language		x	
QUALIFICATIONS:			
Minimum of 6 GCSEs at Grade C	x		
Word Processing Skills			x
PREVIOUS EXPERIENCE:			
Experience in dealing with public	x		
SPECIAL REQUIREMENTS:			
Available to work unsocial hours	x		

ACTIVITY

Now go ahead and design a person specification for the post you have selected. Again, you may get some help from the details in the advertisement.

File your person specification with your other work.

EXAMINATION QUESTION

Explain the differences between a job description and a person specification.

(4 marks)

(CCEA Business Studies, GCSE, Paper 2 Higher Tier, 2000)

Tips for answering this question:

a When answering this question, you should show that you understand the features of both documents.

b You are asked to 'explain the differences' so a suitable wording in your answer would be ' A job description gives details of ...... whereas a person specification gives details of ......

c For 4 marks, you would be expected to explain two differences between the documents.

Contract of employment

Purpose of a contract

The main purpose of a contract of employment is to set out the rights and duties of both the employee and the employer. It is an agreement between the two parties and can be enforced by law. Therefore, it gives protection and security to both the employee and the employer. It begins when the employer makes an offer of work with payment of money and the employee accepts the offer at that rate and agrees to work. By law, a full-time employee must be given a contract of employment within eight weeks of starting to work for that employer.

Content of a contract

The following details must appear on the contract:

- names of the employer and the employee
- date of commencement of the job
- title and description of the job
- hours of work
- agreed rates and method of payment
- details of any pension schemes
- arrangements for the payment of any commission, bonuses or overtime
- length of paid holiday entitlement
- level and duration of sickness, injury and maternity pay entitlement
- length of period of notice to be given
- details of grievance and disciplinary procedures
- name, job title and location of the business's grievance officer.

EXAMINATION QUESTION

A company prepares a contract of employment. State when this must be presented to the employee and show the relevance which it has for the employee.

(7 marks)

(Adapted from CCEA Business Studies, GCSE, Paper I Higher Tier, 2001)

Tips for answering this question:

You are asked to 'state' when the contract is to be presented. This is a straightforward 'recall of knowledge' question and all that is required is for you to name when it must be done. No explanation is necessary and there will not be any marks for an explanation.

The main marks will be given for the relevance (or importance) which the contract has for the employee. You would be expected to give details of two or three reasons why it is important for an employee to have a contract. Do not waste time showing its importance to the employer – that is not asked for.

A typical contract of employment would look like this:

CONTRACT OF EMPLOYMENT

Between

Employer _____

Employee _____

Title of position held _____

Date of commencement _____

Hours of work _____

Payment rate (including commission, bonuses and overtime) _____

Method of payment _____

Pension schemes which apply _____

Holiday entitlement _____

Sickness, injury and maternity pay entitlement _____

Period of notice of employment termination _____

Details of grievance and disciplinary procedures, including the details of the firm's grievance officer are set out in the Employee Handbook.

This contract may be altered only after consultation between the two parties named.

Signed on behalf of the Employer   Employee's Signature

_____   _____

Date _____   Date _____

ACTIVITY

a   Use a computer to make a copy of the contract of employment shown above.
b   Assume that you have got the post you selected earlier from the newspaper. Call up your copy of the contract and complete it as a contract of employment between yourself and the business named in the advertisement.
c   File your contract of employment with your other documents.

Main Methods of Recruitment

> When the employer has completed the first four documents, the next step is to contact possible candidates and invite them to apply for the post.

The employer may do this inside the business – known as internal recruitment – or outside it, which is external recruitment. The most commonly used methods of recruitment are discussed below.

The employer's choice of recruitment method will depend on several factors:

- the size of the business
- the amount of money available for advertising
- the type of work being offered
- where the business is situated
- how many employees are required
- how quickly the new employee is needed.

Internal recruitment

The usual methods of internal recruitment are to advertise the post:

- on notice boards
- in internal news sheets
- by sending memos or e-mails to all employees.

Advantages of internal recruitment

a The applicants are familiar with the business
b Existing employees are given the opportunity to gain promotion within the business
c It improves staff morale and provides motivation
d It is a cheaper method than advertising externally
e The process should take shorter time to complete.

Disadvantages of internal recruitment

a The range of applicants is limited
b It does not bring new skills and ideas into the business
c It could lead to staff discontent if one colleague is promoted over the other employees.

ACTIVITY

There is a vacancy for a sales assistant in your school tuck shop. The person appointed will be required to work in the shop from Monday to Friday during term time. Anyone interested in the post should apply to the School Secretary for further details regarding duties and pay.

Using a computer, if possible, design an advertisement for the post. The advertisement should be eye-catching and suitable for display on the school's notice board.

External recruitment

External recruitment may have to be used. There are several reasons for the use of external recruitment:

- there may not be a suitable candidate within the business
- none of the present employees may be interested in the post
- sometimes a business may wish to introduce 'new blood' who will bring in fresh ideas and up-to-date training.

Methods of External Recruitment

The four main methods are:

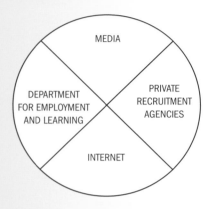

The term 'media' includes a range of methods:

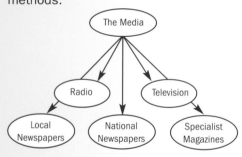

The media

Advertising in local newspapers is less expensive but does not reach a wide audience. It would be suitable for jobs which are not very highly paid and for which people would not travel long distances.

Advertising in national newspapers is more expensive but is read by a greater number of people. Newspapers such as the *Belfast Telegraph* have special Job Finder supplements. This method of advertising would be suitable for jobs which are more highly paid and for which people would be more willing to travel.

Figure 2.5

Specialist magazines are read by certain groups of workers and are used to recruit highly skilled or specialist workers. For example, *The Lancet* is a magazine for doctors, the *Nursing Times* is of interest to nurses and the *Times Educational Supplement* is read by teachers and other people working in the field of education.

From time to time, some television and radio stations broadcast details of job vacancies. This is usually done on a local basis and would have similar features to advertising in local newspapers.

The Internet

There are several websites on the Internet which advertise a range of jobs and which businesses may use. Many businesses also have their own websites on which they advertise their vacancies.

The main advantages of using the Internet are that it:

- is not expensive
- has a wide audience
- attracts candidates who are up to date with the latest technology.

Figure 2.6

ACTIVITY

Imagine you are looking for a job. Write down details of two disadvantages which using the Internet would have for you.

Department for Employment and Learning

Part of the work of the Department for Employment and Learning is to help employers to find suitable employees.

JobCentres are found throughout Northern Ireland and are situated in:

Belfast (4)	Antrim	Armagh	Ballymena
Ballymoney	Ballynahinch	Banbridge	Bangor
Carrickfergus	Coleraine	Cookstown	Downpatrick
Dungannon	Enniskillen	Kilkeel	Larne
Limavady	Lisburn	Londonderry (3)	Lurgan
Magherafelt	Newcastle	Newry	Newtownabbey
Newtownards	Omagh	Portadown	Strabane

JobCentres are run by the Government and display notices about available work on behalf of employers. They do this on notice boards in the centres, via the Internet, on local radio, and in newspapers. Job vacancies may also be viewed at www.jobcentreonline.com.

People who are unemployed, or are interested in a change of job, visit the JobCentres to find information and obtain advice about job vacancies and training courses. The JobCentres will help people to apply for suitable jobs and the big advantage is that the service is free.

This method of recruitment is often used for finding workers who are skilled or semi-skilled, such as factory workers, shop assistants and cleaners.

Many JobCentres now share the same premises as the Social Security Offices. These joint offices are known as Jobs and Benefits Offices where people can not only look for work but also find out about state benefits to which they may be entitled.

ACTIVITY

If you have access to the Internet, search the JobCentre website (www.jobcentreonline.com.) and make a list of any vacancies which would be of interest to you.

Private recruitment agencies

There are several private recruitment agencies in Northern Ireland which offer the service of finding suitable candidates for available positions. Some examples are Grafton Recruitment, Diamond Recruitment Employment Agency and Lynn Recruitment.

People looking for work register with the agency and employers contact the agency with details of available work. The agency matches the candidate with the most suitable work available. When a person is appointed, the business pays the agency for the service.

The advantage is that time is saved by the employer which is very useful when a temporary worker is required quickly, for example to fill an absence due to illness in an office. However, the service is expensive.

ACTIVITY

In your notebook, write the name of the most suitable method of recruitment for each of the following positions:

a A part-time office cleaner in Limavady
b The Principal of Belfast Royal Academy
c A forklift operator in a hardware business in Enniskillen
d A qualified physiotherapist in Daisy Hill Hospital, Newry
e A sales assistant for a supermarket in Coleraine
f A clerical officer, needed for two weeks, in an office in Strabane.

EXAMINATION QUESTION

Candy Box Ltd is a small company that specialises in the production of chocolates. It needs to recruit a new Personal Secretary to the Managing Director. The Human Resources department has been told to place a job advertisement in the *Belfast Telegraph*.

a Give details of factors which would have influenced the choice of medium used to advertise the post.
(4 marks)

b Identify one other medium which Candy Box could have used to advertise the post.
(1 mark)

(Adapted from CCEA Business Studies, GCSE, Paper 2 Higher Tier, 2000)

Tips for answering this question:

a In this case you would be expected to name and give details of two factors.
b In Part B you should simply name one other suitable method, making sure that it is suitable for use in Candy Box Ltd. Do not take time to explain the method – there is only one mark for Part B.

Types of Employee

Employers need to recruit several different types of employee. For this purpose, employees may be classified as skilled, semi-skilled or multi-skilled

Skilled

A skilled employee is defined as one whose job requires a high level of training and for which the worker needs qualifications. Examples of such occupations are mechanics and computer operators.

Semi-skilled

A semi-skilled employee is one whose job is only partly skilled. Various processes in the job may require training while other processes may not require training.

An example would be a person responsible for stocking shelves in a supermarket. The actual stacking of goods on the shelves would not require qualifications. However, the employee may also have to complete stock records on the computer and this aspect of the job would need training.

Figure 2.7
A mechanic at work

Multi-skilled

Modern industry requires very different roles and skills than were required in the past. Routine jobs on an assembly line for example, are now done by machine so fewer workers are needed to do these tasks.

As a result, there is a move away from unskilled manual work into more highly skilled and specialised work. This has meant that each worker now needs to be able to undertake a number of separate tasks within a business. This is known as multi-skilling.

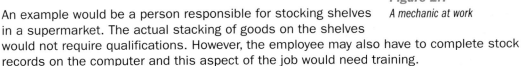

ACTIVITY

a   Make a list of four occupations which need skilled employees. Give details of the skills required in each occupation.
b   Make a list of four occupations which need unskilled employees.

Factors affecting job satisfaction

> Job satisfaction is defined as the degree of happiness a person gets from his or her work.

If an employee is to reach his/her full potential and do his/her best work, it is extremely important that he/she enjoys his/her work and gets a high degree of job satisfaction from it.

There are several factors which increase a person's job satisfaction:

- Wages/salaries
  Money is obviously a very big factor in any job. People work in order to earn enough money to buy the goods they need and to be able to have some luxury in their lives. However, money alone is not enough!

- Responsibility

  Employees need to be given responsibility in the business. They want to achieve some status so they also need to have opportunities to apply for and be given promotion.

- Fulfilment

  People get job satisfaction from doing a good piece of work, so a sense of achievement is important.

- Enjoyment

  Enjoying the work is also an important factor in job satisfaction and it is vital to find work which you are happy doing.

- Good working conditions

  The conditions in the workplace can also affect job satisfaction. Such conditions could include a pleasant environment with warm, well-lit buildings for example.

  The other people in the workplace also can have a major effect. Liking the people working with you makes the job much more enjoyable and increases job satisfaction to a significant degree.

- Praise

  Everyone responds to praise and wants to feel valued as an employee. Job satisfaction improves if the employer has a good relationship with his staff and recognises their effort and contribution to the business.

ACTIVITY

Make a list of the factors which give you job satisfaction in your GCSE work.
What steps could you take in order to improve your job satisfaction?

REVISION

At this stage you should understand:

Retirement	Resignation	Promotion
Dismissal	Recruitment	Needs analysis
Job analysis	Job description	Person specification
Applications	Shortlist	Contract of employment
Internal recruitment	External recruitment	Skilled employee
Semi-skilled employee	Multi-skilled employee	Job satisfaction

As revision, look each one up in the Glossary at the end of the book.

Legal Controls on Recruitment in Northern Ireland

UNIT 2.3

> Certain legal controls have been introduced to prevent discrimination at work. The following laws must be observed and are designed to protect minority groups such as women, the disabled, and people coming from other countries and cultures.

All recruitment in Northern Ireland is controlled by:

- Sex Discrimination (Northern Ireland) Order 1976 (amended 1988)
- Disability Discrimination Act 1995
- Race Relations (Northern Ireland) Order 1997
- Equal Pay Act (Northern Ireland) 1970 (amended 1984)
- Fair Employment and Treatment (Northern Ireland) Order 1998.

Sex Discrimination (Northern Ireland) Order 1976 (amended 1988)

The Sex Discrimination (Northern Ireland) Order 1976 and its 1988 amendment forbid discrimination on the basis of a person's gender.

It is also unlawful to discriminate against someone because he/she is married.

This Order states that men and women should have equal treatment and opportunity:

- when employers are advertising for applicants for jobs
- in the recruitment and selection of employees
- in the promotion of employees
- when employers are setting rates of pay and other conditions in jobs.

Other issues such as pregnancy and maternity rights, training, sexual harassment, terms and conditions of employment, retirement and pensions are also covered by this legislation.

The employer would also be breaking this law if he/she knowingly allowed employees to discriminate against other employees on the ground of their gender.

Disability Discrimination Act 1995

The Disability Discrimination Act 1995 makes it unlawful to treat disabled people less favourably than other people in employment.

This Act defines disability as: 'a physical or mental impairment which has a substantial and long-term adverse effect on a person's ability to carry out normal day-to-day activities'.

Under the Disability Discrimination Act 1995, discrimination occurs where:

- a disabled person is treated less favourably than someone else
- the treatment is for a reason relating to the person's disability
- the treatment cannot be justified.

Discrimination also occurs when there is a failure to make a reasonable adjustment for a disabled person and that failure cannot be justified.

Race Relations (Northern Ireland) Order 1997

Under this Order, people of all races, colours, nationalities or ethnic origin must be treated equally during the recruitment process, in employment and in training

It is racial discrimination to treat a person less favourably on racial grounds than another person would be treated in the same circumstances. For example, if an employer set conditions or requirements which would be difficult for a person of another colour or race to meet, then he/she would be guilty of racial discrimination.

The Race Relations (Northern Ireland) Order makes particular mention of Irish Travellers and makes it illegal to discriminate against them.

As with the Sex Discrimination Order, the employer would be liable if he/she allowed any of his/her employees to discriminate against other employees in the business.

There are exceptions to the Race Relations (Northern Ireland) Order 1997. In each of the following circumstances, the Order would not have been broken where:

- a person of a particular racial group is required for a job – for example, in a dramatic performance or as a photographic model
- welfare services are being provided to a particular racial group and those services can best be provided by a person of the same racial group – social workers, for example.
- the employment is in a private household
- the employment is in a small business where there are fewer than six partners
- the employment involves working outside Northern Ireland for most of the time.

Equal Pay Act (Northern Ireland) 1970 (amended 1984)

This Act states that women performing the same, or broadly similar, work to men must be treated in the same way as men.

They must be paid the same, and must have the same conditions of service as men.

The Equal Pay Act applies to all full-time and part-time work and to all sizes of business.

It is important to note that, to receive equal pay, the woman's work need not be exactly the same as the man's work. It must be of 'equal value'. This means that it must be equally demanding or equally skilful and require equal levels of knowledge, decision-making and responsibility. This idea of equal value was introduced by the amendment regulations in 1984.

Fair Employment and Treatment (Northern Ireland) Order 1998

The Fair Employment and Treatment (Northern Ireland) Order 1998 updates the Fair Employment Acts of 1976 and 1989.

This Order was passed to ensure that people of all religious beliefs and political opinion in Northern Ireland have equal opportunities in employment.

In order to comply with fair employment rules, employers must:

- register with the Equality Commission if they employ more than 10 people
- annually submit information about the religious composition of the workforce – including part-time employees
- submit information on people who have applied for jobs
- retain all information for three years so that their practices can be examined over a period
- review their practices at least once every three years
- create a 'neutral area' in the workplace. This means that they must prohibit the display of flags, emblems, posters and graffiti or the circulation of materials or the singing of songs which would give offence or cause fear.

Not all types of employment are covered by the fair employment laws. The main exceptions are:

a any occupation where the nature of the job requires it to be done by a person holding a particular religious belief or political opinion – a minister of religion, for example
b employment which is wholly outside Northern Ireland.

Responsibility for implementing the fair employment legislation now rests with the Equality Commission (before the 1998 Order that responsibility was undertaken by the Fair Employment Commission).

It is the duty of the Commission to:

- work to eliminate religious discrimination
- give advice to employers on their practices
- help anyone who has a complaint and requests advice.

The Equality Commission has powers to investigate any employer any time and, if necessary, to bring an employer before a fair employment tribunal. The Commission may also issue directions on measures which must be taken by employers. (For further details, refer to the section on the Equality Commission on pages 134–5.)

The court to which the Equality Commission would bring its legal cases is called the Fair Employment Tribunal.

This Tribunal has two functions:

a It decides on individual cases of discrimination. It has power to award damages for financial loss, for loss of opportunity or for injury to feelings.
b It hears appeals against directions of the Equality Commission. The tribunal has power to take steps to force employers to comply and can impose fines on them if necessary.

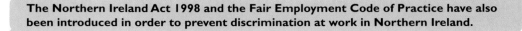

The Northern Ireland Act 1998 and the Fair Employment Code of Practice have also been introduced in order to prevent discrimination at work in Northern Ireland.

Northern Ireland Act 1998

The Northern Ireland Act 1998 applies to all public-sector employers.

This Act obliges public-sector employers to draw up Equality Schemes and covers equality in the public sector in all employment matters such as recruitment, selection and promotion.

ACTIVITY

Copy and complete the following sentences in your notebook.

a   Legal controls aim to prevent ………….. at work. They are designed to protect groups such as ….. and the ……..

b   The Sex Discrimination (Northern Ireland) Order forbids discrimination on the basis of a person's ……. or because he/she is …….

c   … … ………….. ….. states that men and women should have equal treatment and opportunity.

d   The Disability Discrimination Act 1995 states that it is unlawful to treat …….. people less favourably than other people in employment.

e   … ………. ………….. … would be broken if an employer did not make adjustments to the work premises for a disabled person.

f   … …. ………. …… makes it illegal to discriminate against Irish Travellers.

g   Two exceptions to the Race Relations (Northern Ireland) Order 1997 are when ……. services are being provided or the work is in a ……. …..

h   Under the terms of the …. ………. ….. people of all races must be treated equally in employment.

i   The …… … Act states that women performing the same, or broadly similar, work as … must be paid the same, and must have the same ………. of service as ….

j   The …. ………. … ……… Order was passed to ensure that people of all ……… beliefs and ……… opinion in Northern Ireland have equal opportunities in ………..

Fair Employment Code of Practice

The Fair Employment Code of Practice has been drawn up by the Equality Commission and acts as a guideline for employers in all matters relating to employment. It lays down procedures for employers to follow.

The Code of Practice has no legal standing, however employers would be unlikely to be seen to be acting within the law if they did not follow the Code.

EXAMINATION QUESTION

Explain how government legislation could affect a business's recruitment procedure.

(4 marks)

(Adapted from CCEA Business Studies, GCSE, Paper 2 Foundation Tier, 2000)

Tips for answering this question:

Note that there are 4 marks for this question. To gain full marks, you should name and give details of any two laws which affect recruitment.

ACTIVITY

You have to decide which law has been broken in each of the following situations:

a   No car parking spaces were reserved for disabled employees
b   A woman was not given a job because she was married
c   Irish Travellers were refused part-time jobs
d   The pay structure in a company stated that male secretaries would be paid £1 per hour above the rate paid to female secretaries
e   The business's main building had no wheelchair access
f   The business refused to employ any Chinese workers
g   Political slogans were allowed on factory walls
h   A job advertisement stated that only women need apply.

Moral and Ethical Issues Underlying Anti-Discrimination Legislation

All the laws you have just studied have been introduced so that proper rules of conduct are applied to recruitment, and that discrimination at work is prevented.

The moral foundation of the legislation is that the most vulnerable groups in society – women, the disabled and foreigners – are protected and given their rights.

The government, in passing such laws, is making sure that employers behave in a moral and ethical way. They are obliged to treat all their employees equally and with respect. The underlying principle here is that everyone is equal in the eyes of the law, and therefore each one is entitled to equal treatment. In recruitment terms, the result should be that the best person is employed or given promotion regardless of that person's gender, religion, political opinion or physical ability.

The Sex Discrimination (Northern Ireland) Order makes sure that men and women are given equal opportunities in employment. A woman who has good qualifications and experience must be given the same chance to gain promotion as the men in the business. She cannot be refused a job, for example, because she may have to take maternity leave.

The Equal Pay Act (Northern Ireland) makes sure that a woman is treated in a morally correct way, and is given pay equal to that of her male colleagues where the work she does is of equal value.

Figure 2.8

The Fair Employment and Treatment (Northern Ireland) Order was passed to make sure that people of all religions or political beliefs are given equal opportunities to get employment.

The Disability Discrimination Act was introduced to ensure that people who are disabled are given opportunities to work. Where their qualifications are adequate, disabled people must be treated equally with able-bodied people in the recruitment process. Employers are obliged to overcome any physical difficulties in their premises by installing ramps, lifts and special toilets. In this way, the legislation recognises the contribution which the disabled make to the business world and ensures that their disability does not prevent them from making that contribution.

The Race Relations (Northern Ireland) Order was designed to make sure that it would be possible for people from other cultures and races to get employment in Northern Ireland. As well as people from other cultures and races, this Act covers people of all skin colours and members of the Irish Travelling Community.

Role of the Equality Commission for Northern Ireland

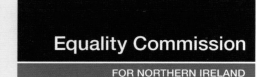

The Equality Commission for Northern Ireland was established under the Northern Ireland Act 1998. Its aim is to help build a more equal society in Northern Ireland.

The Commission's mission statement illustrates this aim:

Combating discrimination and promoting equality of opportunity through advice, promotion and enforcement.

How does the Equality Commission do this?

Its duties include:

- working to eliminate unlawful discrimination
- promoting equality of opportunity and encouraging good practice
- promoting good relations between people of different racial groups
- keeping the relevant laws under review.

The Commission's main work is to give advice and assistance to people who believe that they have been treated unfairly or discriminated against on grounds of their:

- colour
- race
- nationality
- ethnic or national origin (including being an Irish Traveller)

- religious belief
- political opinion
- gender
- sexual orientation
- married status
- disability.

In cases where legal action is needed, the Commission will arrange legal representation. It can take legal action against individuals and organisations in some circumstances – for example, if they have published an advertisement which discriminates against someone from one of the groups shown in the above list.

The Commission also sees that the law on equality is enforced in order to bring about greater equality in the world of work and in society in general. The Commission has powers to ensure that employers monitor and review their employment practices as well as the composition of their workforce. For example, employers must show that they are willing to employ:

- both men and women
- both single and married workers
- people with different religious or political opinions
- people of any race or ethnic origin
- people with disabilities.

In addition, the Commission will:

- provide information, advisory and training services
- publish Codes of Practice which set standards for fairness and equality in employment, pay, housing and the provision of goods and services
- make sure that public sector organisations take equality into account
- undertake research into equality issues
- award grants for promotional and educational work and
- carry out public education campaigns to raise awareness of equality issues.

ACTIVITY

Copy and complete the following sentences in your notebook.

a   The Equality Commission works to eliminate .... discrimination. It has powers to bring an employer before a ....

b   In order to comply with the rules of the .... Commission, employers must register with the Commission if they employ more than ... people and must retain all information for ..... years.

c   Employers also must create a .... in the workplace so they must not allow the display of ..... or the singing of ..... which would cause fear.

d   The Northern Ireland Act 1998 applies to all .... employers who must draw up ....

e   The Fair Employment Code of Practice has been drawn up by the .... and acts as a guideline for ....

ACTIVITY

Study the following and answer the questions at the end:

A woman was absent from her company on maternity leave. During her absence, two promotion posts were advertised internally and filled without her being told about the positions.

She said that the company was guilty of discrimination against her because of her sex and pregnancy. She argued that because she was not told about the posts, she had not been able to apply for promotion.

a   In your opinion, is the woman's allegation of discrimination reasonable?
b   If so, which law was broken?
c   What action would you have advised the company to take when advertising the post?

REVISION

At this stage you should understand:

The provisions of the:

- Sex Discrimination (Northern Ireland) Order 1976 (amended 1988)
- Disability Discrimination Act 1995
- Race Relations (Northern Ireland) Order 1997
- Equal Pay Act (Northern Ireland), 1970 (amended 1984)
- Fair Employment and Treatment (Northern Ireland) Order 1998
- Fair Employment Code of Practice.

The work of the:

- Equality Commission for Northern Ireland.

As revision, read over the details of each one again.

Selection

Methods of selection

After the recruitment stage, the next step is for the employer to choose the new employee from the list of applicants who have applied for the position. This is known as the selection process.

In order to choose the most suitable applicant, it is important for the employer to find as much information as possible about all the applicants.

To do this, the following six methods of selection are most commonly used:

When you become involved in the selection process, remember that this is the first impression the employer will have of you, and first impressions do count. You never get a second chance to make a first impression!

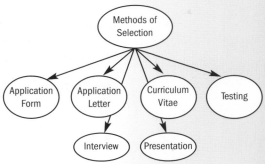

Application form

Sometimes an employer asks the applicants to complete a form on which they must answer all questions. An application form may be used because it has the advantage that the applicant is giving exactly the type of information the employer needs, making it easy for the employer to compare applicants.

When completing an application form it is important to:

- work neatly and accurately
- complete all sections
- work in black or blue ink – NEVER in pencil
- sign and date the form
- check that all details are correct – untrue information would rule out your application.

Application letter

Sometimes the advertisement states that the applicant should reply by writing a letter of application. An employer may ask for an application letter because it shows the employer the level of the applicant's communication skills.

An applicant for a job has to show in the application letter that he/she is suitable for the post. The letter should make the employer want to meet the applicant.

To do this, an application letter should include the applicant's:

- personal details
- educational background
- qualifications and work experience
- names of previous employers

- names and addresses of two referees
- details of personal hobbies, interests and achievements.

All the rules for completing an application form also apply when writing a letter of application – work neatly and accurately, complete all sections, use black or blue ink and check all details.

Figure 2.9
Dungannon and South Tyrone Borough Council headquarters

ACTIVITY

Dungannon and South Tyrone Borough Council

Tourist Information Receptionist
Required for
Killymaddy Tourist Information Centre,
Ballygawley Road, Dungannon.

37 hours per week
Salary Scale £9,267 – £12,390 per annum

Applicants for the above post should have a minimum of:
6 GCSEs (Grades A–C) including English Language
Ability to speak a foreign language desirable

Application by letter to be received by the Human Resources Section
Dungannon and South Tyrone Borough Council
Circular Road, Dungannon BT71 6DT
by 5 December 20..

You should now write a letter of application, on your own behalf, for the position in the Tourist Information Centre.

Curriculum vitae

Sometimes the advertisement asks the applicant to include a curriculum vitae (CV).

A curriculum vitae is simply a list of all the applicant's qualifications, work and achievements to that date. An employer may ask for a CV because it shows all the applicant's details and it also shows how well the applicant can organise and display information.

There is a standard format for a curriculum vitae and it includes the applicant's:

- personal details – name, address, telephone number, nationality, marital status and date of birth
- educational background
- qualifications
- work experience
- positions of responsibility
- previous employers
- two referees
- personal hobbies and interests
- other achievements.

ACTIVITY

You are now ready to design your own curriculum vitae. Begin by listing all the results of examinations you have sat, sports awards you have achieved, trips you have gone on, details of your work experience and any school positions you hold or have held such as prefect or librarian.

Use a computer to arrange all that information, plus your personal details, under the headings given above. Later, you can add to the CV as you pass more examinations etc.

EXAMINATION QUESTION

TRAVEL CONSULTANT
required by
MILLIKEN TRAVEL

The applicant should have 2 years' experience in an ABTA travel agency and be competent in the use of computers

Applications by letter enclosing CV to
4 Castle Street, Bangor, Co Down, BT20 4ST

Examine the extent to which a curriculum vitae is a suitable method of selection for the above position.

(6 marks)

(Adapted from CCEA Business Studies, GCSE, Paper I Higher Tier, 2002)

Tips for answering this question:

Here you are asked to 'examine' the extent to which the curriculum vitae is suitable. To 'examine' is to use one of the higher order skills, so there are 6 marks allocated in total. To gain those 6 marks you should select at least two reasons why the curriculum vitae is suitable, giving details and reasons.

If you feel the CV is unsuitable you may state this, but you should also back up your view with two reasons.

When the employers receive all the application forms, letters and CVs they will sort them into two groups – suitable and unsuitable applicants. The 'suitable' group will include those who meet all the criteria in the advertisement, and the 'unsuitable' group will include those who do not meet the criteria.

Unsuitable applicants are then informed by letter that they have been unsuccessful and suitable applicants are invited to undertake a test or an interview or give a presentation.

Figure 2.10

Testing

Two types of tests are frequently used – practical tests and psychometric tests.

Practical tests are more usual in the selection process for manual, practical jobs. In a practical test the applicant would be asked to undertake a piece of work which would test skills required in the business. For example, an applicant for the job of a computer operator may be asked to key in a letter or construct a database. This shows the employer whether the applicant's computer skills reach the level required in the business.

Psychometric tests are usually used when management level positions are being filled. Psychometric tests provide a description of the personality of the applicant, and the results are compared with the person specification. The applicants have to answer multiple choice questions about themselves which are designed to show what they like or dislike and how they would react in certain situations.

Figure 2.11

Interview

Interviews are very frequently used in the selection process. The applicants who have been shortlisted are invited to an interview where they meet representatives of the business to answer questions and discuss the post.

At the interview, all interviewees are asked the same questions and given the same time so that the employer can later compare the answers given.

Interviews are useful because they give employers the opportunity to meet applicants and to judge how suitable they would be in that particular job.

It is important for the applicant to:

- prepare thoroughly for an interview
- do research on the company
- dress suitably
- act naturally in the interview
- show a genuine interest in the business
- arrive in good time.

ACTIVITY

Refer back to the position in the Tourist Information Centre for which you wrote an application letter. You have just heard that you are being interviewed for the job.

a   Draft three questions which you think you may be asked.
b   Draft one question which would be appropriate for you to ask at the interview.
c   What else might you do to prepare for the interview?

EXAMINATION QUESTION

Explain the benefits of using interviews to select the successful applicant from those shortlisted for the position of Travel Consultant in Milliken Travel.

(4 marks)

(Adapted from CCEA Business Studies, GCSE, Paper I Higher Tier, 2002)

Tips for answering this question:

You are required to 'explain' the benefit of using interviews. To be awarded the 4 marks, you should name two benefits and state why they would be useful in selecting the successful candidate – this question is really asking for the advantages of an interview, from the employer's point of view.

Presentation

It is now common for applicants for management positions to be asked to give a presentation as well as be interviewed.

In this situation, the applicant would be given a title in advance and told the length of time the presentation should last.

The applicant would be expected to talk on the prepared subject which would be related to the work of the particular post. For example, applicants for a shop manager's post may be asked to speak on their ideas for motivating staff or increasing turnover.

Presentations are used by employers because they show the personality of the applicants as well as their communication skills, level of preparation and ideas about the job.

Figure 2.12

ACTIVITY

You have been asked to make a presentation when you attend the interview for the position in the Tourist Information Centre. You have been given the topic in advance and the title is 'The importance of the role of the Tourist Information Receptionist'. You have to speak for a maximum of five minutes and may use Powerpoint or an overhead projector if you wish.

Prepare your presentation for use at the interview.

Responsibilities of employers and employees in the selection process

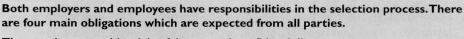

> Both employers and employees have responsibilities in the selection process. There are four main obligations which are expected from all parties.
>
> They are honesty, objectivity, fairness and confidentiality.

Honesty

It is expected that both employer and employee would be totally honest with each other. For example, documents provided by the employer, such as the job description or advertisement, must be accurate and clear. All other information given about the job – for example pay or holidays – would be expected to be totally honest.

The employees must also provide honest information regarding such details as their qualifications and experience. No information should be left out by the employee if it would influence the final decision – a criminal record, for example.

Objectivity

Both parties are expected to be totally without prejudice about each other. For example, the employer could not reject applicants simply because of their religious, political or social background. The employer has a responsibility to find the best person for the position, regardless of any other consideration.

Fairness

Total fairness is required by all parties. The employer, for example, must allocate equal time and consideration to each candidate in an interview and must ask the same questions to everyone. The same conditions must be applied to each person.

The employee must also be totally fair by disclosing full and accurate information.

Confidentiality

Both employee and employer must treat all information learned about each other as strictly confidential. The employee must not talk to others about details of the business and the employer must not give personal details of the applicants to third parties.

ACTIVITY

In the following wordsearch, find the words shown in the list. The words can be read in straight lines, horizontally, vertically or diagonally, either backwards or forwards. There is no overlap of words in the grid.

selection	applicant	form	letter	curriculum
vitae	interview	test	job	psychometric
shortlist	honesty	objectivity	fairness	confidentiality

Activity continues on next page

Activity continued

```
S M H T I N T E R N A R E T T E L
E U O P J W E N G A D A O R B A K
L P N I E R O B J E C T I V I T Y
E W E L I U A A S B R O C H S K G
C L S R S H O R T L I S T L P D S
T A T X S L E K C C G T I C M P O
I L Y C J O B E I N T E R V I E W
O U P E N C T T P Q I P Y C M U A
N X Y E P S Y C H O M E T R I C
X O D D E R Y N N H O S M T D E I
C U R R I C U L U M B C U T I K L
E B R V Y T I O I U Q B V I T A E
C O N F I D E N T I A L I T Y R P
E I I X A I P R T U E M A U T U Y
T E S T U N A L B S S E N R I A F
P X C V B E U F H H K J L I O O B
A P P L I C A N T I R E G M R O F
```

REVISION

At this stage you should understand:

a Details of the various methods of selection:

application form	application letter	curriculum vitae
testing	interview	presentation

b Responsibilities of employers and employees in the selection process.

As revision, look each one up in the Glossary at the end of the book.

UNIT 2.5

Training

Training is defined as 'the acquisition of knowledge and skills which can be applied to a particular job'.

Regular training is needed in modern industry because:

- constant changes in technology need updated skills
- introduction of new methods needs new information
- a highly trained workforce is more efficient
- it helps the business to keep ahead of its competitors
- it provides motivation for employees
- it decreases the possibility of accidents in the workplace
- it decreases the supervision required for employees.

Employees who do not retrain and keep up to date with modern trends risk becoming redundant.

Purpose of Training

There are four major purposes in training:

1. to introduce new employees to the business
2. to introduce employees to new equipment or methods
3. to improve the efficiency of the employees
4. to lessen the possibility of accidents in the workplace.

Employers realise that their most valuable resource is their employees. Therefore they are anxious to have a highly trained and well motivated workforce and are willing to invest considerable sums of money into training programmes.

The Chairman of the Northern Ireland Skills Task Force makes the point in a recent article in the *Belfast Telegraph*:

Purpose of training

| to introduce new employees | to introduce new equipment or methods |
| to improve efficiency | to lessen possibility of accidents |

It pays to develop workforce

The chairman of the Northern Ireland Skills Task Force insists developing workforce skills is a must for Ulster businesses.

Bill McGinnis said that it was clear that Northern Ireland employers needed to develop a world-class workforce as their key competitive asset.

"The biggest impact we can make on workforce skills is through those currently in employment, most of whom will still be working by 2010," he said.

"Workforce development and excellence in human resource practices are critical elements in helping employers develop the

skills sets they need, in helping individuals achieve their career goals, and in helping the economy compete and thrive in the information age.

Importance of Training

Businesses undertake constant training which they consider important from the point of view of both the business and the employees for the following reasons:

- multi-skilled workers are flexible and can undertake different jobs in the business
- training keeps employees up to date with new technology and new methods
- training enables employees to learn new skills and become more effective
- having more effective employees improves the quality of the business's products which will lead to increased sales and profits for the business

Figure 2.13

- highly trained employees have better opportunities for promotion in the business
- highly trained employees are better motivated
- a business which has a highly trained staff and uses up-to-date methods earns a good reputation both as an employer and as a competitor in the marketplace.

Types of Training

Induction training

Can you remember your first days in your present school? it is likely that you spent the first days being shown around and becoming familiar with the new surroundings. You were told how things were done in the new school and were introduced to the people you needed to know. That process was your 'induction'.

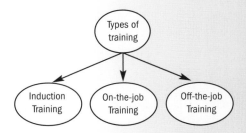

Induction also happens in business, and is the name given to the training of new employees. It is designed to make new employees feel comfortable in the new workplace and to help them to fit in to their new surroundings. Induction enables new employees to understand the ethos and work of the organisation and to play their part more efficiently.

The content of the induction programme would vary from business to business. It usually includes:

- a guided tour of the buildings
- an introduction to work colleagues and line manager
- a talk or video on the business's rules
- explanation of the business's health and safety procedures.

Write the answer to the following questions in your notebook

a   Name two benefits which induction has for a new employee in a business.

b   Give details of one benefit which induction has for the company.

On-the-job training

On-the-job training is the most common form of training for unskilled and semi-skilled workers. It is training given at the employee's normal place of work during his/her normal working hours.

On-the-job training may be done in a variety of ways:

1. Internal courses

   Sometimes employers run courses inside their own business and use their own machinery and equipment. This means that the content of the course is designed specifically for that business.

   This method is very effective because the employee is shown how to do the work and can practise it under supervision.

2. Work shadowing

   Sometimes the new employee 'shadows' an experienced employee. This means that they work alongside one another and the trainee learns from the experienced worker.

3. Role play

   Sometimes role play is used. In this method a 'make believe' situation is created, and the employees have to work out how they would solve the problem.

Figure 2.14
On-the-job training in hairdressing

the employees have to work out how they would solve the problem.

On-the-job training has several advantages:

a the content of the course is designed specifically for the business
b it is usually more economical because the work of the business is not interrupted
c training is given to each individual

ACTIVITY

In certain circumstances, on-the-job training can have one major disadvantage. Think what this disadvantage might be and write it down in your notebook, giving it the title 'Disadvantage of On-the-job training'.

d everyone knows one another
e employees feel at home in their own surroundings.

Off-the-job training

Off-the-job training is training provided by a specialist and takes place outside the business – perhaps at a training centre, college or university. The training is paid for by the business and may be on a day release basis or for a longer period of attendance at a full-time course for a term or longer.

Figure 2.15

Off-the-job training may be done in a variety of ways:

1. Lectures
   Sometimes employees attend lectures where they are given information which they can later apply in their work.
2. Demonstrations
   Demonstrations are effective for showing how tasks should be done. The trainee watches the expert but then must be given an opportunity to practise the skill.
3. Role play
   Role play is used in both on-the-job and off-the-job training and is undertaken to imitate a real-life situation.

Off-the-job training has the following advantages:

a since the training is done by specialists, it usually is of a higher quality
b employees meet people from other organisations and can exchange ideas
c employees visit a new environment and perhaps are introduced to new equipment
d employees can attend evening classes which means they do not miss their work and this reduces the cost.

ACTIVITY

Write down the most appropriate method of training for each of the following situations:

1. A business has replaced all 10 of the office computers. All 10 of the office workers need to learn how to use the new computers.
2. An engineering firm has installed one new machine. The firm has no experience of this type of machinery. Pearl will be working on the new machine but is unfamiliar with it.
3. A school is introducing a new subject to its curriculum and two teachers – Miss Todd and Mr Kenny – have been told they will be teaching the subject next year. They need help.
4. Brian is starting work as a hotel waiter next month. He has not done this type of work before.
5. Joan is working as a hairdresser but would like to extend her hairdressing skills in order to get promotion in the salon.
6. Billy is tired of his work as a civil servant and has decided to open a garden centre. He needs to learn more about growing garden plants.
7. Lillian has decided to join Billy in the garden centre to look after the office work. She has been a housewife for many years but had done clerical work before her marriage.

EXAMINATION QUESTION

Quality Doors Ltd has a factory in Co Fermanagh and is a hi-tech business manufacturing doors for kitchen and bedroom furniture on a large scale. The business has a highly trained workforce and takes pride in using the latest technology.

Recommend the methods of training which Quality Doors should use for its production staff.

(6 marks)

(Adapted from CCEA Business Studies, GCSE, Paper 2 Foundation Tier, 2002)

Tips for answering this question:

In this question you are asked to 'recommend' methods. To do this you have to name at least two training methods which would be useful and beneficial to the business. You must then give your reasons why these methods would work well in that particular business.

REVISION

At this stage you should understand the following terms:

Induction	On-the-job training	Off-the-job training
Internal training	External training	Work shadowing

As revision, look each one up in the Glossary at the end of the book.

Motivation

> Motivation is the way in which a person can be encouraged to make an effort to do something.

> Many studies have been carried out on what makes people want to work. Probably the most famous of these studies was by Abraham Maslow, an American psychologist who died in 1970.

Maslow concluded that people have five levels of need which he illustrated in a 'Hierarchy of Needs' pyramid. He placed the most basic needs at the bottom of the pyramid and the most advanced needs at the top of the pyramid. According to Maslow, when people satisfy one level of need, they then move up to the next level.

In his theory, the most basic need is to survive – to have enough money to buy food, shelter and necessary clothes. When they have satisfied the need for **survival**, they then need to feel safe and secure – perhaps from unemployment – so the second level of need is for **security**. After that, people need to belong to a group and to have friends – these are their **social** needs. They then move on to needing **status**. At this stage they need to be respected in the community, to be esteemed, and to be given recognition for what they do. When all these needs have been satisfied, people finally have **self-actualisation** (**or self-fulfilment**) needs. This is ambition to achieve as much as they possibly can – perhaps to be promoted to a high-level position with more responsibility.

Maslow's Hierarchy of Needs

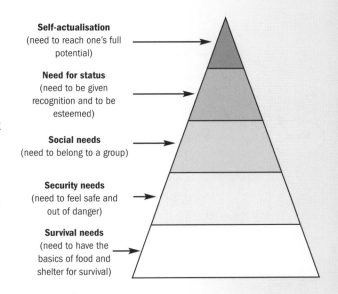

Self-actualisation
(need to reach one's full potential)

Need for status
(need to be given recognition and to be esteemed)

Social needs
(need to belong to a group)

Security needs
(need to feel safe and out of danger)

Survival needs
(need to have the basics of food and shelter for survival)

Importance of Motivation

Obviously, it is very important for a business to have well-motivated employees. This is because highly motivated employees:

- will probably work harder
- are likely to produce a higher quality of work
- are less liable to take time off.

ACTIVITY

A generous pay system is a good incentive for workers, but money alone is not enough! Maslow's theory has shown that employees need to feel valued in the workplace, they need to feel they belong, and they need to be rewarded for good work.

For these reasons, employers introduce a variety of methods of motivation which offer rewards to employees usually in addition to their basic pay. These methods of motivation may or may not be for money – in other words, they may be either financial or non-financial.

Financial Methods of Motivation

Bonus

A bonus is an extra payment made to employees who work well and help the business, for example, to complete its orders on time or to meet its sales targets. It is paid as a lump sum, usually either at Christmas or at the beginning of the summer holidays.

Bonus payments encourage employees to work harder. The advantage for the employees is that they can increase their income while the employer has the advantage of greater production, resulting in higher sales and profits.

Commission

Commission is an extra financial reward which is most suitable for a sales person. It is calculated as a percentage of the sales which that person makes. For example, if the commission is 10% and the sales person's sales amounted to £8,000, then the total commission that person would earn would be £800 on top of his salary.

Commission payments encourage sales staff to increase their sales. In this way the sales staff increase their income while the business sells more goods and makes more profit.

Profit sharing

Under a profit-sharing scheme, employees receive a share of the profit made by the business in addition to their basic salary.

Profit sharing acts as a good motivator for employees because it encourages them to increase the business's output and profits of which they can then own a share. It also has the advantage that the employees feel a greater sense of belonging to the business and take a greater interest in its success.

Profit sharing is most usually found in the service sector because, in that type of work, it is not possible to estimate any single employee's contribution to the profits made in the business. A slight unfairness of the system is that all employees benefit from the profits made in the business – even those who have worked less well and are less deserving.

In August 2002, B&Q made a record payment to their employees after the company's annual profits increased by 14% to £300 million. Around 30,000 employees received 8.25% of their salaries as part of a profit share scheme.

The B&Q Human Resources Director said 'People are the key to B&Q's success. We want to share incentives across the company so that the hard work of every one of our employees is recognised as contributing to the company's success'.

Piece work

In piece work, employees are paid according to the number of products they make. Therefore the harder they work, the more they earn which acts as a motivator to work harder. Usually a basic wage is paid and extra money is paid according to the amount of work completed.

Piece work payment is only possible in the type of job where products can be counted and where the product can be made fairly quickly – in a factory, for example.

Piece work has the advantage for the employer that more goods are likely to be produced while for the employee, it has the advantage of increased earnings.

Figure 2.16

The major disadvantage of piece work is that employees may rush their work and produce poor quality articles which would not sell and would give the business a poor reputation.

ACTIVITY

Thomas, Jane, Beryl and Marina all work for the same company. Study the following details and then write down the method of financial motivation each one receives.

a   Thomas has a management position and each year he receives some of the profits made by the company.
b   Jane is a salesperson for the company and receives a percentage of the sales she makes.
c   Every Christmas, Beryl receives a welcome addition to her wages because the employees have worked hard all year.
d   Marina gets a basic wage but can increase that by producing more goods each week.

EXAMINATION QUESTION

Justify an appropriate financial method of motivation the sales team might receive in addition to their basic salaries.

(4 marks)

(CCEA Business Studies, GCSE, Paper 2 Higher Tier, 2001)

Tips for answering this question:

In your answer you must first decide on, and name, an appropriate method of motivation for sales staff. Then you have to 'justify' your decision. This means you must show **why** that method of motivation is suitable for the sales team.

2 marks would be given for choosing a suitable method and 2 marks would be given for justifying your choice. Notice that the question asks for **an** appropriate method so do not waste time on more than one method – you will not get marks for them.

Non-Financial Methods of Motivation

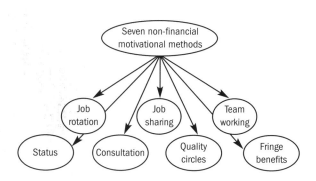

Job rotation

Job rotation is a system in which employees move around different jobs in the business in order to avoid the possibility of them getting bored by doing the same work all the time.

The system has the added advantage of giving opportunities for workers to learn more jobs. Job rotation is suitable for unskilled work and is frequently used for factory workers on production lines.

Job sharing

Job sharing, as the name indicates, is dividing a full-time job between a number of part-time workers – usually two workers. It is becoming very popular, especially in administration, where one worker might, for example, work two days per week and the other might work three days per week.

For job sharing to work efficiently, it is vital that each one pulls his/her weight and that they keep each other informed of the tasks they have undertaken and decisions made.

Team working

In a team-working system, employees are grouped together in teams, making sure that the team has the full range of abilities and skills required to make the product or carry out whatever task they have been set. The team may be given responsibility for how they carry out the work and organise it.

This system has the advantage of making the employees feel more responsible for their own team's decisions. In addition, employees feel committed and will be anxious to make their own team successful so will work hard to make that happen.

Team working increases job satisfaction for employees and improves morale in the workplace.

Status

Employees feel motivated if they have the opportunity to progress to higher-level positions within the business and to take on more responsibility.

To meet this need for status, businesses offer opportunities for employees to improve their education or training by funding them to attend courses which will improve their promotional prospects.

Consultation

Consultation is the process by which management discusses with employees and seeks their views and advice. This consultation might be on matters relating to shop floor practice or the proposed introduction of new procedures or machinery, for example.

Businesses benefit from spreading decision making in this way since they get new ideas and employees feel better motivated and can take ownership of the decisions.

Quality circles

Quality circles originated in Japan where they are used widely and successfully. They have now become very common in this country, possibly because of the spread of Japanese business in the British Isles.

Figure 2.17

The introduction of quality circles is really another approach to team working. Employees are organised into work teams and meet regularly to examine the quality of what they are doing and to try to find ways of doing the job better and improving the quality of the product even further.

Fringe benefits

Fringe benefits – sometimes referred to as perks – come with many occupations and are usually related to the seniority of the employee.

For example, directors and senior managers may be entitled to benefits such as company cars, free use of houses, education fees paid for their children, expense accounts, private health care for themselves and their families, pension schemes and trips abroad.

Factory floor workers may be entitled to benefits such as transport to work, free uniforms, discounts on the business's products, recreational facilities, savings schemes, company shares and luncheon vouchers.

ACTIVITY

Copy out the following diagram of Maslow's Hierarchy of Needs and, inside the brackets, write down which method of motivation would satisfy that need.

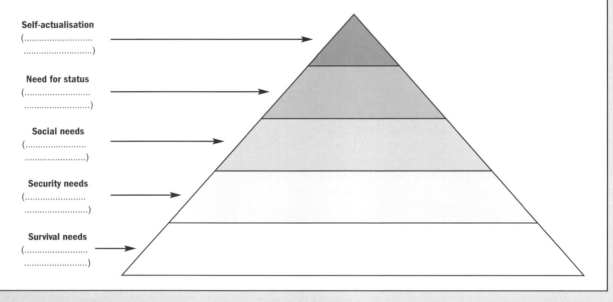

Self-actualisation
(............................
............................)

Need for status
(............................
............................)

Social needs
(............................
............................)

Security needs
(............................
............................)

Survival needs
(............................
............................)

ACTIVITY

You are employed by an agency which has been asked for advice on the type of motivation to offer the following workers. State which method of motivation you think is most appropriate in each case, giving reasons for your decisions.

a Catherine is a sales representative for a fashion company and needs encouragement to increase the company's sales.
b David has been working as a swimming instructor in a leisure centre for several years. He feels that he is 'stuck in a rut' while many of his friends have become leisure centre managers.
c Joyce is a factory supervisor and is good at her job. However she often feels de-motivated because she works hard and she thinks her bosses get all the rewards.
d Patrick is the financial director of the Northern Ireland branch of a multi-national organisation. He agrees that he is very well paid but needs some further encouragement.
e Elizabeth loves her work as a dentist but has a young family and cannot cope with all the demands made on her time.
f George is bored because for years he has been doing the same work on a production line in a toy factory.

EXAMINATION QUESTION

Recommend two non-financial methods of motivation which the business might use to encourage the sales team to increase sales.

(4 marks)

(Adapted from CCEA Business Studies, GCSE, Paper 2 Higher Tier, 2001)

Tips for answering this question:

In your answer you must decide on and name **two** appropriate non-financial methods. Remember that they must be suitable for sales staff.

You are asked to 'recommend' the methods, which means you must show that they are the best methods in the circumstances. This requires an explanation of why they are the best. One mark would be given for choosing each suitable method and one mark would be given for your recommendation or explanation of each method.

REVISION

At this stage you should understand:

Motivation	Bonus	Commission
Profit sharing	Piece work	Job rotation
Job sharing	Team working	Status
Consultation	Quality circles	Fringe benefits

As revision, look each one up in the Glossary at the end of the book.

UNIT 2.7

Appraisal

> Appraisal is the process of assessing an employee's performance in his/her job.

Reasons for Appraisal and its Importance

Employers are always anxious to know how to use their employees most effectively and to be aware of their strengths and weaknesses. Performance appraisal is used to discover this information.

In summary, the reasons for appraisal are:

Appraisal provides feedback to an employee on his/her performance. The system shows how performance could be improved and considers how the employee's career could be developed.

After identifying the employees' strengths and weaknesses through the process of appraisal, the employer may decide to reward employees who are performing well, or possibly to offer training to other employees where appraisal has shown weaknesses.

Appraisal is also frequently used to decide on the level of an employee's salary. In this case, the employee's effectiveness in the business is linked to his/her pay – a system known as 'performance related pay' – which is not appropriate for all types of work.

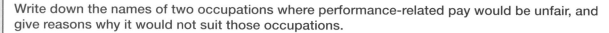

ACTIVITY

Write down the names of two occupations where performance-related pay would be unfair, and give reasons why it would not suit those occupations.

Benefits of Appraisal for Employees and Employers

Appraisal is beneficial for employees because it:

- gives them opportunities for promotion and sets pay levels
- makes sure that they receive training if necessary
- allows them to achieve their full potential

- lets them communicate with the employer on a one-to-one basis
- gives them an opportunity to discuss problems
- provides clear objectives and acts as a motivator.

Appraisal is beneficial for employers because it:

- helps in the planning and development of the business's human resource provision
- shows up staff strengths and allows the business to use the best employees efficiently
- identifies staff weaknesses and helps the business to plan an effective training programme
- increases staff competence and overall productivity
- improves the profitability of the business as a result.

Figure 2.18

ACTIVITY

Andrew is an employee in the accounts section of a large company. He has just been told that his appraisal interview will be held next week. He is nervous, and has come to you for help.

Write down the benefits which Andrew could get from appraisal.

EXAMINATION QUESTION

Explain the benefits for any business of introducing appraisal.

(4 marks)

(adapted from CCEA Business Studies, GCSE, Paper 2 Foundation Tier, 2002)

Tips for answering this question:

You are asked to 'explain' the benefits. In this case there are 4 marks so you should give details of two benefits for a business in introducing appraisal. You are not asked to consider appraisal from the employee's point of view.

Methods of Appraisal and Their Evaluation

There are many methods of staff appraisal and the choice of method depends on the individual business and the type of work it does. The most commonly used ones are discussed here.

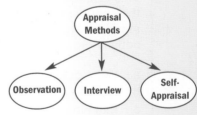

Observation

Observation is where the employee is watched doing his/her work, usually by the person who is that employee's immediate superior. For example, a shop floor worker would be observed by a supervisor and the supervisor may be observed by a manager.

Observation is a useful method of appraisal because:

- it allows employees to be observed in their usual surroundings
- it gives a true picture of employees' work.

However, some employees may find it off-putting to be observed doing their work.

Observation is usually accompanied by an interview.

Interview

An appraisal interview is a one-to-one discussion between the employee who is being appraised (the appraisee) and the supervisor or manager who is carrying out the appraisal (the appraiser).

The interview is a very useful method of appraisal because:

- it gives both parties a private opportunity to discuss the employee's work and progress
- it allows the employee to put forward his/her own ideas
- it diagnoses problems in work and tries to find solutions.

At the end of the interview, the appraiser completes a form which shows such qualities as:

- employee's level of initiative
- employee's ability to cope with pressure
- employee's leadership skills.

Self-appraisal

Nowadays employees are encouraged to undertake self-appraisal, which is simply looking critically at one's own work and seeking ways to improve its quality or finding easier, more efficient ways of performing it.

Self-appraisal has the advantage of making the employee more responsible for his own work. However one disadvantage is that the worker may not be aware of his/her own faults or know how to improve.

Figure 2.19

ACTIVITY

This is an opportunity for you to carry out self-appraisal of your own performance in school for the school year so far. Take the exercise seriously because it could help you to improve your standard. Include all areas of your school life – examination subjects, sport, extra curricular activity etc.

a   Write down what you feel you have done well.
b   List the areas where you have not done so well.
c   Examine why you did not perform so well in those areas.
d   Finally, think of ways in which you could improve your weak points. It may be useful to get the help of your teacher to do this.

ACTIVITY

Match the appropriate sections in the following table. The first one has been completed for you.

Appraisal is	training requirements for staff
Performance-related pay	is watched doing his/her work
Appraisal is used to identify	is known as the appraisee
Employees benefit from appraisal as it	profitability should improve
Employers use appraisal to help them	assessing an employee's performance
As a result of appraisal the business's	an interview
Observation is where the employee	is known as the appraiser
Observation is usually accompanied by	is not suitable for all types of work
The employee who is being appraised	to increase staff competence
The person carrying out the appraisal	allows them to achieve their full potential
An appraisal interview is a one-to-one	at one's own work
Self-appraisal is looking critically	discussion between appraiser and appraisee

EXAMINATION QUESTION

Name and describe the most suitable method of appraisal for production staff.

(3 marks)

(CCEA Business Studies, GCSE, Paper 2 Foundation Tier, 2002)

Tips for answering this question:

In this question you have to 'name and describe' the method. You would get 1 mark for naming one method which would be appropriate for the type of staff named. You would get the remaining 2 marks for describing the features of that method. One method is all that is asked for.

REVISION

At this stage you should understand:

- the importance of appraisal
- benefits of appraisal for employees and employers
- methods of appraisal.

Make sure you understand the following terms:

Appraisal   Observation
Self-appraisal   Interview

As revision, look each one up in the Glossary at the end of the book.

UNIT 2.8

Employer/Employee Relations

Trade Unions

A trade union is an organisation which has been formed to look after the interests of the employees who are its members and to make sure that they are being treated fairly by their employers.

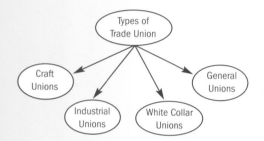

Trade unions first came into existence during the Industrial Revolution when factory workers were not always well treated by the factory owners. At that time workers had no rights and any worker who complained about this treatment risked being dismissed.

The workers realised that they had a better chance of being listened to and of improving their pay and conditions of work if they joined together in a union which would speak with one voice on behalf of them all.

There are four types of trade union which all represent different types of employees:

- Craft unions — Craft unions are usually small and consist of skilled workers who all work at the same craft.
- General unions — These are very large unions and have members who are workers in one area of work but come from a wide range of industries. For example, the Transport and General Workers' Union represents all employees working in transport.

Figure 2.20
A local trade union office

- Industrial unions Members of industrial unions all work in one industry irrespective of the type of work they do in that industry. For example, the National Union of Railwaymen represents anyone working on the railways.
- White collar unions All members of white collar unions are non-manual workers and work in technical, clerical, supervisory or managerial jobs – for example, in Northern Ireland, the majority of teachers belong to the UTU, INTO or the NAS/UWT.

NASUWT

Closed shop

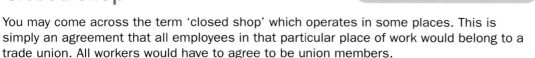

Here are two other terms which you should know:

You may come across the term 'closed shop' which operates in some places. This is simply an agreement that all employees in that particular place of work would belong to a trade union. All workers would have to agree to be union members.

Operating a closed shop means that all employees are paying union subscriptions. Otherwise, union members sometimes feel annoyed that non-union members gain the advantages the union has fought for but they did not contribute to the union.

Single-union agreement

You will also hear of a 'single-union agreement'. This is an agreement that management in that business will negotiate with only one named union. This agreement does not force employees in that business to join the union but, if they wish to have union membership, then it must be that particular union which they join.

Employers are in favour of single-union agreements because negotiations are easier with only one set of union officials to deal with. Talks take less time and disputes are generally more easily resolved.

Employees gain the advantage of being in a more powerful position because the union has greater strength representing most of the workforce. It also means that there is no inter-union disagreement which can delay agreements and weaken the employees' position.

ACTIVITY

You are an employee in a factory which does not operate a single-union agreement. You feel that this is a disadvantage to everyone working in the factory.

Using a computer, prepare a memo for the notice board listing the advantages both workers and management would gain from having a single-union agreement.

Role of Trade Unions

So, why do workers join a trade union?

They join for four main reasons. Unions help them to get better pay and conditions, they advise and inform them, they defend their rights if there is a dispute with management and they work to resolve conflict.

Giving advice and information

Unions are frequently required to give advice and information. Members may wish to check their entitlement to holidays or overtime pay, for example, and would expect their unions to advise them on the proper course of action if they were not being treated fairly in these cases.

Union advice and information might be required by members on:

- matters relating to levels of pay
- the improvement of conditions at work – hours of work, sick pay, fringe benefits etc
- health and safety legislation
- recruitment policies
- training entitlements
- redundancy payments
- pension rights.

Defending employees' rights and resolving conflict

Where employees are being treated unfairly or are having some of their rights withheld, unions would be expected to defend their members. It would be the duty of the union concerned to speak to the firm's management, to draw the employer's attention to the way in which its members were being treated unfairly, and to have their rights restored.

Where conflict had arisen between workers and management, the unions are also expected to undertake talks with management on behalf of their members and solve the problems.

Unions would have to defend members in order to:

- safeguard their rights
- protect promotion opportunities
- see that employees get fair treatment in job applications
- protect them against any other form of unfair action by the employers
- obtain and maintain job security.

Negotiating pay and conditions

Negotiating pay for employees and conditions under which they work is a particularly common area of work for trade unions. This is done through a process known as 'collective bargaining'.

Collective bargaining is where officials from trade unions, on behalf of employees, have talks with representatives of the employers to negotiate agreements for increased pay for employees or improvements in their conditions of service. Conditions of service would include such topics as fringe benefits, holidays, hours of work, sickness and maternity pay, pensions or training and promotion opportunities.

The trade union will probably come to the talks demanding a higher pay increase than is necessary and the employers would make an opening offer which is lower than they are really prepared to pay. After discussion, they hope to be able to agree on a figure somewhere between the union's demand and the employers' offer.

Collective bargaining may be conducted locally – for example, where talks are on behalf of one factory. Where talks are being held to reach agreements for an entire profession – such as teachers or doctors – collective bargaining would be done nationally.

ACTIVITY

You are a member of a trade union but some of the people who work with you are not. You are all going to have a chat about the pros and cons of union membership over lunch tomorrow.

Write notes showing the arguments which you plan to put forward in order to convince your friends that they should become members.

ACTIVITY

You are the trade union official who has been called in to negotiate with the management in the Quick Print Factory. The factory has had several very successful years and the owners are full of praise for their workers who have worked very hard to get orders out on time.

Your members have not had a pay increase for three years. They feel they are entitled to an annual pay increase and also believe they have contributed to the business's success in a very significant way.

The meeting has been planned for later in the week.

Hold the negotiation meeting in class. Up to three students should play the part of the management and up to three should be union officials. Take time to prepare your arguments before the meeting.

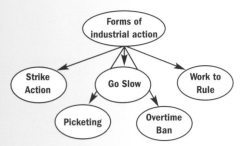

Industrial Action

Agreement is not always reached in the process of Collective Bargaining and sometimes talks break down. In this event, the unions may instruct their members to take industrial action which is a method of bringing the dispute to the attention of the general public.

Strike action

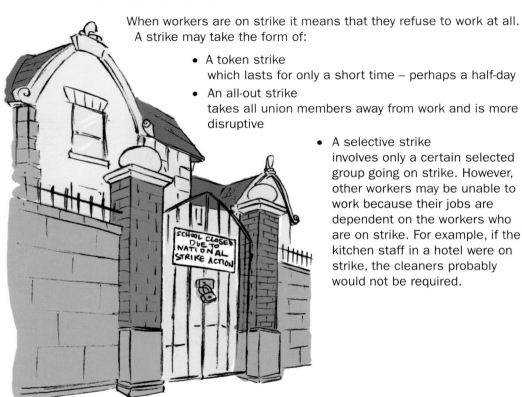

When workers are on strike it means that they refuse to work at all. A strike may take the form of:

- A token strike
  which lasts for only a short time – perhaps a half-day
- An all-out strike
  takes all union members away from work and is more disruptive
- A selective strike
  involves only a certain selected group going on strike. However, other workers may be unable to work because their jobs are dependent on the workers who are on strike. For example, if the kitchen staff in a hotel were on strike, the cleaners probably would not be required.

Figure 2.21

When labour is withdrawn, workers will lose their pay during the period of the strike (unless the unions can afford to pay them) and production is lost in factories. This may result in orders being late or even lost altogether.

Go slow

On a 'go slow', workers simply take their time and therefore slow down production without actually going on strike. For example postmen might deliver letters one at a time. In this case workers protect their pay but production can be slowed down seriously, resulting in delayed or lost orders.

Work to rule

In this situation, workers will observe every little rule in an exaggerated way. For example, in a bakery they might run tests to check the safety of the ovens after every batch of baking instead of every day or every few days as is normal. This action also protects the workers' pay but disrupts production and results in lower profits for the business.

Picketing

Sometimes workers on strike will take action to discourage other workers from going to work. Picketing takes the form of standing with placards at the entrance to the workplace, thus causing other workers to walk through their lines. This action can be very intimidating for workers who wish to go to work.

Picketing secures publicity for the workers, disrupts work, and also gives the organisation a poor public image.

Figure 2.22

Overtime ban

When an overtime ban is in force, all workers refuse to do any overtime hours. An overtime ban has the effect of reducing the work being done in the factory, slows down production and results in profit cuts.

It also lowers the workers' take-home pay in the short term but they hope to gain longer-term increases.

ACTIVITY

There are many disadvantages associated with industrial action.

Using a computer if possible, make three lists of the disadvantages associated with industrial action.

Use the following headings for your lists and then attach them to your business studies notes:

a   Disadvantages of Industrial Action for the Business
b   Disadvantages of Industrial Action for the Employees
c   Disadvantages of Industrial Action for the Customers

Moral and Ethical Issues Associated With Industrial Action

It is impossible to make a judgement of the rights and wrongs of industrial action without knowing the circumstances of each example. If employers are being unfair then workers have to take some form of action to gain their rights. If, however, workers are already well paid and are simply being greedy then it is unjust that they should cause suffering to other people.

It is true that industrial action affects a greater number of people than those who are directly involved in the strike. Other workers inside the business would be affected because a breakdown in part of the business's operations causes stoppages in other departments. Similarly, workers in other businesses may also be affected because the parts they need are not being produced by the workers taking industrial action. Is it right to put other people's jobs at risk?

Industrial action can also give a business a bad reputation and may eventually lead to loss of orders and export opportunities if customers are unsure of their ability to deliver goods on time. This situation could eventually lead to the loss of work for everyone in the business.

Shortages in production eventually lead to shortages in the shops and so the general public is deprived of the goods they require. Such shortages result in price rises. Any increases in wages gained though the industrial action would also be passed on to the consumer, so once again, the general public would be affected adversely. The action had, however, nothing to do with them.

Industrial action, if prolonged, would eventually have an effect on the economy of the country as a whole. Consumers would have less money to spend because a number would have lost their jobs, so businesses would need to produce fewer goods.

This is the beginning of a downward spiral because eventually employees would be made redundant and there would be less money available generally in the shops. The government would not only gain less revenue in taxes but it would also have to pay increased unemployment benefits.

There is a fundamental moral issue associated with industrial action and those involved in the action need to consider the effects of their action on other people.

Class discussion

> You should discuss in class the moral questions and issues raised here and then decide how you feel about the wider implications of industrial action.

Impact of Legislation on Trade Unions

Trade unions have now lost much of their former power. This decline started in the 1980s and was triggered by the Conservative Government, when Margaret Thatcher was Prime Minister. At that time a number of laws were passed which were designed to undermine the position of the unions and reduce their power.

As a result, union membership has fallen over the last 20 years and continues to decline up to the present time. For example, there were 13 million trade union members in the United Kingdom in 1980. At present, that figure has been reduced to just over 8 million.

There are several reasons for this decline:

- periods of high levels of unemployment when workers do not stay in union membership
- rising numbers of part-time workers who feel less need to be unionised
- fewer workers in the manufacturing sector. The heavy industries were always strongly unionised
- the growth of self-employment; the self-employed do not join unions
- increasing numbers of women in the workplace; fewer women than men join unions
- modern working conditions are protected by a series of laws such as the Health and Safety at Work Act. As a result, workers do not have as much need of unions to protect their conditions
- poor treatment of workers is less common in modern workplaces
- laws which curtailed union activities and power.

Details of the legislation

The most up-to-date and relevant pieces of legislation applying to trade unions in Northern Ireland are:

a Industrial Relations (NI) Order 1992
b Trade Union and Labour Relations (NI) Order 1995
c Employment Rights (NI) Order 1999.

These Orders in Northern Ireland largely reflect various Acts in English law, and impact on union activities in the following ways:

- picketing is restricted to an individual's own place of work, making secondary picketing illegal
- a worker cannot be dismissed for union membership
- closed shops can only come into existence with the support of the vast majority of the employees of that organisation
- a secret ballot must be held before a strike is called and the action must be supported by the vast majority of the employees of that organisation
- workers have the right to choose for themselves which union they wish to join
- union members have the right to decide whether or not to have their union subscriptions deducted from their pay
- unions may not hold political funds unless given permission by their members in ballots which must be held every 10 years.

ACTIVITY

As you would expect, trade unions were very unhappy when the Industrial Relations (NI) Order 1992, the Trade Union and Labour Relations (NI) Order 1995 and the Employment Rights (NI) Order 1999 became law.

a State three reasons why the unions were displeased.
b Give details of one way in which the above Orders would impact on employees.

Role of the Labour Relations Agency (LRA)

It sometimes happens that agreement cannot be reached between trade unions and business organisations. In that case, they may decide to bring in the Labour Relations Agency.

The Labour Relations Agency (LRA) is an independent body in Northern Ireland and was established under the provisions of the Industrial Relations (Northern Ireland) Order 1976.

It is the equivalent of the Advisory Conciliation and Arbitration Service (ACAS) in Great Britain. (ACAS does not operate in Northern Ireland.)

The functions of the Labour Relations Agency are to:

- improve industrial relations in Northern Ireland
- provide impartial and confidential advice and assistance on industrial relations
- foster good employment practices throughout Northern Ireland
- work to resolve disputes on employment issues.

In order to try to resolve disputes on employment issues, the LRA undertakes a conciliation and arbitration service.

Conciliation

This is where the LRA brings the two parties in the dispute together so that they may listen to each other and understand each other's position. The LRA acts totally independently – it is not working for either side, but is there to act as a third party to find a resolution of the problem.

During the conciliation stage, it often happens that the two sides can reach a compromise arrangement with which they both can agree. However, if such agreement cannot be reached, they then move into the arbitration stage.

Arbitration

During arbitration, the LRA provides another neutral (independent) person to act as an arbitrator. Both parties must agree on the selection of this person.

The arbitrator listens to both sides of the dispute and then suggests a solution which is usually a 'middle ground' between the two points of view. For example, if the employees' side is demanding a pay increase of £10 per week and the employer has offered £6, the arbitrator would suggest an increase to £8 in the hope that they could both agree to that figure. It is usual for both sides to agree in advance to accept the arbitrator's decision.

The two parties cannot be forced to accept the arbitrator's solution. If they fail to agree after the arbitration stage, the dispute continues but the LRA has no further part to play in it.

The following table shows the success rate of the conciliation process in Northern Ireland during the year 1 April 1999 to 31 March 2000:

Type of case	Number of cases settled by conciliation	Total number of cases dealt with
Unfair dismissal	1274	1838
Wages order	184	507
Sex discrimination	85	402
Breach of contract	186	498
Equal pay	11	63
Disability discrimination	19	61
Race discrimination	2	30
Other employment rights	99	227
TOTAL	1860	3626
Percentage	51	100

Source: Labour Relations Agency

ACTIVITY

Using the above table, answer the following questions:

1. Which type of case has been settled most frequently by conciliation?
2. Why do you think that so few race discrimination cases were brought to the LRA?
3. What type of problem might the 'Other employment rights' cases have been about?
4. Using a spreadsheet package on the computer, draw a bar graph to show the data in the table.

EXAMINATION QUESTION

If a dispute occurred in a firm, describe one role that the Labour Relations Agency (LRA) might play.

(3 marks)

(Adapted from CCEA Business Studies, GCSE, Paper I Higher Tier, 2001)

Tips for answering this question:

You are asked for one role only. Name one of the LRA's roles – this will get 1 mark. 2 marks will be given for describing (in this case, this means giving the details of) whichever role you have named.

The Trades Union Congress (TUC)

The Trades Union Congress is an umbrella organisation for trade unions – sometimes referred to as the unions' union. It speaks on behalf of the entire trade union movement to government.

At present the TUC has over 70 unions in its membership, representing 7 million working people throughout the United Kingdom. This makes it a very powerful organisation.

The role of the TUC is to:

- bring unions together to draw up common policies
- lobby the government to implement policies that will benefit people at work
- campaign on economic and social issues
- represent working people on public bodies
- represent British people on international bodies such as the European Union and United Nations
- carry out research on employment-related issues
- run training programmes for union representatives
- help unions to develop new services for their members
- help unions to avoid clashes with each other
- build links with other trade union bodies world-wide.

The Irish Congress of Trades Unions (ICTU)

> The Irish Congress of Trades Unions (ICTU) is the Irish equivalent to the Trades Union Congress in the United Kingdom. It is the single umbrella organisation for trade unions in Ireland, and has a Northern Ireland Committee, based in Belfast.

The ICTU represents a wide range of 734,842 working people both in the Republic of Ireland and in Northern Ireland. At present there are 64 unions affiliated to the Irish Congress of Trades Unions. 215,478 people in Northern Ireland are represented by the Congress.

The role of the Irish Congress of Trades Unions is to:

- support trade unions in their day-to-day business
- protect and improve living and working standards of workers
- improve wages, hours of work and working conditions in particular
- monitor the implementation of national agreements on conditions of employment
- support and encourage effective organisation of workers in unions
- assist closer co-operation between unions and unity within the trade union movement
- assist in research, information, legal advice and general guidance on behalf of member unions.

The Confederation of British Industry (CBI)

> The Confederation of British Industry (CBI) is a very large organisation for employers and acts as a pressure group on their behalf

Founded in 1965, the CBI is a non-profit making, non-party political organisation funded by the subscriptions paid by its members. It is a United Kingdom organisation but has a regional office in Belfast. It is estimated that CBI members employ over 4 million of the workforce.

The Confederation's mission statement and aims and objectives are shown here to illustrate the purpose of the organisation:

The CBI Mission Statement

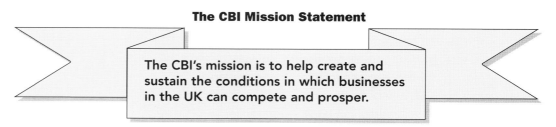

The CBI's mission is to help create and sustain the conditions in which businesses in the UK can compete and prosper.

Overall aims and objectives of the CBI

To influence public policy in Britain and in Europe and elsewhere, to ensure that it creates the conditions in which businesses can best flourish and in which growth and employment are maximised.

To promote best practice in British business whether in specific functions and techniques which generate immediate improvements in business performance, or in business practices which build the long-term capabilities and reputation of the business community

To provide information services and networking opportunities which support trade, investment and sound business decisions.

Role of the Confederation of British Industry

How does the CBI actually fulfil these aims, and what is its role?

- It ensures that the government, the European Commission and the wider community understand the needs of British business.
- It helps to create and sustain the conditions in which business in the UK can compete and prosper.
- It tries to influence government policy regarding the domestic business environment.
- It is also active in international trade policy.

The CBI offers its members:

- a chance to shape public policy
- a voice on policy in Europe and internationally
- professional information on the public policy issues which affect business
- regular economic forecasts and surveys of business trends
- conferences and other networking opportunities enabling members to debate public policy with those who make it, whether in the UK or overseas.

R E V I S I O N

At this stage you should understand the work of the:

- Trade unions and the impact of legislation on trade unions
- Labour Relations Agency
- Trades Union Congress
- Irish Congress of Trades Unions
- Confederation of British Industry (CBI).

You should understand the meaning of:

Trade unions	Craft unions	General unions
Industrial unions	White collar unions	Closed shop
Single-union agreement	Collective bargaining	Strike action
Go slow	Work to rule	Picketing
Overtime ban	Conciliation	Arbitration

As revision, look each one up in the Glossary at the end of the book.

SECTION THREE

Production

Learning Objectives

To develop a knowledge and critical understanding of

- the types of production
- the changing trends in type of production in Northern Ireland
- the trends in the scale of production
- the main factors influencing product development
- economies of scale
- the main methods of production
- the importance of quality assurance
- social and environmental considerations in production
- the factors influencing the location of production
- impact of technology on production
- the implications of relevant legislation on production.

UNIT 3.1 Types and Scale of Production

Types of Production

You will recall that, in the very first section of this book, you learned that 'production' refers to the creation of either goods or services. We used the example of the teachers in your school being involved in production – producing the service of education.

You should return to that section to revise the different types of production – primary, secondary and tertiary. The following diagram should remind you of their details.

Changing Trends Across the Types of Production in Northern Ireland

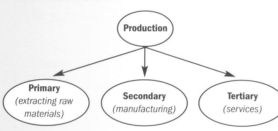

The modern trend in employment is for a shift away from the primary and secondary sectors towards employment in the tertiary sector. The service sector is the fastest growing sector of production at present. This trend, known as de-industrialisation, is affecting most developed countries although it is less noticeable in Northern Ireland than in any other part of the United Kingdom.

The following table illustrates the changes in Northern Ireland in the number of employees engaged in secondary sector occupations and the changes in the number of employees engaged in the tertiary sector between March 1990 and March 2001.

The figures for the United Kingdom are also shown so that you can draw comparisons between them.

Employee Jobs March 1990 to March 2001						
	Northern Ireland			United Kingdom		
	1990 (000s)	2001 (000s)	% change	1990 (000s)	2001 (000s)	% change
Secondary (manufacturing)	104	103	−0.7%	4,819	3,862	−19.9%
Tertiary (services)	373	485	+30.1%	17,298	19,824	+14.6%
Other (taken as primary)	27	21	−22.8%	721	466	−35.4%

Source: ONS and Department of Enterprise and Investment, August 2001 (adapted)

The figures for the 10 years show that:

- the tertiary sector has grown much more in Northern Ireland than in the rest of the United Kingdom during this particular period
- the decrease in the secondary sector is less pronounced in Northern Ireland than in the rest of the United Kingdom
- the 'other' sector – understood to be primary – shows the greatest decrease overall. The very poor conditions experienced by the farming industry recently could account for some of this decrease.

De-industrialisation is caused by several factors:

- manufactured goods are imported cheaply from countries such as Japan, China, Malaysia and Taiwan
- people are spending more on leisure activities so entrepreneurs have moved into that market
- there is now more demand for services such as education, personal banking, insurance for property and cars, investment and legal advice, therefore increasing numbers of employees are needed in these areas.

The following table shows the number of people employed in Northern Ireland in each of the primary, secondary and tertiary sectors at March 2002.

Number Employed in Different Industrial Sectors in Northern Ireland in March 2002		
Sector of Industry	Number of Employees	Percentage of Total Workforce
Primary	19,620	3.01%
Secondary	132,250	20.33%
Tertiary	498,700	76.66%
Total	650,570	100%

Source: DETI – Quarterly Employment Survey (adapted)

ACTIVITY

a   Copy the above table on to a spreadsheet.
b   Display the information as two pie charts. Give the charts suitable labels.
c   Display the information on two bar graphs. Label the graphs.

ACTIVITY

a On a computer, create a table with four columns and 22 rows.

b In the first row, label the four columns: occupation, primary, secondary, tertiary.

c In column 1, rows 2–21, write the occupations of 20 people you know well – members of your family or other close friends.

d In columns 2, 3 and 4, classify each occupation as primary, secondary and tertiary by ticking the appropriate list.

e On row 22, total the number of occupations in each of the three sectors.

f Study your results and say whether they reflect the percentages shown for Northern Ireland in the table above.

g What do your results show about the area you live in?

The following table shows the percentage which each sector contributed to the total production in Northern Ireland in 1999.

Origins of Production in Northern Ireland by Industrial Sector	
Sector of Industry	Percentage Contribution
Primary – Agriculture (4.7%) Electricity, Gas, Water (2.94%) Mining, Quarrying (0.53%)	8.17%
Secondary – Manufacturing (20.11%) Construction (6.22%)	26.33%
Tertiary – Services	65.5%
Total	**100%**

Source: Northern Ireland Annual Abstract of Statistics (adapted)

ACTIVITY

The total production in Northern Ireland in 1999 amounted to £17,003 million.

a Copy the above table on to a spreadsheet.

b Insert a third column on the right–hand side, entitled 'Value of Contribution'. Calculate the value in money for each sector and insert the figures on the spreadsheet.

c Display the information as a pie chart and give the chart a suitable label.

d Display the information as a bar graph and label the graph.

Small- and Large-Scale Production

Officially, businesses are classified in nine size bands according to the number of employees working in each business. The bands are:

0	1–9	10–19	20–49	50–99	100–199	200–249	250–499	500+

Businesses have to decide whether they wish to produce on a small scale, whether they wish to become medium size, or whether they are aiming to expand and become large enterprises. All have advantages.

Small businesses:

- can offer a more personal service
- are more flexible
- may undertake a specialist service.

On the other hand, **large** businesses:

- can take advantage of economies of scale
- have the facilities to go into the export market.

Every business has a certain capacity for production. This is the number of products which it has the resources to make and which are likely to be sold.

If it makes fewer products, than its capacity then it has wasted resources and is making less profit than it is capable of making.

If, on the other hand, it makes more products than its capacity, it risks being left with excess unsold stock.

Usually the size of a business is determined by the capital available, but in some cases the owner has made a conscious choice to remain small.

Susanna runs a small catering business from home. She has built up a very good reputation and has as many customers as she can cope with. She caters for business lunches in companies' own premises, dinner parties in private houses and small family parties to celebrate events such as birthdays, christenings and anniversaries.

Susanna likes to do all the buying and cooking herself but employs Rebecca and Emma sometimes to help as waitresses at the functions.

Susanna has learned from experience that she has the capacity to cater each week for a maximum of four lunches for 12 people each, as well as a maximum of two evening parties of approximately the same size. This capacity is based on the amount of freezer space she has, the size of her cookers and other kitchen equipment, and on the room in her car for transporting her food.

The quality of her catering is so high that she is having to refuse work and some customers are anxious to employ her for larger functions such as wedding receptions.

Sometimes Susanna wonders if she should increase her capacity for production.

ACTIVITY

Read the case study above and then answer these questions:

1. Give details of two major items of expenditure Susanna would have if she decided to take on extra work.
2. What risk would Susanna take if she does decide to expand her business?
3. Name two advantages Susanna would gain by expanding.
4. What advice would you give Susanna about the future of her business? Give your reasons.

Trends in Scale of Production in Northern Ireland

The majority of businesses in Northern Ireland are small. In January 2002, 89% of businesses in the province had fewer than 10 employees while only 2.1% had more than 50 employees, as can be seen from the following table:

Businesses in Northern Ireland at January 2002										
Employee Numbers	0	1–9	10–19	20–49	50–99	100–199	200–249	250–499	500+	Total
Business Numbers	27,875	30,895	3,720	2,125	675	375	65	130	135	65,995

Source: NI Statistics and Research Agency

ACTIVITY

a   Copy the above table on to a spreadsheet.
b   Display the information as a line graph and label the graph.
c   Add a third row at the bottom of the table and insert the percentage of businesses in each size band.

ACTIVITY

You should answer the following questions in your notebook:

1. Which size band had the largest number of businesses in January 2002?
2. Which size band had the smallest number of businesses in January 2002?
3. 27,875 businesses had no employees. Describe the type of businesses these might be.
4. Name a business in your area which has between one and nine employees.
5. Name a business in your area which has over 500 employees.

Statistics also show that, in January 2002, half of all businesses in Northern Ireland had no business premises while 45% of businesses had one site and the other 5% had two or more business premises.

> To be able to comment on trends in the scale of Northern Ireland's production, you need to study statistics from previous years. Here are the figures from 2001 and 2000.

Businesses in Northern Ireland at April 2001										
Employee Numbers	0	1–9	10–19	20–49	50–99	100–199	200–249	250–499	500+	Total
Business Numbers	28,605	30,225	3,710	2,180	685	355	70	135	135	66,100

Source: NI Statistics and Research Agency (adapted)

ACTIVITY

You should answer the following questions in your notebook:

1. Which size band had the largest number of businesses in April 2001?
2. How does that figure compare with the number in the same size band in January 2002?
3. What is the change in the number of businesses which had no employees?
4. Comment on the trend shown in the total number of businesses operating in Northern Ireland between April 2001 and January 2002.

Businesses in Northern Ireland at March 2000										
Employee Numbers	0	1–9	10–19	20–49	50–99	100–199	200–249	250–499	500+	Total
Business Numbers	11,368	26,461	3,348	2,041	639	313	64	133	123	44,490

Source: NI Statistics and Research Agency

You should note that, in March 2000, 85% of businesses in the province had fewer than 10 employees while 2.9% had more than 50 employees.

ACTIVITY

a Copy the above table on to a spreadsheet.
b Display the information as a pie chart and label the chart.
c Add a third row at the bottom of the table and insert the percentage of businesses in each size band.

ACTIVITY

Which of the following statements are true?

a   The total number of businesses in Northern Ireland increased between 2000 and 2002.
b   The total number of businesses in Northern Ireland decreased between 2000 and 2002.
c   The total number of businesses in Northern Ireland stayed the same between 2000 and 2002.
d   There is a large number of small businesses in Northern Ireland.
e   There is a small number of large businesses in Northern Ireland.
f   The number of businesses employing 10–19 people has steadily increased.
g   The number of businesses employing 10–19 people has steadily decreased.
h   The number of businesses employing 10–19 people has stayed the same.
i   The most popular size of business in Northern Ireland has no employees.
j   The most popular size of business in Northern Ireland has 1–9 employees.
k   The most popular size of business in Northern Ireland has 500+ employees.
l   More employees worked in the largest-size businesses than in the smallest-size businesses.
m   Businesses with 500+ employees are likely to be owned by limited companies.
n   Businesses with 500+ employees are likely to be owned by sole traders.

Economies of Scale

> Economies of scale are gained when an increase in production causes a decrease in production costs.

Economies of scale can be illustrated by an example from the newspaper industry. It would be very expensive to produce a single copy of a newspaper because all the major costs in newspaper production – costs of research, writing, designing and laying out the newspaper – would have to be met even for one copy.

However, when several thousand copies of the newspaper are printed, the costs do not multiply in proportion to the number of copies. The costs of researching, writing, designing and laying out the newspaper are the same regardless of the number printed, and the only additional costs are extra paper, ink and electricity.

There are three main types of economies of scale (although there are several others as well):

Marketing economies of scale

Marketing economies of scale are gained in situations where the business can save in expenses associated with marketing such as advertising and distribution.

For example, it costs the same sum to deliver 10 boxes of goods in one lorry load as it does to deliver a single box of goods. For this reason, businesses try to combine goods in one consignment and pick up other goods to use the vehicle economically on the return journey.

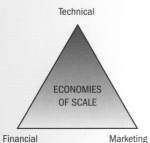

A large business is charged the same rate for advertising as a small business. However, in a large business advertising expenditure is less per unit of production than it is in a small business which is producing on a smaller scale. For this reason, a large business can afford to undertake more advertising than a small business can. The larger business is also likely to increase its sales, as a result of the advertising, by more than the small business.

Figure 3.1
Large businesses such as Marks & Spencer can take advantage of economies of scale

EXAMINATION QUESTION

Cable Electrics is a large manufacturing firm producing televisions and other electrical goods. Increased specialisation has resulted in a rise in output. Productivity has been improved by using new technology.

Explain how Cable Electrics might benefit from marketing economies of scale.

(4 marks)

(CCEA Business Studies, GCSE, Paper 2 Foundation Tier, 2000)

Tips for answering this question:

When you are asked to 'explain' something, the examiner wants to see if you understand the topic. In this question, you should show that you understand marketing economies of scale by showing two ways in which this particular firm could benefit from them.

Technical economies of scale

Technical economies of scale are gained in situations where the business can cut its production costs by introducing upgraded technology or by altering its production methods. Increased mechanisation will speed up production and allow the business to use the mass production method. In this way, costs of labour and power are lowered and overhead expenses such as rates are more effectively used.

Large businesses usually can afford more advanced technology than small businesses, so technical economies of scale are often of more benefit to larger businesses.

Financial economies of scale

Financial economies of scale are gained in situations where the business can borrow money or otherwise gain finance by cheaper methods.

Large businesses, in general, provide better security and fewer risks for banks therefore banks are willing to allow them to borrow larger sums for longer periods of time and at better rates of interest.

The opposite of an economy of scale is a diseconomy of scale.
This would occur when a business becomes too large to be run effectively and efficiently.

ACTIVITY

Write down the name of the type of economy of scale which is described in each of the following:

1. Fleet Delivery Ltd uses vans instead of lorries when small loads are being delivered.
2. The Premier Furniture Company has installed computerised machinery in its production plant.
3. A large group of supermarkets, Finest Foods, has been offered a lower rate of interest on a bank loan than Gillian Little who runs a small grocery shop.
4. Paul Kennedy, the manager of Finest Foods, uses the same advertisements to promote all shops in the chain.
5. The Fresh Bakery merged with The Daily Bread Company and increased its product range by using the flow production method.
6. The City Book Store is able to purchase books on credit from its main supplier because of the large size of its orders.

REVISION

At this stage you should understand:

- changing trends across the types of production in Northern Ireland
- small and large scale production
- trends in scale of production in Northern Ireland.

You should also know the meaning of:

Production capacity
Marketing economies of scale
Financial economies of scale

De-industrialisation
Technical economies of scale
Diseconomy of scale

As revision, look each one up in the Glossary at the end of the book.

Methods of Production

> **Every business will research the quickest, most efficient and the most profitable way in which to manufacture its product.**

There are four methods of production, and the method chosen by any business depends very much on the type of product being made, and on the quantity which is required

Although we shall study each of these methods separately, it should be understood that, in practice, very often a business may use a combination of the methods for some of its work.

Main Methods of Production and Their Use in Particular Circumstances

Job production

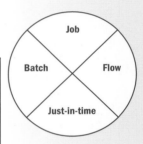

Joan Johnston is a talented dress designer in Ballynahinch who especially enjoys designing and making wedding dresses. She works alone in a large room at the back of her house. Although her dresses are expensive, they are in great demand because they are expertly handmade and unique. Each girl comes to her with a vague idea of the design of the wedding dress she would like, and Joan draws the final design and makes the dress to suit the customer's individual requirements.

Joan gets tremendous job satisfaction from her work, and produces only one dress at a time so that it gets her full attention. Very often, she changes little details of the dress during its production because the customer sometimes changes her mind. Joan is happy to do this because she wants the customer to be really pleased with the dress which is a 'one-off' and individually produced for her.

Joan Johnston's work is a good example of job production.

Job production is where one single item is made at a time and is often produced to the customer's individual specification. Each product is unique and a long time would usually have been spent on it. For this reason, goods produced by this method are expensive to buy.

Job production would not be suitable for factories but would be found in craft shops where emphasis is placed on the hand-made, interesting and individual character of the product.

Examples of goods made by the job production method are:

- craft goods
- luxury cars

Figure 3.2

- designer clothes
- double glazing
- stained glass windows
- landscape gardening
- house plans
- antique furniture.

The **advantages** of job production are:

- each piece is made to the customer's exact requirements
- job satisfaction is high for the worker
- quality of the goods is very high
- the design is flexible and can be changed.

The **disadvantages** of job production are:

- the products are very expensive
- the work is very time consuming
- the advantages of economies of scale are lost.

Batch production

Cupid's is a shop in Ballynahinch which sells wedding dresses. The Sales Manager, Margaret Wilson, has been looking at the wedding photographs in the local newspapers. She has been very impressed with the dresses which the newspaper reports of the weddings say were made by Joan Johnston.

Margaret approaches Joan and asks her to make 10 dresses – all the same design, but in different sizes – for sale in Cupid's. She promises that another order will follow for 10 dresses of a different style.

Joan agrees with this arrangement and has to employ two temporary dressmakers, Hazel and Joyce, to help with the additional work.

Joan has now moved into batch production.

Batch production is used where several of the same product are made in a batch. When the first batch is completed, production continues with a number of a second product, and so on. All the items made in a batch are the same, so production is speeded up. This reduces the cost of labour and results in the final product being less expensive for the customer.

Batch production would be suitable for businesses such as bakeries which bake a number of the same loaves and cakes every day, and where the products do not have to be individual. Newspapers are also produced by this method. The papers are printed every day and each batch must meet a deadline.

Examples of goods made by the batch production method are:

- newspapers
- bread
- clothing
- furniture
- motor car components
- books
- building of housing estates where all the houses are the same.

Figure 3.3
These houses are all identical – an example of batch production

The **advantages** of batch production are:

- workers may specialise to some degree
- labour costs are reduced so the final price is lower
- machinery may be used
- production is faster
- begins to take advantage of economies of scale.

The **disadvantages** of batch production are:

- the work is less interesting than in job production and is repetitive
- more space is required for working and storage
- larger stocks of raw materials must be kept
- machines may have to be re-set between batches, which loses time.

Flow production

Other shop managers in Cookstown, Ballyclare, Newcastle and Maghera have been contacting Joan Johnston to ask if she would supply wedding dresses for their shops.

Joan is certainly interested in this extra work but realises that her production method would have to change. She rents larger premises, buys additional sewing machines, makes Hazel and Joyce permanent, and employs three additional people – Evelyn, Robert and Mervyn. Joan names the business 'Wedding Belles'.

Joan organises the operation on an assembly line basis and each of the six people working in the business is responsible for his/her own separate part of the production of the wedding dresses.

Although her profits are higher, Joan regrets the fact that the larger number of dresses she now produces are all the same. She also misses the personal contact with her customers which she once enjoyed.

Joan has now moved into flow production.

Figure 3.4
Mass-produced goods – made by the flow production method

Flow production is also sometimes known as mass production or assembly line production. It is the method used in factories and most modern production would employ this method.

In flow production, one product is made continuously and in large numbers. A conveyor belt or assembly line is organised and, as the product moves along the line, parts are added to it. In this way, the item starts at the beginning of the line as raw materials and is packaged and ready for sale when it reaches the end of the line.

Operation of an assembly line requires numbers of employees to sit at their particular places and perform their allocated tasks as the product moves along the line. Each employee's task is very repetitive and simple so those engaged in flow production tend to be unskilled or semi-skilled. Motivation of workers is often a problem, and strategies such as job rotation are often used in order to relieve the monotony.

Flow production is suitable for use where large numbers of identical products are being made. This method is very dependent on machinery, therefore a large amount of capital is needed to establish the factory.

However, since large quantities are being produced in the shortest possible time, wages and other costs are kept to a minimum and the finished product is usually not expensive for the customer.

Examples of goods made by the flow production method are:

- motor vehicles
- machinery
- Televisions
- inexpensive clothing
- toys.

The **advantages** of flow production are:

- final product is inexpensive
- large quantities can be manufactured
- the quality of the product is standardised
- machinery can be used so labour costs are reduced
- unskilled wages further reduce costs
- assembly lines can run continuously
- production is fast
- takes full advantage of economies of scale.

The **disadvantages** of flow production are:

- the work is repetitive and boring
- there is an increased risk of accidents

- employee motivation is low
- the products are all identical
- large capital investment is required
- large buildings are usually needed
- large stocks of raw materials must be kept
- machinery breakdown can halt production
- there is a loss of traditional skills.

Just-in-time production

Just-in-time can also be thought of as a method of stock control. The system originated in Japan and is widely used in that country and in Japanese factories in other parts of the world.

Using the just-in-time method:

- products are manufactured just in time for them to be sold. This prevents large stocks of finished goods having to wait to go to market
- the raw materials or parts which are needed for making the final product, are ordered and arrive just in time for use in its manufacture. Large stocks are not held in warehouses waiting to be used.

In this way the just-in-time production method saves money being tied up for long periods in unused stocks of raw materials and unsold finished products. It is therefore effective in reducing costs for the manufacturer.

On the other hand, mistakes in deliveries could hold up production because there are no reserve stocks to go on using.

The **advantages** of just-in-time production are:

- capital is used very effectively
- warehousing is not needed for storage
- if faults occur in supplies, the business does not have a large number of the faulty items
- there is no waste by having excess stocks
- the finished product should be cheaper for the consumer to buy.

The **disadvantages** of just-in-time production are:

- the business is very dependent on having a very efficient ordering system
- production could be halted if the wrong goods were delivered at the last minute
- it puts severe pressure on suppliers
- the company and its suppliers must work together closely.

ACTIVITY

Imagine that you are a Japanese manager of a new car factory being set up in Northern Ireland. You have experience of the just-in-time method of production and you wish to introduce the system into the new factory.

You plan to give a talk to the employees tomorrow to explain the system to them. Using the computer, produce the talk which you have prepared for the meeting.

EXAMINATION QUESTION

Quality Doors Ltd has a factory in Co Fermanagh and is a hi-tech business manufacturing doors for kitchen and bedroom furniture on a large scale. The business has a highly trained workforce and takes pride in using the latest technology.

a **Explain two methods of production which would be suitable for use by Quality Doors Ltd**

(4 marks)

b **Describe one method of production that this business is unlikely to use.**

(2 marks)

(CCEA Business Studies, GCSE, Paper 2 Foundation Tier, 2002)

Specialisation

Joan Johnston has had to allocate separate responsibilities to each of her employees in 'Wedding Belles'.

Joan has retained responsibility for all design work. Mervyn is the cutter, and passes on the prepared parts of the dresses to Hazel and Joyce who make them up into dresses on the sewing machines. The dresses are then passed to Evelyn who is responsible for the finishing work of sewing on buttons and decorations and pressing the finished garments. Robert is responsible for packing, labelling and transporting the finished products to the shops. Robert also does all the clerical work.

Joan has now started to use specialisation.

Specialisation occurs when an employee concentrates on one particular operation, and does it all the time. It is where each worker, or group of workers, undertakes only a small section of the total work and specialises in that particular part of making the product.

It also occurs when a country concentrates on producing one particular type of goods. For example, areas of France specialise in making wine because the climate there is suitable for vineyards and wine making.

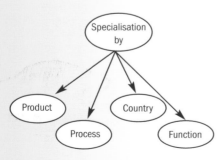

There are four types of specialisation:

- Product For example, the 'Wedding Belles' business specialises in the product of wedding dresses.
- Process For example, in 'Wedding Belles', Hazel and Joyce have specialised in the process of machining the dresses.
- Function For example, in the 'Wedding Belles' business, Robert has specialised in distribution and clerical work.
- Country For example, France specialises in the production of wine.

Advantages of specialisation
- People can work constantly at jobs which suit their special skills or training. In this way, each person becomes an expert.
- The finished product should be of higher quality because of this expertise.
- Resources can be used effectively and concentrated in one place.

Disadvantages of specialisation
- Specialised workers are trained in only one skill so other work may be difficult to find if they become redundant.
- Any business concentrating on a small range of work becomes very dependent on other businesses.
- An area concentrating on a single industry is very badly affected if that industry should fail. For example, parts of France would suffer greatly if poor weather caused the vines not to grow.

ACTIVITY

If you are a student at a large school you will already be used to specialisation. Your teachers have all specialised in certain subjects which they concentrate on and teach all the time.

a   What is the main advantage for you, as a student, of having specialised teachers?
b   Which disadvantages, from the teachers' point of view, can you see in specialisation?
c   Design a table with two columns, naming the subjects taught in your school and the names of the teachers who specialise in those subjects.

EXAMINATION QUESTION

Cable Electrics is a large manufacturing firm producing televisions and other electrical goods. Increased specialisation has resulted in a rise in output. Productivity has been improved by using new technology.

a   **What method of production is likely to be used at Cable Electrics?**

(1 mark)

b   **Apart from increasing output, suggest one other advantage to the firm of using specialisation.**

(2 marks)

c   **Suggest one disadvantage to the firm of using specialisation.**

(2 marks)

(CCEA Business Studies, GCSE, Paper 2 Foundation Tier, 2000)

Tips for answering this question:

This is a straightforward 'recall of knowledge' question.
a   In Part A you are required simply to name the method which would be most appropriate in Cable Electrics. No further explanation is necessary.
b   In Part B you need to state, and briefly describe, one advantage of specialisation. Make sure that it is an advantage taken from the firm's point of view.
c   In Part C you should name and briefly explain one disadvantage of specialisation – again taken from the firm's point of view.

Division of labour

Flow production usually leads to division of labour which is a particular type of specialisation. In division of labour, the manufacture of the product is divided into a number of small stages and each employee is given a single task which may be very narrow.

I once visited a toy factory which used the practice of division of labour. I stood behind a girl whose job was to attach the heads to the bodies of dolls as they moved along the conveyor belt. That was the task which she was given, and she spent the entire day lifting a doll's head from a box with her right hand, lifting the doll's body from the conveyor belt with her left hand and attaching the two in the time the belt had halted in front of her.

Advantages of division of labour

- Each worker becomes very practised at one particular task.
- Workers have to be trained for only one small task so lengthy training is avoided.
- The work is faster so the costs per unit of production are reduced.
- Reduced costs can be reflected in lower prices to the consumer.
- Lower prices will raise sales and profits.
- Time is saved because workers do not have to move between jobs.
- Tools and machinery are used economically because each worker will need only the tools which are required for one particular function.

Disadvantages of division of labour

- The work can be very monotonous and boring.
- Bored workers can cause accidents.
- It is difficult for workers to have pride in their work since they do not see the finished product.
- Delays or strikes in one section can cause stoppages throughout the production process.
- There is a loss of traditional skills.
- Goods produced by this method lack variety.
- Workers can feel isolated from each other.
- Redundant employees would have difficulty in finding other work because they are very narrowly trained.

ACTIVITY

You are the manager of a factory which makes television sets. The workers complain of boredom and you have observed that they seem to be very disinterested in their work and half asleep most of the time.

Suggest ways in which you could lessen the boredom and motivate the workers.

The Impact of Technology on Production

Modern technology has been the cause of the greatest changes in modern production and businesses invest large amounts of capital in technology in order to become more successful.

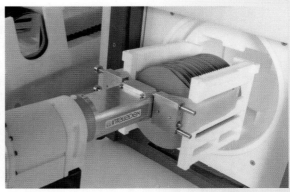

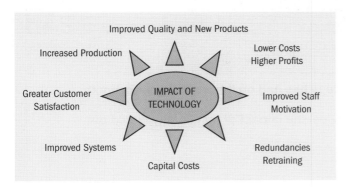

The major impacts of technology on production are:

1 **An improvement of the quality of the finished product**

   As a result of the use of technology, the quality of the products is standardised and the possibility of human error is minimised.

2 **The development of new products**

   Improved methods of research and development would lead to new products being added to the business's range.

3 **An increase in the business's production level**

   A fully mechanised business can work around the clock with no interruptions. This would have the effect of increasing the level of output.

4 **A decrease in the production costs per unit**

   Increases in production lead to the benefits of economies of scale which reduces overall costs per unit of production.

5 **Higher profit levels**

   Increased production and sales, as well as reduced costs lead to improved profits for the business and improved efficiency overall

6 **Greater customer satisfaction**

   An improvement in the quality of the business's product and the speed of its service would lead to a larger number of satisfied customers. Computers can also monitor stock levels which would result in better customer satisfaction.

7 **Improved motivation of workers**

   Workers enjoy being part of an organisation which is progressive and are also motivated by the opportunities provided in the business. They also benefit from constant training.

8 **Improved information and communication systems**

   Internal and external communications are improved by the installation of the Internet and e-mail systems. Access to information is improved by the provision of computer-based systems using databases and spreadsheets as well as word-processing.

9 **Possible redundancies of employees**

   The increase of automated jobs can cause staff redundancies. Previous skills are no longer required and new ones are needed.

10 **Retraining programmes**

A programme of continuous training is required to keep employees abreast with the latest developments in technology. This is expensive for the business to sustain.

11 **Capital costs**

The installation, updating and maintenance of technology requires a substantial capital investment. This costly investment is often impossible for small businesses to fund.

ACTIVITY

Carry out a survey of the impacts which technology has had on the work in your school.

The areas of the school which are most likely to feel the impact of technology would be:

a   The General Office
b   The Principal's and Vice Principal's Offices
c   Some teaching departments such as Business Studies, CDT etc.

If possible, interview the members of staff concerned to find out whether the overall impact of new technology has been advantageous or disadvantageous to their work.

Influences on Product Development

Competition in business is very fierce and businesses need to be constantly either developing new products or modifying existing ones to keep ahead of the competition.

For this reason, businesses spend large amounts annually on the development of new products. It is estimated that, in the year 2000, £13 million was spent in the United Kingdom on research and development of new products.

The normal process of product development goes through several stages. It starts with the generation of a new idea, further studies are done on the idea to see if it is workable and practicable, it is then developed, tested, put into full production and finally launched on the market.

Many ideas are abandoned at an early stage because they may be too expensive, may not be feasible or are too similar to other products on the market.

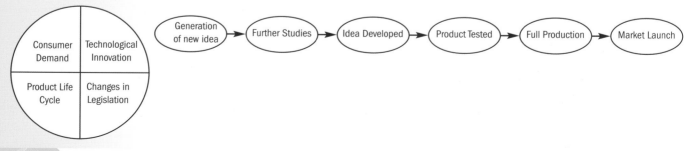

Four of the influences on product development are:

Consumer demand

Markets change rapidly and the demands of consumers alter as fashions change or according to seasonal changes, for example. Timing is important if the new product is to be successful. It is essential that products are developed and ready for market at the time when consumer demand is at its highest.

Businesses carry out exhaustive market research to discover the needs of consumers in order to develop a product which fits those needs as closely as possible and therefore would be successful after it is launched.

Technological innovation

Changes in technology take place on a continuous basis and alter the design and capabilities of products very quickly. Newly developed products are expected to incorporate the latest innovations.

The market for computers is a good example, as is the music industry. Methods of listening to music today bear no similarity to 10 years ago, and the life of a computer is very short because computer users want to have machines which are up to date. For these reasons, product development is greatly influenced by innovations in technology.

Product life cycle

It is important that new products are developed quickly because the life cycle of products in general is getting shorter. Businesses develop new products all the time but special efforts are made to have new products ready for introduction to the market when others have entered the decline stage.

Changes in legislation

New laws also influence the development of products, especially legislation which affects health and safety.

Legislation controls the ingredients which may be used in food products and it also controls the design of toys and children's wear. For example, nightwear must not now be made from inflammable material following several accidents where children's pyjamas caught fire as they played by the fireside. In this case children's wear had to be redesigned in a different material to conform with the new law.

ACTIVITY

Answer the following questions in your notebook.

a   Why is it necessary for businesses to develop new products or modify existing ones?
b   Name the six stages in product development
c   In what way does consumer demand influence product development?
d   What is meant by 'technological innovation'?
e   Why is it important to have a new product developed when others have entered the decline stage of the product life cycle?
f   Give one example of an effect which a change in legislation has had on the development of a product.

UNIT
3.3

Factors Influencing Location of Production

Several different factors influence the location of production. Although much of the decision of where to situate a business depends on the type of business being opened, other factors need to be considered as well. Before we go any further, think about the following situation for a moment.

Colin Smith has always wanted to run a service station, and now has the required capital.

Three sites are available for him to buy and he could afford any of them. He simply wants to go to the site where he would sell the most fuel and has no other considerations in mind. The sites are:

1. At the Belfast end of the M1 where drivers have to travel approximately 40 miles to the next service station unless they leave the motorway.
2. In the small seaside town of Castlerock which has a small population but has sizable numbers of visitors during the summer months.
3. In the very busy city of Newry which is situated on the main Belfast to Dublin route, has a large population and is a good commercial centre. However, Newry is situated on the border with the Republic of Ireland, where fuel is very much cheaper than in Northern Ireland.

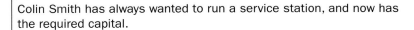

ACTIVITY

You are asked to give Colin your opinion on the best choice of site for his proposed business.

Copy and complete the following table to list the advantages and disadvantages of each site.

SITE	ADVANTAGES	DISADVANTAGES
Belfast end of M1		
Castlerock		
Newry		

I would advise Colin to locate in:	
because:	

In your consideration of Colin's problem, you have looked at the type of business he hoped to run and then decided on the location where he would achieve the highest sales. However, decisions about location are never as straightforward as this, and other factors have to be considered.

The other influences on location are:

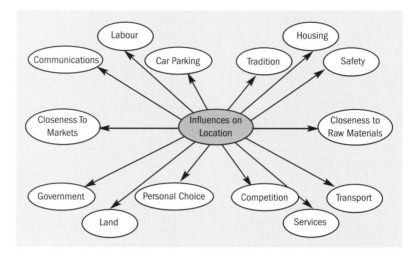

Services

All businesses need to have available the basic services of:

- electricity
- water
- waste disposal
- telephone
- drainage.

In the case of manufacturing businesses, other ancillary services are also required such as technological back-up for machinery and computers.

If these services are already available, the business considering locating to that area will save time and money, and will consider that site before one which does not have the basic services.

Different types of business require services in different proportions. For example, businesses engaged in food production usually require a large quantity of water, while waste disposal would be extremely important in the case of an abattoir.

Land

A major consideration is the price of land. The cost of land varies greatly from area to area, and the success of the new business could be seriously affected by this capital cost.

The cost depends on:

- how central the site is. Sites in the centre of towns are the most expensive to buy or rent and also have a higher rates valuation. In addition, they are usually smaller so are suitable for use by retailers rather than manufacturers.

Figure 3.6

196 GCSE Business Studies for CCEA

- the area of the country in which it is situated. As a general rule, land becomes more expensive near large towns or cities. It is cheaper to buy or rent in more remote areas or in areas which are considered to be less prosperous.
- the competition for the site. Having a number of parties interested in the site will increase its price considerably.
- the availability of land. Land is a very scarce resource and planning restrictions are rigid.

However, other factors also have to be considered regarding the suitability of the land:

a at some time in the future the business may wish to expand, so the business has to be sure that there is available land for future expansion.

b whether the land must be purchased or is available for renting is also relevant.

c the amount of the rates payable to the local authority will also influence new businesses.

Government influences

The influence of the Government is very significant in the location of industries. Some parts of the country suffer greatly from unemployment as a result of the decline of traditional industries. Government policy is to try to cure employment black spots and to even out wealth and resources throughout Northern Ireland

In order to do this the Government:

- encourages businesses to locate in certain areas by providing advance factories at reduced rates in those areas
- offers financial incentives such as grants and tax relief
- sets up industrial estates
- attracts foreign investment
- bids for EU investment.

Transport costs

The cost of transport is a major consideration. If the business is a manufacturing business requiring heavy and bulky raw materials from another country, it is more economical to locate the business near a seaport in order to reduce costs of transporting over land. Similarly, if the finished product is a heavy one and is mostly exported, a location near the port would further reduce costs.

However, Northern Ireland is a very small country and therefore the distance to be travelled overland is relatively small to any part of the province. The consideration of transport overland in Northern Ireland is much less important for this reason, than it would be in a large country such as Canada, for example.

Communications

A sound infrastructure of good roads or a reliable rail network encourages businesses to choose to move to an area. Having these in place would assist the business to deliver goods more quickly to its customers and would also help it to receive its deliveries more easily.

Nearness to a seaport or airport may also be important, depending on the type of product being made, and on whether or not raw materials have to be imported.

Figure 3.7
Large sums have been invested in roads in Northern Ireland

Labour

Skilled labour is an important element in any business. If a supply of skilled labour already exists in an area, that area immediately becomes more attractive to new businesses. This might occur, for example, in an area where a business has closed down and left skilled labour redundant.

Businesses are also attracted to areas where there is an available labour supply of people who can be trained.

Businesses sometimes choose to establish in areas of high unemployment because wages there are likely to be lower than in areas where competition for workers is strong. However, the introduction of the minimum wage has narrowed the difference in the wage levels to a large degree.

Housing

Figure 3.8
Some areas provide housing for key workers

New businesses frequently have to bring a number of key workers with them – workers who have been trained by the business in some of their other plants. This practice means that those key workers can be used to provide on-the-job training for local employees.

If houses are easily available for the key workers coming into the area, it is a positive feature of the area for the business locating there.

Closeness to raw materials

In examples of manufacturing businesses where the raw material is heavy, it makes economic sense to place the business near the source of the raw materials. For instance, timber businesses frequently locate in heavily forested areas.

Some of Northern Ireland's traditional industries were originally started in places where a supply of the required raw materials was available. However, in some cases, the supply of those raw materials has been exhausted for many years and the industries continue with imported materials. (See the case study on Belleek Pottery in this unit.)

It is therefore true to say that closeness to raw materials was more important in past centuries than at present because transport systems are more developed now.

Closeness to markets

As in the case of closeness to raw materials above, closeness to markets is now less important than it once was for manufacturing businesses.

However, this factor is of great importance in the case of retail businesses. They need to be located centrally in areas which are popular with shoppers and where they are obviously going to get customers.

Shopping centres usually have one major retail store as the anchor shop and a series of other smaller outlets and boutiques. The large store attracts large numbers of shoppers and all the other retail outlets in the centre benefit from the passing trade.

For example, Marks and Spencer is the anchor shop in the Foyleside Shopping Centre in Londonderry but all the other shops and restaurants in Foyleside are also busy because of the large numbers of visitors to the centre.

Competition from other businesses

If the new business is a retail business, it will decide to locate where there is not a lot of competition and where its market will be strongest. For example, a chemist would choose to open a shop in a village or an area of town where there are no existing chemist shops.

Safety

Business activity which causes health risks would not be permitted to be located in an area where it would provide a danger. This would be particularly important in the case of nuclear stations, petrol refineries or chemical plants.

In examples such as these, it is important that the business is sited far away from dwelling houses and public places.

Car parking

Available car parking facilities are very important for retail businesses, but most particularly for those selling groceries or goods such as DIY materials. These goods are heavy and difficult to carry so customers need to be able to park near the shop.

There is also the added fact that town-centre parking is expensive and limited. These are the main reasons why large out-of-town retail centres such as Sprucefield outside Lisburn are so popular.

Car parking facilities are also important for manufacturing businesses in order to accommodate employees, delivery vehicles, visitors and trade representatives.

Personal choice

For small, family-owned businesses the decision about location is very often based on where the family wants to live. Family-owned businesses are sometimes passed down through the generations of one family and therefore the business is located in the area where the family has always lived.

Tradition

Frequently we find the continuation of an industry in an area after the original reason for being there has disappeared. The case study on Belleek China is also an example of tradition. The china clay is no longer available locally but the industry remains in Belleek because there is a supply of very skilled labour in the area and a tradition of china making.

ACTIVITY

The food retailer Iceland has said that it would like to set up new supermarkets in Armagh, Ballyclare, south/west Belfast, Cookstown, Downpatrick, Kilkeel, Limavady and the suburbs of Londonderry.

Iceland said the stores would be located to provide easy access for shoppers. It is targeting high streets or main roads in populated areas for the outlets and wants sites which are easy to access by foot as well as by car or public tranport.

Read the above report on Iceland Supermarkets and answer the following questions:

a   Which influence on location is most important to Iceland?
b   Why is Iceland targeting high street or main road sites?
c   Why do you think Iceland has named these eight towns in Northern Ireland?

ACTIVITY

Details of 14 influences on location are given in this unit. In the spaces provided below, state the three most important influences for each of the businesses named.

A supermarket   ....

                                       ....

                                       ....

A meat processing factory   ....

                                       ....

                                       ....

A garden centre   ....

                                       ....

                                       ....

An old people's home   ....

                                       ....

                                       ....

EXAMINATION QUESTION

Sandwich Ltd has been established for over 10 years. Originally it was located in Belfast. Five years ago it opened four new outlets.

Give details of two factors which might have influenced the location of the new outlets.

(4 marks)

(CCEA Business Studies, GCSE, Paper 2 Higher Tier, 2002)

Tips for answering this question:

Details of two factors are required. In this case name the factors (for 1 mark each) and then give a short description of each one for the further 2 marks.

The world famous Belleek China is manufactured in the small village of Belleek which is situated on the banks of the River Erne and on the border between Counties Fermanagh and Donegal.

In 1849 John Caldwell Bloomfield inherited the Castlecaldwell estate which included the village of Belleek. This was shortly after the potato famine in Ireland and the new landlord, concerned about his tenants, was anxious to find work for them.

A geological survey of the area revealed the presence of feldspar, kaolin, flint, clay and shale – the necessary raw materials for the production of pottery.

In 1858, using his own capital plus that of two wealthy friends who were interested in the project, John Caldwell Bloomfield opened a pottery on a site at the side of the village where the river would provide power to drive a mill wheel. He used his influence to get the railway service to build a railway to Belleek so that coal could be brought in to fire the kilns and also provide a method of transport for the finished product to be taken to markets.

The new pottery provided a much-needed source of employment for local people. However, experienced potters were also required and they were brought to Belleek from Stoke-on-Trent – one of the most famous and established pottery areas.

The Belleek Pottery became very prosperous and by 1865 it had established a steady market throughout Ireland and England as well as America, Canada and Australia.

Belleek Pottery continues to operate on the same site although obviously its structure and methods have had to be updated. A major capital investment, partly funded by the Industrial Development Board in 1983, made this possible. The building has been modernised, all the kilns are now powered by electricity and the water wheel is no longer in use.

One of Belleek Pottery's world-famous products

Belleek Pottery

ACTIVITY

Read the case study on Belleek Pottery Ltd and answer the following questions:

a   What was the major reason for opening the pottery in Belleek?
b   Name three other influences for choosing the site in Belleek.
c   Give details of two reasons why china is still manufactured in Belleek.

Social and Environmental Considerations in Production and its Location

We have already seen how businesses have to take a variety of factors into consideration before they locate their businesses. In addition, they must consider the social and environmental issues of their position. These issues are very individual to the type of business and to the nature of the area being chosen, and each one of you will be able to give examples of influences in your own districts.

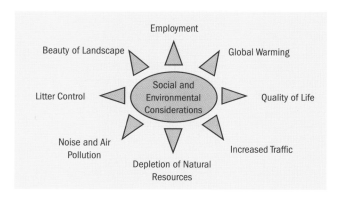

Employment

The most important social issue is the effect on the employment of the area. Positive effects occur when a business establishes in a district by the new jobs it creates for production workers and clerical workers, as well as catering, cleaning and security staff. In addition, employment may be created in other subsidiary businesses by the need for extra components for the main business. This increased employment has wider spin-off benefits for the shops, hotels and places of entertainment in the area which are all positively affected by the increased wealth and higher standard of living in the district. This general improvement in the area encourages other businesses to locate there and the benefits continue to grow.

All these effects are reversed if a business decides to relocate away from the area and redundancies occur as a result of the move of the business to another place.

Quality of life and beauty of the landscape

Environmental issues must also be considered in order not to damage the quality of life for the people of the area by ruining the surrounding landscape. Consideration is being given to the environment in recent times because of the evidence of environmental damage of past generations in some parts of the British Isles.

Northern Ireland was never as heavily industrialised as parts of England and Wales, so fortunately it escaped most industrial damage. We have a beautiful country and the vast majority of businesses take their responsibility for it very seriously.

Global warming and pollution

People today are concerned about global warming, about the depletion of natural resources, about holes in the ozone layer and about modern farming methods. It is important to protect:

- the beauty of the landscape
- natural habitat for wildlife
- the quality of the air
- the quality of the water in rivers and lakes
- the beauty of the coastline.

In addition, it is important to control:

- noise
- litter.

Figure 3.9

Planning is strictly controlled by the government and local authorities. No building development is permitted in areas of natural beauty or in green belts of the countryside, and plans must be submitted for all building work to ensure that it fits in with the surrounding area.

Further strict legislation protects the environment from air and water pollution and also controls litter. Emissions into the air of smoke and fumes from factories are monitored so that further damage to the ozone layer would not be caused. A business's waste disposal policy must ensure that no chemicals or other dangerous substances are released into the drainage system where they eventually would find their way to the rivers and lakes.

Increased traffic

Nevertheless, there would be increased traffic in the area as a result of the location of manufacturing businesses there. This creates congestion on the roads, the heightened possibility of accidents, damage to the road surface and fuel emissions from vehicles.

Restrictions are put on the noise levels from factories and on the night hours when goods may be transported through residential areas.

Depletion of natural resources

Farmers are given encouragement to delay hedge and grass cutting until young birds have been reared and not to use chemicals on their land which would be injurious to wildlife. They are also prohibited from cutting down trees for the same reason.

Most businesses have environmental policies which show their commitment to the environment.

The following case study gives details of the work done by Phoenix Natural Gas in respect of the environment.

Phoenix Natural Gas is highly aware of its environmental responsibilities. Its product, natural gas, has huge environmental benefits to the consumer by improving air quality. In six years of being in Northern Ireland, the company has connected over 45,000 customers which it estimates has caused a 2.3% reduction in the carbon dioxide in the atmosphere. The use of gas has also reduced the level of sulphur dioxide by 42%.

Other steps which Phoenix has taken to protect the environment are:

- The company has undertaken a major recycling project. Where possible it has used new polyethylene pipes inside the old gas network in Belfast. This has been done in order to cut down excavation in the area.
- The main Phoenix building makes maximum use of natural light and natural ventilation cutting down costs of heating and lighting.
- The company recycles paper, batteries, printer cartridges and toners. It also recycles old mobile telephones and IT equipment.
- It uses only environmentally friendly products.
- The company has a no-smoking policy.

ACTIVITY

Match the businesses named on the left with their most suitable locations. The first has been done for you to start you off.

BUSINESS	LOCATION
A chemical factory	At the entrance to a hospital
A toy shop	In the centre of population near several large towns
A leisure centre	In a remote area but convenient to farms
A newspaper and confectionery shop	In an area far away from houses
An abattoir	Attached to a hotel
A hospital	In the middle of the orchard country
An apple juice factory	In a high street shop
A flower shop	Beside a bus station

R E V I S I O N

At this stage you should make sure that you understand and are able to name:

- all the factors influencing location of production
- all the social and environmental considerations in production.

If you are uncertain, go back over the unit and make sure that you have worked through all the activities.

Quality Assurance and Safety in Production

UNIT 3.4

> Quality is defined as 'the constant achievement of all that customers require'.

Importance of Quality Assurance in Production

Modern businesses whether they produce goods or services – are extremely conscious of the need to maintain high standards of quality if they are to retain their places in the market. Competition is fierce between producers, and consumers demand quality therefore they will go to the producer who offers the highest-quality items at the best prices.

For this reason, most businesses undertake the process to obtain recognised quality standards. Being awarded a recognised standard is an assurance to members of the public that the business organisation has met the high standards required and this gives consumers confidence in dealing with that business.

Four of the principal awards are:

Charter Mark

A Charter Mark is for public service organisations and is a part of the Government's plan to modernise public services. A Charter Mark is awarded to those organisations providing the highest possible quality services to their customers.

CUSTOMER SERVICE EXCELLENCE

To achieve the award, the service has to demonstrate that it has:

- set standards and performed well
- actively engaged with its customers, partners and staff
- been fair and accessible to everyone and promoted choice
- continuously developed and improved
- used resources effectively
- contributed to improving opportunities and quality of life in the community it serves.

In 2001 there were 63 Charter Mark winners in Northern Ireland. A selection of these (from various parts of the province) are:

Belfast City Hospital – Regional Cardiology Unit
Newcastle Tourist Information Centre
Ballynahinch Family and Child Care Services
Mater Hospital – Eye Outpatient Department
NI Housing Executive – Ballymena District Office
NI Housing Executive – Portadown District Office
Mid Ulster Hospital – Children's Unit

Belfast Zoo
Omagh Leisure Complex
Cookstown Job Centre
Limavady Job Centre
Strabane Job Centre
Translink – Armagh Operations
Translink – Newry Operations

ACTIVITY

Answer the following questions in your notebook:

a   Why did the Government introduce the Charter Mark?
b   As a member of the public, what would you expect of the service in an organisation which had been awarded a Charter Mark?
c   What would your reaction be if you were an employee in one of the organisations which had been awarded a Charter Mark?

ISO 9001

ISO 9001 is a Business Management Standard award designed to help organisations to manage their processes, and is subject to regular validation by external assessors. It concentrates on process management, checks that documented systems are in place and that everyone is sure of his/her role in the organisation.

ISO 9001 looks at how the business:

- trains its staff
- checks that its products or services are correct
- handles mistakes
- tries to improve its products or services
- uses its resources.

Before being given the award, the business has to go through external assessment procedures.

Having this award enables the business to:

- meet its customers' requirements
- have low levels of customer dissatisfaction
- continually improve its working practices
- be confident in markets where high quality is essential.

Customers of an ISO 9001 business have confidence that its products have successfully passed rigorous standards and that the risk of failure is greatly reduced.

The Northern Ireland Council for the Curriculum, Examinations and Assessment (CCEA) has been awarded an ISO 9001.

Listen to some of the comments which two CCEA employees made after their organisation had achieved the award:

Rewarding Learning

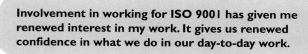

Involvement in working for ISO 9001 has given me renewed interest in my work. It gives us renewed confidence in what we do in our day-to-day work.

What we had to do to achieve this award touched all staff to a greater or lesser degree. We now have documented and reliable systems in place which assure the quality of our operations. We'll also be reviewing and updating these on a regular basis as we're retested for the award every six months.

ACTIVITY

Answer the following questions in your notebook:

a   What is the main difference between a Charter Mark and the ISO 9001 award?
b   What is the guarantee of continued high standards in the ISO 9001 award?
c   One of the CCEA employees said that the award gave her renewed confidence in her day-to-day work. Why would this be so?

European Foundation for Quality Management (EFQM)

The European Foundation for Quality Management (EFQM) was created in 1988 by the presidents of 14 major European companies. The reason for its establishment was to encourage European business organisations to improve their standards so that European businesses would be world leaders and achieve total advantage over their competitors.

The EFQM model has nine criteria which look at what the business does and what it achieves:

- leadership
- policy and strategy
- people
- people results
- partnership and resources
- processes
- customer results
- society results
- key performance results.

Businesses have to measure their performance continually in each criterion and find ways to solve problems and improve performance.

Investors in People

At the very centre of the award 'Investors in People' (IIP) is the importance of the people who work in the business and the need to invest in their training and development.

IIP establishes a level of good training practice so that the people in the business can help the business to achieve its goals. Employees feel motivated by the process; resulting in all-round and continuous improvement.

INVESTORS IN PEOPLE

The idea behind the Investors in People Award is that if the people who work in an organisation are improved, they will improve the organisation's systems which, in turn, will improve the performance of the entire organisation.

IMPROVE PEOPLE → PEOPLE IMPROVE SYSTEMS → IMPROVES BUSINESS PERFORMANCE

The Investors in People scheme is also externally assessed and is about:

- resolving all the people issues in the organisation
- improving the skill levels of all staff
- supporting the development of everyone working in the organisation
- getting people to take responsibility for their own development
- encouraging people to improve their own performance
- getting everyone to understand the business's aims.

ACTIVITY

Answer the following questions in your notebook

a What effect is an Investors In People award in a business likely to have on the careers of its employees?

b Getting employees to understand the business's aims is an important part of the Investors in People Award. What benefit would this be to the business?

Value to an organisation of attaining a recognised quality standard

The following quotations are taken from employees in businesses which have been awarded one of the recognised quality standards. They illustrate the benefits to be gained in getting an award.

- IBM — 'We reduced our error rate 165 fold in four years'
- Ericsson — 'We cut our lead time from 52 to 27 days in three years'
- TNT — 'Our responsiveness has improved to the extent that 99.4% of the newspapers we deliver are on time'
- Ulster Carpet Mills — 'Our productivity increased by 77%'

ACTIVITY

You should do some research in businesses in your area. Find out if they have been awarded any recognised quality standard or are working for one at the present time.

a Find out the details of their award(s).

b Ask about the benefits which they believe the award has, or would have, for their business.

The Health and Safety (Northern Ireland) Order 1978

The Health and Safety (Northern Ireland) Order 1978 applies to all places of work and sets out the responsibilities of both employers and employees to ensure that the work environment is safe.

Rights and responsibilities of **employers** in the area of health and safety

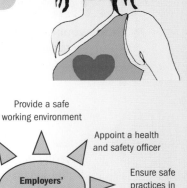

Employers have a general duty to ensure, so far as is reasonably practicable, the health, safety and welfare of their employees at work. They also have a duty towards people who are not their employees but use their premises.

Employers are expected to:

- ensure the safe use of articles and substances
- provide health and safety training for employees
- appoint a health and safety officer
- carry out regular fire drills
- provide protective clothing, such as goggles, where necessary
- maintain all machinery and systems in efficient working order
- provide safe premises with clear signs and enough space for people to move around with ease
- ensure safe practices in the workplace
- have the premises adequately ventilated and well lit
- provide suitable workstations with supportive seating for office-type work
- maintain an indoor temperature of at least 16 degrees Celsius (or 13 degrees Celsius if the work involves physical activity)
- carry out cleaning and the removal of waste regularly
- equip the premises with drinking water, clean washing facilities and toilets
- provide storage space for employees' clothing
- provide facilities for rest periods and to eat meals.

Provide a safe working environment

Provide health and safety training

Appoint a health and safety officer

Carry out regular firedrills

Employers' Responsibilities

Ensure safe practices in the workplace

Have healthy premises

Provide facilities for employees

Carry out regular cleaning and waste removal

Rights and responsibilities of **employees** in the area of health and safety

Employees have a duty to support the health and safety procedures in their workplace and to take reasonable care of their own health and safety as well as the health and safety of other people.

Employees are expected to:

- take all reasonable care for their own health and safety as well as the safety of others
- co-operate in meeting the business's health and safety requirements

Co-operate with the
business's health and
safety policy

Take care of their own
health and safety

Take care of others'
health and safety

Use all
equipment
carefully

**Employees'
Responsibilities**

Wear the
protective
clothing provided

Undergo health
and safety
training

Report all faults
and dangers

Be conscious of health and
safety issues

- use all equipment carefully to keep it in good working order
- wear the protective clothing and equipment provided
- undergo health and safety training
- report all faults and dangers.

ACTIVITY

Study your school's health and safety policy and use it to write notes on your own health and safety responsibilities as a pupil in that school.

EXAMINATION QUESTION

Describe the responsibilities which Health and Safety legislation places on a business.

(8 marks)

(Adapted from CCEA Business Studies, GCSE, Paper 2 Higher Tier, 2002)

Tips for answering this question:

This question carries a large number of marks. To gain those marks you have to name, and show the main features of, approximately four of the things which an employer is expected to do in order to comply with the Health and Safety at Work Act. This question should be looked at only from the employer's point of view.

REVISION

At this stage you should understand:

- the meaning of 'quality assurance'
- the need for quality assurance in modern business
- outline details of the principal awards
- value to an organisation of attaining a recognised quality standard
- requirements of the Health and Safety (Northern Ireland) Order 1978 for employers and employees.

SECTION FOUR

Marketing

Learning Objectives

To develop a knowledge and critical understanding of:

- the process of identifying and satisfying customers' needs in a changing and competitive environment
- the determination of marketing policy by size and nature of the business
- the implications of legal constraints on marketing
- the implications of ethical constraints on marketing
- marketing issues for firms in Northern Ireland operating in a global economic environment
- the cultural dimension in international marketing.

Market Research

What Do We Mean by 'Market Research'?

Market research is the collection of information from consumers, and people who may become consumers, finding out whether they like or will buy the business's products. Such research may be about existing or new products.

Businesses are market driven and therefore consumers' opinions are most important to them.

Businesses spend large sums of money in finding out about their market because:

- the information ensures that they are providing the products which consumers are most likely to buy
- it enables them to price the products at an acceptable level for consumers
- it can show if the packaging is attractive to consumers
- it indicates the type of people who would be their target market
- it shows the area in which sales are likely to be more successful
- sometimes it gives information about competitors
- it makes businesses aware of any changes in consumers' tastes or requirements
- having all this information gives the business confidence to develop the most appropriate marketing strategy
- it can also prevent the business from making expensive mistakes.

ACTIVITY

Rory is a Year 12 student who will be leaving school in June after he has finished his GCSE examinations.

He is planning to set up a window cleaning business in his home town.

Make a list of the information Rory would need about the market before he establishes the business.

Methods of Market Research

Secondary research

> Secondary research is also known as 'desk research' which gives a clue how it is worked. Secondary research is done by using published statistics, data and other information which had been collected previously. This makes secondary research very suitable for use by smaller businesses.

This information may come from government publications, from external sources such as newspapers, trade journals, government publications or the Internet. Information may also come from the business's internal sources such as its own sales and financial records.

This diagram shows the various ways in which secondary research can be done:

Advantages of secondary research

- The information is cheap to obtain.
- The information is available immediately.
- The information will have been well researched and will be accurate.
- The data available covers a wide range of sources.

Disadvantages of secondary research

- The data is unlikely to have been collected for exactly the same purpose as the business requires so may not meet the business's needs exactly.
- The information may be out of date.
- The information is available to every other business in the market.

ACTIVITY

Copy the following table and complete it to show the advantages, disadvantages and uses of internal and external secondary research.

ADVANTAGES, DISADVANTAGES AND USES OF SECONDARY RESEARCH

Method	Advantages	Disadvantages	Suitable For:
Internal Sources			
External Sources			

Figure 4.1

Primary research

Primary research is also known as 'field research' which gives a clue about how it is carried out. Primary research is the collection of original information and is carried out by making direct contact with consumers and members of the public who may become consumers.

Advantages of primary research

- The business can design the research in the best way to discover the particular information it needs.
- The business can be sure that the information gathered is up to date.

Disadvantages of primary research

- Designing the research, gathering the information and analysing it can be slow.
- For this reason, businesses often employ specialist researchers but this can be expensive.

The diagram on the left shows the various ways in which primary research can be done.

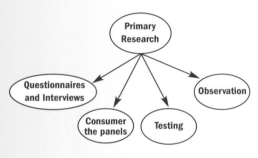

Questionnaires and interviews

This is probably the most common method of primary research. You may have been stopped on the street or in a shop yourself and asked questions about a certain product. Questionnaires can be conducted by telephone or by post as well as face to face.

Advantages of questionnaires and interviews

- Information is taken directly from the people who are, or will be, the business's consumers.
- The questioner can help the member of the public to understand the questions.

Disadvantages of questionnaires and interviews

- Some people resent being stopped and questioned.
- Sometimes people misunderstand the questions and give misleading responses which makes the results less accurate.
- It is a slow method.
- Postal questionnaires are not always returned.

Observation

As its name suggests, this method of primary research involves watching or observing the reactions of people to products. For example, people may be observed making their selection of goods in supermarkets.

Advantages of observation

- It is not costly for the business.
- It is unobtrusive for the consumers.

Disadvantages of observation

- It is less accurate and is open to interpretation.
- It is not suitable for all products.

Consumer panels

The use of consumer panels involves taking responses from people who regularly sit on panels and give their opinions on given products or other consumer information. Panel members are paid and have been selected for their expertise or knowledge in this area.

Advantages of consumer panels

- Very detailed information can be gathered.
- The panel members are skilled and impartial.

Disadvantage of consumer panels

- It is an expensive method.

Testing

Testing involves members of the public being given samples of the product and being asked for their opinion of it. This is frequently used in supermarkets when a new variety of a food, such as cheese, is being launched on the market.

Advantages of testing

- Tests are straightforward to organise.
- Consumers' first-hand opinions are given.

Disadvantages of testing

- It may not test a cross-section of the public.
- It is not suitable for all products.

Interpretation of Results of Market Research

The CCEA specification also expects its candidates to carry out an interpretation of results of market research. This is a very practical activity and is an ideal topic to incorporate into your coursework.

EXAMINATION QUESTION

CC Computers produce computer games. They have learned that their major competitor has just launched a new game.

Describe a suitable method of market research for this business.

(4 marks)

(Adapted from CCEA Business Studies, GCSE, Paper 2 Foundation Tier, 2001)

Tips for answering this question:

The command word in this question is 'describe', which means that you must first name one suitable method of market research and then you are expected to write a statement which shows the main features of that method and how the method would work for CC Computers.

ACTIVITY

ACTIVITY

Let's return to Rory who plans to set up a window cleaning business.

He now needs you to advise him how he might find the information he needs about the window cleaning market in his home area

Write down the names of the methods he might use and tell him how to find the information he needs.

ACTIVITY

Copy and complete the following list to show the best method of primary research to use to collect information in each example:

1. A new flavour of cheese ....
2. Detergent ....
3. Television programmes watched ....
4. A new soft drink ....
5. Trainers ....
6. Golf balls ....
7. Baby wipes ....
8. Computer software ....
9. Bathroom tiles ....
10. Cars ....

Sampling

Sampling is a part of primary research. Instead of asking opinions from a large number of people, this method questions a selection – or sample – of people. For accuracy of results, it is estimated that any sample should consist of approximately 2,000 people. The people questioned would be chosen as being representative of the population as a whole.

Sampling has the advantage of being manageable for the business which would find it impossible to survey everyone. It is also within its financial means and time limitations.

Methods of sampling

There are several methods by which sampling can be done and the most commonly used are:

Random sampling

A random sample is where people are randomly selected and asked for their opinions. The random sample may be taken as every tenth person who walks down the street or every fiftieth name in the telephone directory, for example.

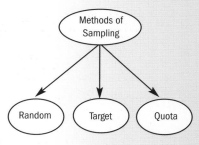

There is a possibility that some of the people questioned may not be familiar with the product or even be interested in it. For instance, there is not much point in questioning a very elderly gentleman about trainers! Therefore the results of random sampling are of most use where the product is one which nearly everyone uses.

Advantages of random sampling

- Personal opinions are given by those surveyed.
- Everyone has a chance of being chosen.

Disadvantages of random sampling

- Results are not very accurate unless a very large sample is used.
- Random surveys are the most expensive type of survey.
- The method is unsuitable for some products.
- It does not necessarily reach the most appropriate people.

Quota sampling

Quota sampling is where interviews are held with a set number of people who fall into pre-determined categories. For example, a quota sample might consist of 50% males and 50% females or one-third teenagers, one-third middle-aged people, and one-third elderly people.

As in random sampling, these people's views are taken to reflect the views of everyone in their gender or age group.

It is important that the sample also reflects the composition of the people in the area, so, if there were more elderly people living in the area than teenagers, then the sample should contain more elderly people than teenagers.

Advantages of quota sampling

- Results are more accurate than in random sampling.
- It is more likely to reach the appropriate people.
- Personal opinions are given by those surveyed.
- Everyone in the particular category has a chance of being chosen.
- Quota surveys are considerably cheaper than random surveys.

Disadvantages of quota sampling

- The composition of the population must be known in order for the correct proportions to be interviewed.
- The method is unsuitable for some products.

Target sampling

Target sampling is where people from only a particular market segment are questioned. This narrows down the people questioned to include only those who are really going to be interested in the particular product being researched.

The survey might be limited, for example, to a particular area, or to people who work in a particular profession, or share a particular sport or hobby. Target sampling would be carried out wherever and whenever these people are likely to be present.

For example, people who fish for a hobby could be targeted by a business producing fishing rods while everyone living in Draperstown could be sampled to get their views on the proposed opening of a casino in the town. If the researchers were gathering information about sportswear they might question people in leisure centres, or they might question people at a motor show for their views on a new car.

Advantages of target sampling

- Results are more accurate than in other methods of sampling.
- It is more likely to reach the appropriate people.

Disadvantage of target sampling

- Target samples may be small.

ACTIVITY

Your school is considering the formation of a chess club. You have been asked to undertake a quota sample of both boys and girls from all year groups in order to find out their level of interest in the new club.

The following information about the school population has been supplied to you. The information gives the total number of boys and girls in each year group and the percentage which that represents of the total school population of 500 pupils. It has been decided to exclude Year 14.

WHOLE SCHOOL POPULATION					
YEAR	BOYS	% BOYS	GIRLS	% GIRLS	% TOTAL
8	45	9	48	9.6	18.6
9	35	7	40	8	15
10	40	8	30	6	14
11	45	9	45	9	18
12	50	10	50	10	20
13	35	7	37	7.4	14.4
TOTAL	250	50	250	50	100

1. Make a copy of the table, leaving out the figures for the numbers and percentages of the pupils.
2. Complete your table to show the numbers and percentages of pupils in each year group you plan to interview.
3. Write a first draft of the questions you plan to ask the pupils.
4. State whether you agree or disagree with excluding Year 14, and give your reasons.
5. How would you have carried out this survey if you had been allowed to conduct a random survey?

Market Segmentation

Market segmentation is a very useful method by which businesses may study the market for their products. Market segmentation is the selection of the groups of people who would be most interested in a particular product so that the product may be targeted at them. Targeting the correct segment of the market is vital to the business if it is to achieve sales.

This method involves dividing the market for a product into different groups and types of consumers. Examples of the groups are given in the list below. While all groups differ from one another, members of groups are seen to share tastes and to have similar spending patterns. For example, most teenagers share tastes in clothes and music while the majority of wealthy people tend to go to the same restaurants and drive similar cars.

Markets are commonly segmented according to:

- Age

  Each age group has its own choice of product. Think of the differences in preferences in music and clothes as examples. Do your parents like the music you listen to? Does your granny like your clothes?

- Gender

  In some products, males and females choose differently. For example, research has shown that males and females have different tastes in the cars they buy. Females are more influenced by the shape and appearance of the car while males tend to be more influenced by its performance.

Figure 4.2

- Ethnic/cultural background

  Each race or ethnic grouping of people has its own taste in food, music and clothes.

- Geography

  Consumers living in different areas of the country, or in different countries, like different foods and often have different hobbies, for example.

- Socio–economic class

  This classification looks at the occupation of the head of the household and places the occupations in nine different bands. Obviously, the occupation will determine the level of income of the household which in turn will determine the type of spending of the family.

  A new classification called the 'Standard Occupational Classification 2000' was published in 2000 which reflects the changes in modern society.

Standard Occupational Classification 2000	
Socio-economic Group	Occupations
1	Managers and senior officials
2	Professional occupations
3	Technical occupations
4	Administrative and secretarial occupations
5	Skilled trades occupations
6	Personal service occupations
7	Sales and customer service occupations
8	Process, plant and machine operatives
9	Elementary occupations

ACTIVITY

Copy and complete the following list to indicate the market segment which should be targeted in each example.

a   A top of the range car   ....
b   Naan bread   ....
c   Farming equipment   ....
d   Rock music   ....
e   Trainers   ....
f   Caviar   ....
g   Toys   ....
h   Computer software   ....
i   Tickets for a city fashion show ....
j   Walking sticks   ....

EXAMINATION QUESTION

Explain what is meant by 'market segmentation'.

(2 marks)

(CCEA Business Studies, GCSE, Paper I Foundation Tier, 2001)

Tips for answering this question:

Here you are asked to 'explain', so you have to show the examiners that you understand what the term means. You should write your explanation in a simple sentence starting 'Market segmentation is ....'

R E V I S I O N

At this stage you should understand:

Market research	Target market	Secondary research
Primary research	Questionnaires	Consumer panels
Testing	Sampling	Random sampling
Quota sampling	Target sampling	Market segmentation

As revision, look each one up in the Glossary at the end of the book.

Marketing

Before you can understand the Marketing Mix you should be sure that you understand what marketing is. The word 'marketing' is used frequently, but could you define what marketing really is?

Let's take the definition used by the Chartered Institute of Marketing:

> **'Marketing is the process which identifies, anticipates and satisfies customers' requirements profitably'.**

In other words, marketing finds out what products or services customers want, either now or in the future, and provides those products or services to them at a price which leaves a profit for the business. You should be aware that marketing is about much more than simply selling.

Modern marketing focuses very clearly on the customers and always looks at the business from their point of view. It asks what customers really need and if the business is meeting that need. Market-driven businesses will change the product or service to suit the customer.

Sainsbury's and Tesco are two businesses which are very committed to marketing and are now the most profitable retailers in Northern Ireland. Compare their position with that of Marks and Spencer who, until recently, were less aware of their customers' needs. They became criticised for selling clothing which many people thought dull and uninteresting. As a result, Marks and Spencer's profits plummeted and they are now having to work very hard to regain their position in that particular market.

Sainsbury's
making life taste better

Competitive marketing

'Competitive marketing' is another frequently used term and simply describes any market in which there are many businesses competing for customers.

ACTIVITY

Copy the following list and give the name of a competitor for each of these well-known retailers in Northern Ireland.

Business   Name of Competitor

Computer World   ....

Activity continues on the next page

Debenhams	....
McDonald's	....
Woolworths	....

The Marketing Mix

The Marketing Mix is all the key activities which are used in marketing a business's products. This is frequently referred to as the four Ps: Price, Promotion, Place and Product

Some people argue that two other Ps should be added to the marketing mix: P for People who are, as we have seen, such an important part of marketing, and for Packaging, but packaging is really part of Promotion.

The idea of the Marketing Mix is the same idea as when mixing a cake. A baker will alter the proportions of ingredients in a cake depending on the type of cake he/she wishes to bake. The proportions in the Marketing Mix can be altered in the same way and differ from product to product.

A new brand of detergent, for example, would be marketed very differently from a new range of expensive jewellery.

Figure 4.3

The mix will also vary at different times throughout the life of a product. The price would be lowered or advertising might be increased at times when sales are falling off.

A business will manipulate the four elements of the Marketing Mix in whatever way it has to, in order to keep ahead of its competition.

In the next four units we shall study each of the elements of the Marketing Mix.

EXAMINATION QUESTION

Define the term 'Marketing Mix'.

(2 marks)

(CCEA Business Studies, GCSE, Paper 2 Foundation Tier, 2001)

Tips for answering this question:

This is a straightforward 'recall of knowledge' type of question in which you simply need to say what the Marketing Mix is, giving the names of the four elements of the mix.

Price

Pricing policies

There are a number of pricing policies which a business may adopt. The choice of policy depends on:

- the type of product being marketed
- the competition in that market
- the price which people would be willing to pay
- the costs of production which must be covered.

Market-led pricing

Market-led pricing is also referred to sometimes as 'competitive pricing'.

This method simply accepts the price which competitors are charging for a product and then prices its product at the same level or slightly lower in order to gain some advantage over the competitors.

Market-led pricing would operate in a market where there is strong competition and involves close monitoring of competitors and any changes they make to their prices.

This strategy is operated for products such as washing powder where customers will buy their favourite brand in whichever shop offers it at the lowest price.

Cost-based pricing

Cost-based pricing, also sometimes referred to as 'cost plus pricing', involves working out the business's total fixed and variable costs and then adding on a percentage profit. The business also has to consider the total number of items which it plans to produce and sell.

The calculation is simple:

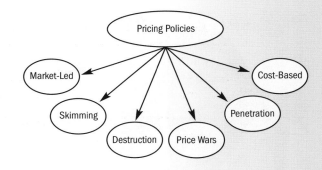

Figure 4.4 *Market-led pricing*

$$\text{Cost-Based Price} = \frac{\text{Total Costs} + \text{Profit}}{\text{Total Sales}}$$

The big advantage of cost-based pricing is that the business is guaranteed to make a profit on its sales since it has covered its costs.

However, the danger is that the business may not be able to sell the expected quantity of the product, perhaps because competitors are offering the same goods at a lower price. Therefore, in operating cost-based pricing it is vitally important to be aware of competitors' prices and what the market will bear.

Skimming

Skimming is most often used in the case of new products when there is little competition in the market.

This strategy sets a relatively high price initially, in an attempt to 'skim' the market – like skimming the cream off the milk! Some people would be willing to pay the higher price because the product is new and unique and few other people would own it. Later on, other businesses will enter the market, setting up competition so, in order to maintain sales, the price would be reduced.

Figure 4.5 *Price wars*

The high initial price gives the impression of high quality and is justified by the manufacturers because the product usually would have had high costs in research and development. The danger of skimming is that some people would be deterred by the high price and prefer to wait until the price falls.

Pricing of mobile phones is an excellent example of skimming. When mobile phones were first produced they were expensive and few people owned them. Initially, they were something of a status symbol. Later they were produced in large numbers by a variety of manufacturers and the price fell to such an extent that today most people own mobile phones.

Penetration pricing

Penetration pricing is where a low price is set at the beginning in order to gain entry to an existing market, and where the price increases when the place in the market has been secured.

Penetration pricing would be used by a new business trying to break into – or penetrate – a market where other competitors already are well established. Obviously, this pricing strategy is suitable for a competitive market.

In order to attract customers to the new store, and away from the competitors, they have to be lured by low prices. The basic idea is that, once the customers have been lured by the lower prices, they will become regular customers. It is at that stage that prices would be raised.

This method of price setting ensures sales, at least in the short term. It is possible, however, that the price has to be set so low that profits may be minimal.

Figure 4.6 *Destruction pricing*

Destruction pricing

Destruction pricing is also known as 'destroyer pricing'. It is a ruthless strategy which is designed to destroy competitors' sales or even drive them out of business altogether.

This method operates by reducing the price of an existing product or selling a new product at an artificially low price. Sometimes this new low price may be below cost level so the business would be sustaining a loss for a period of time. Once the competitors have been driven out of the market, the prices would be raised again.

If the competitor is a small business it would be unable to reduce its prices in this way and may be forced to close. This has been the fate of so many of our corner shops and village stores in Northern Ireland.

Price wars

In very competitive markets such as the grocery market, businesses sometimes engage in price wars in which prices of some goods are cut to a very low level in order to secure sales.

The idea is to attract customers to their particular supermarket to buy the marked-down goods and encourage them to buy other goods while they are there.

Price wars are not popular with businesses, however, even though they often happen. They are risky because advantages gained over other businesses are short-lived and rival businesses tend to respond by slashing prices even further.

If pursued long enough, price wars would cut profits seriously and, in the end, only the customer benefits by the low prices.

ACTIVITY

Study the following situations and name the pricing strategy which is being described in each example.

1. A new hardback book is published at £20. Two months later, it is sold in paperback for £10.
   ....

2. A new supermarket in Lisburn opens selling a particular chocolate bar at 50p. Existing supermarkets in the town lower their prices of the chocolate bar to 40p.
   ....

3. Several stationery companies in Belfast keep lowering their prices of computer paper to take sales away from each other.
   ....

4. A bicycle manufacturer introduces a new model at a low price in order to attract sales.
   ....

5. A chemist shop in Lurgan researches the price of particular brands of toothpaste in all local outlets and then charges the same prices as they are charging.
   ....

6 A florist in Lisnaskea sets her prices to cover her total costs plus a little profit.
   ....

EXAMINATION QUESTION

CC Computers produce computer games and their major competitor has just launched a new game. Sales of their most popular game are declining.

Explain two pricing policies which CC Computers could use if they decide to introduce a new game.

(6 marks)

(Adapted from CCEA Business Studies, GCSE, Paper 2 Higher Tier, 2001)

Tips for answering this question:

You are asked to 'explain' two pricing policies. This means that you should give as much detail about two policies as you can in order to show that you fully understand them. You would be given 1 mark for correctly naming each suitable policy, and 2 marks for a good explanation of each one.

ACTIVITY

Six pricing policies are described in the column on the left. You should link each one to the appropriate name in the column on the right. The first one is done for you.

Activity continues on the next page

Activity continued

Description	Pricing Policy
This policy is based on the prices charged by competitors	Destruction pricing
This policy charges a high price at the beginning and reduces it later	Market-led pricing
This policy cuts prices very low in order to take sales away from competitors	Cost-based pricing
This policy tries to put other firms out of business	Penetration pricing
This policy sets a low price at the beginning and increases it later	Skimming
This policy is based on the costs incurred in making and selling the goods	Price wars

Factors that affect price

Price has to be carefully worked out for every item put on the market. Several factors have to be considered:

Costs of production

The producer has to calculate the total costs incurred in manufacturing the goods. These costs would include factory overheads and raw materials.

The retailer has to calculate the costs incurred in offering the goods for sale such as transport charges, wages to sales staff and shop overheads.

The price charged to the consumer has to be set at a level which would cover all these costs.

Need to make a profit

The overall aim of any business owner is to make a profit from the business, so the goods must be priced at a level which not only covers the total costs but also leaves a margin of profit for both the manufacturer and the retailer.

The owners would expect the level of profit on their investment in the business to be at least as much as the interest they could have earned if they had left their money in the bank. A healthy profit margin also encourages other investors to buy into the business.

The highest level of profit, however, will not necessarily be made by charging the highest prices since this could discourage sales.

Competition in the market

We have already seen in this unit how competitors' prices are monitored in order to increase sales. The aim in business is to set the price at a level which would encourage customers away from competitors.

To do this, the price has to be slightly lower than that charged by the competition if the goods are exactly the same.

Price which the market could bear

It is most important that the business is sensitive to the price which customers can afford and are willing to pay. This is also linked to the type of product.

If the goods being sold are luxury items they would be targeted at a wealthier market so that particular market could bear a higher price. Goods being sold in a shop in a less well-off area will have to be priced at a level which the customers there could afford.

Whatever the circumstances, the price charged has to be the one at which the highest level of sales would be made.

Season of the year
The demand for certain items rises at particular times of the year. The highest sales of toys are made in November and December, for example, for the Christmas market. At these times of greatest demand the price is at its highest and falls immediately after the event. This is why it is possible to buy Christmas cards very cheaply in January.

The red rose you bought for your girlfriend or boyfriend for St Valentine's Day was very expensive, but the next day the price would have been considerably lower!

Quantity of stock in hand
At times when there is a glut of goods in stock a retailer will hold a sale in order to reduce stocks. The price charged to the consumer obviously is affected.

This also happens with airline tickets which can be bought much more cheaply immediately before the date of the flight. In this case, it is better for the airline company to sell the remaining seats at a reduced price rather than fly with a half-empty aeroplane.

In business, this is referred to as 'underused capacity'.

ACTIVITY

Six factors which affect prices are described on the left. You should link each one to the appropriate name in the column on the right. The first one is done for you.

Description	Pricing Policy
The price charged has to cover all costs of production and selling the goods	Season of the year
The price is set so that the owners make some money for themselves	Price the market could bear
The price depends on the time of the year	Cost of production
The price depends on how much people can afford to pay	Need to make a profit
The price depends on what other firms are charging for the same goods	Quantity of stock in hand
The price is determined by how much of the goods the business has	Competition in the market

Relationship between Price and Demand

Before exploring the relationship between price and demand, you should be sure that you understand the business meaning of 'demand' and how it differs from 'needs'.

We all have needs and wants.

We **need** food, basic clothing and shelter in order to survive.

We **want** a range of fashionable clothes, a more luxurious house or a bigger car but these items are not essential for our survival.

The total of our wants become 'demand' when those wants are backed up by money or when we are able to pay for them. So we can now define demand:

> **Demand is the quantity of goods which will be bought at a given price.**

Successful businesses are those who can satisfy consumer demand and can get:

> **the right goods to the right place at the right time and at the right price.**

There are many factors which cause a change in the demand for particular goods:

- The price being charged for the goods
  Usually, the higher the price being charged, the lower the demand for the goods.
- Customers' tastes
  People buy what they like or according to the prevailing fashion. For example, even if alcohol were free, some people would still not buy it because they are teetotal.
- Level of income
  Customers usually buy what they can afford. As income increases, people would not necessarily buy more goods but they probably would buy better-quality goods.
- Price of other goods
  Some goods act as substitutes and can be bought instead. For example, if potatoes were very expensive, people might eat pasta instead.
  Other goods are complementary goods which means they are often used together. For example, if the price of fish fell, people would eat more fish. This might cause extra demand for potatoes because we often eat fish and chips together.

- Advertising

  Increased advertising, if successful, would cause an increase in demand.

- Credit rates

  At times when the lending rate is low, people will be able to borrow more from banks and building societies and demand for goods will increase as they buy more goods.

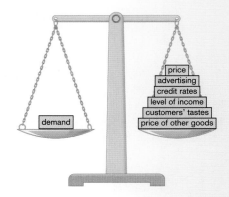

Figure 4.7

ACTIVITY

Damien is a butcher who has a large stock of beef in his shop. Unfortunately, there has been a recent health scare which has put some people off buying beef.

a   Advise Damien on ways to increase demand for beef

b   What else might Damien do in order to increase trade generally in his shop?

The relationship between price and demand is best illustrated graphically, with price on the vertical axis and quantity demanded on the horizontal axis.

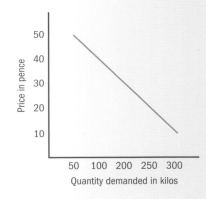

As price falls, demand rises.

This fact can be shown on a demand line which always slopes downward to the right:

This graph illustrates the demand for potatoes:

50 kilos are demanded at 50p per kilo.

300 kilos are demanded at 10p per kilo.

ACTIVITY

Study the above graph showing the demand for potatoes.

a   Read off the number of kilos of potatoes which would be demanded if they were priced at 40p per kilo.

b   Find out how many kilos would be demanded if the potatoes were priced at 30p per kilo.

c   What do your answers prove about the relationship between price and demand?

REVISION

At this stage you should understand:

- factors which affect price
- relationship between price and demand
- factors which cause a change in demand for goods.

You should also know the meaning of:

Marketing	Marketing Mix	Demand
Market-led pricing	Cost-based pricing	Skimming
Penetration pricing	Destruction pricing	Price wars

As revision, look each one up in the Glossary at the end of the book.

The Marketing Mix – Promotion

The second part of the marketing mix which we will study is **promotion**. This is another commonly used term, but could you define it?

> **Promotion is the process by which businesses inform customers about their products and encourage them to buy those products.**

Promotion is a very important element of the marketing mix because even the best products will not be sold if consumers do not know about them.

Promotion is important not only at the introduction of a new product, but as an ongoing process throughout its life, because customers need to be reminded about it if sales levels are to be maintained.

Promotion also keeps the name of the company and the name of its product(s) at the forefront of customers' minds. This creates an image for the company and also helps to keep it ahead of its competitors.

ACTIVITY

Study the above information, then copy and complete the following statements to show what effective promotion does for a company.

a   Promotion is important at the .... of a ... product.
b   Promotion makes .... aware of ... products.
c   Promotion keeps customers .... about products.
d   Promotion maintains .... for the company.
e   Promotion creates an ..... for the company.
f   Promotion helps to keep the company ....

There are many methods of promotion, but the four types illustrated on the right are the most usual:

Methods of Promotion

Advertising | Sales Promotion
Public Relations | Sponsorship

Sponsorship

It is quite common for businesses to sponsor sporting events, charity events or school events. All of these activities portray the business as being public spirited and interested in its local community. The business donates the funds necessary to run the event, and, in return, the players wear kit displaying the company logo. The company name also is usually emblazoned around the sports field. This provides wide publicity for the business, especially if the event is being televised.

Two annual Northern Ireland sponsored, sporting events are the Schools' Rugby Cup, and the Belfast Marathon. At present, the Ulster Schools' Rugby Cup Competition is sponsored by Renault and, in 2002, the Belfast Marathon was sponsored jointly by Belfast City Council and the Ulster Pork and Bacon Forum.

Figure 4.8 *The 2002 Belfast City Marathon (sponsored by Belfast City Council and the Ulster Pork and Bacon Forum)*

On a much larger scale, and involving much larger sums of money, you will notice on television that the UEFA Champions League is sponsored by Ford and Mastercard, currently, the Six Nations Rugby Championship is sponsored by Lloyds TSB, while 'Coronation Street' is sponsored by Cadbury. These programmes all have large followings so, by association, the names of the sponsors are linked with success and popularity.

ACTIVITY

Class debate

The members of your class are all directors of Ford which is one of the multi-national companies sponsoring the UEFA Champions League. Two of the directors are concerned about the amount of money being spent on this sponsorship and wish to pull out of it. Those particular directors feel the money should be saved but they would accept it if the company decided to sponsor a local league instead.

Elect two speakers to propose and second the following motion, and two main speakers to propose and second the opposition of the motion:

'We believe that this company should cease to sponsor the UEFA Champions League. Instead we propose that the company should sponsor a local league.'

All other members of the class should make contributions to the debate from the floor.

Public Relations

Any activity under the heading of 'public relations' is one where the public's awareness of the company is raised and the company is seen to be generous. Creating a good impression in this way creates a loyalty with members of the public who will then be more likely to buy from the business.

Examples of public relations activities are where companies donate sizeable sums of money to charity or perhaps contribute cash or products towards famine relief or a war-torn area.

The *Belfast Telegraph* recently reported:

Eight daredevil staff members from Mivan, the Antrim-based specialist engineering company, reached new heights to help Ulster charity Mencap.

The Mivan group took part in a sponsored abseil at BT Riverside Tower in Belfast, raising £1,600 for the charity, which supports and campaigns for people with a learning disability, their families and carers.

The Antrim-based firm donated 50% of the final total and many of its staff sponsored colleagues to do the abseil.

Mivan staff abseil for charity

Sales Promotion

'Sales promotion' is an overall term covering all methods which are used to persuade the customer to purchase the product. The diagram below illustrates the various types of sales promotion.

Sales promotion methods

Special offers
These are very commonly used. Examples are 'buy two, get one free', or 'get 10% extra free'. The customer is attracted by the low price and sales for the shop would be increased.

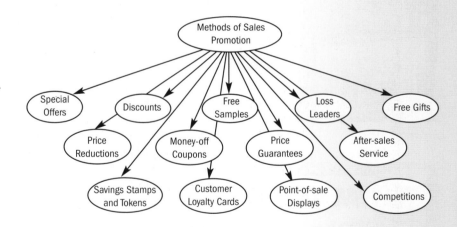

Discounts
This is where 10% or half price, for example, is given off the total price. Again, the customer is attracted by the low price and buys the product

Loss leaders
This is another form of price reduction found in larger shops. The price of one or two items is reduced to a very low level (even to the level of making no profit on those items). These low price goods attract customers in, and the shop hopes to encourage them to buy other, full-price goods while there. Bread is often offered as a loss leader in supermarkets.

Price reductions
In this case the price of the product is reduced for a short period of time. The low price encourages people to buy that particular product which improves its sales.

Figure 4.9

Money-off coupons

Sometimes coupons are printed on the packaging of a product, offering the next purchase of the product at a lower price. Coupons sometimes are sent in the post or can be cut out from newspapers. Customers save the coupons and have to buy the product again to take advantage of the offer. In this way, sales of the product are doubled for the company.

Competitions

Customers are sometimes encouraged to buy a particular product by printing entry forms for a competition on the packaging or including a leaflet at the point of sale. The prize is usually very worthwhile – a luxury holiday or a car – and this encourages people to buy the product.

Customer loyalty cards

Customers' cards are swiped at the check-out point and the totals of their purchases are recorded electronically. Each purchase earns points and the points can later be exchanged for cash or Air Miles. Such cards encourage customers to return to the same store in order to build up their points

Figure 4.10

Free samples

Free samples of some products are given of items such as food, cleaning materials or make-up. Customers are sometimes asked to sample foods in shops. Some products occasionally have free samples of another product attached, and sometimes magazines have free samples of make-up attached to their front covers. All these samples are designed to introduce the product and encourage people to buy it

Free gifts

Some products contain small free gifts enclosed in their packaging. For example, Kelloggs gave small toys in their cereals at one time but were criticised because of the safety factor. Other free gifts are obtained by collecting a certain number of tokens printed on the packaging. Sales are improved because customers have to buy more of the product in order to collect the tokens and get the gift.

Point-of-sale displays

Special displays are sometimes mounted in the shop to encourage shoppers to buy that particular product in that shop. An area is allocated to the product and special display stands erected to draw attention to the product. For some products such as small kitchen appliances, the display may also include a demonstration showing the benefits of those particular appliances.

Figure 4.11

Price guarantees

Customers are encouraged to shop with companies which offer price guarantees such as 'our prices cannot be beaten'. Computer World in Lisburn, for example, challenges customers to find its goods in other shops for less money. If they can find the same goods at a cheaper price, Computer World will refund the difference in the two prices.

After-sales service

Offering an excellent after-sales service is usually an encouragement for customers to choose a particular company when buying an expensive item such as a computer. This gives the customer confidence that assistance would be available if required. For this reason, customers are willing to pay a higher price rather than take advantage of special offer prices in large shops which do not have an after-sales service.

Savings stamps and tokens

In this type of promotion, stamps or tokens are given with purchases and saved. They can then be exchanged for goods which have been displayed in a catalogue or in the store. These are less popular than previously because they take time and the tokens can be mislaid.

ACTIVITY

Write the name of the sales promotional method which you would recommend in each of the following examples and explain your choice of method.

a   Sales of fish have fallen off since a recent health scare about chemicals being dumped at sea.

b   Sales of mobile phones need some help because nearly everyone has already bought the product.

c   A new cereal is being launched on the market by a well-known company which already markets many varieties of cereal.

d   A new luxury car is being launched. The car is very expensive.

e   A cheese manufacturer wishes to improve sales of all types of cheese in order to beat the competition.

f   A small computer retailer is generally having difficulties because people are buying from the large retailers which have a larger variety and can sell at cheaper prices.

g   New tights are being introduced to the market.

h   A firm of soup manufacturers has found that sales of its new soup flavours are not popular.

EXAMINATION QUESTION

CC Computers produce computer games. Their major competitor has just launched a new game.
Recommend the sales promotional methods which could be used to increase sales for CC Computers.

(4 marks)

(CCEA Business Studies, GCSE, Paper 2 Foundation Tier, 2001)

Tips for answering this question:

You are asked to 'recommend' the methods to use. To 'recommend' means that you must choose the methods which are most suitable in the circumstances for this company, and which you think would be most likely to increase its sales. Bear in mind that they have a competitor who could steal their business with the new game. Choose two methods and say why you recommend them.

Advertising

Advertising is an important aspect of promotion and one in which companies invest large sums of money. They do this in order to:

- introduce a new product to the public and encourage sales
- remind the public about an existing product and boost its sales
- target a new segment of the market, thereby increasing their market share
- provide information about products or events.

Figure 4.12
Informative advertising giving details of an auction

Types of advertising

There are three types of advertising and each one has a different function:

1. **Informative** advertising — This type of advertising is purely factual and its intention is to give information. Advertisements about forthcoming events, advertisements giving technical information or advertisements re-calling products because of faults are all examples of informative advertising.

2. **Persuasive** advertising — As its name suggests, the intention of persuasive advertising is to persuade members of the public to purchase the advertised product. This type of advertising aims to convince people that the product being advertised should be selected in preference to the goods produced by rival businesses. It also aims to convince them that the quality of their lives would be improved if they were to buy that particular product.

3. **Generic** advertising — The word 'generic' means 'applied to a large group or class; general, not specific'. Generic advertising is, therefore, advertising for a whole industry or a particular type of goods regardless of where the product is sold. Advertising by the Milk Marketing Board encouraging people to drink more milk is an example of generic advertising.

ACTIVITY

Which type of advertising is described in the following examples?

a   A doctor is telling everyone about the new opening hours at his surgery.
b   Advertising which encourages members of the public that potatoes are good for them.
c   A new perfume is being advertised in the glossy magazines.

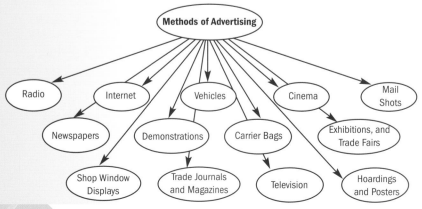

The diagram on the left illustrates the various methods of advertising.

Hoardings and posters

Hoardings are large boards situated at the side of the road. Hoardings have an immediate visual impact on passing traffic and can be seen at a distance. To be effective, they must be large, and therefore are limited to short messages which can be read quickly. This advertising method has no control over its audience so it must be designed to appeal to all tastes and age groups. It is most suitable for advertising goods which are bought by the majority of the population.

Figure 4.13 Hoarding

In cities, large, brightly-lit neon signs are commonly found as modern replacements for hoardings. These neon signs are expensive to maintain and therefore are used only by large multi-nationals such as Coca-Cola.

Neon signs on point-of-sale fridges now frequently replace posters and are also used by companies such as Coca-Cola.

Television
This is the most expensive type of advertising, costing approximately £1,000 per viewing second depending on the time of day. It reaches a wide audience and is highly effective because it can be glamorous and entertaining.

The product may also be seen on television so it can have an important visual impact. Times of advertising are altered to suit the audience, so toys, for example, are advertised during the day or early evening to target children.

Radio
Radio is the advertising method which probably has the widest audience because the radio is listened to at all times of the day and in a wide variety of places. It is cheaper than television advertising and different stations can be used to target different sectors of the market.

Cinema
This type of advertising can reach only those members of the public who visit the cinema. It is therefore more restricted than either radio or television advertising. Cinema advertising is frequently locally based and is often used by shops in the area.

Internet
The Internet is the fastest growing and most recent form of advertising. Advertisements on the Internet have a world-wide audience and can be reached at any time. They are capable of giving vast amounts of information which can then be saved or printed by the customer. It is possible for the customer to link with the advertisers in order to get further information. On the other hand, the Internet cannot be accessed by anyone who does not have the necessary equipment.

Newspapers

Newspapers are bought by the majority of the population so this form of advertising is capable of reaching a wide audience. All newspaper advertising is expensive, however. It is important that the advertisers choose the appropriate newspaper to reach their target market because different sectors of the public read different newspapers. For example, readers of the *News of the World* would have no interest in *The Times* or vice versa.

Newspapers can also cater for small classified advertisements about items for private sale. They may cover a local area – such as the *Portadown Times* – or have a province-wide readership – like the *Irish News*, the *News Letter* or the *Belfast Telegraph*.

Trade journals and magazines

Specialist trade journals are good for advertising items such as specialist equipment since the target market for that equipment is likely to read the journals. Magazines are bought by most people and their vast range caters for all interests and age groups. Advertising in magazines can be accurately targeted at the appropriate age group and is, therefore, very effective.

Exhibitions

Exhibitions are attended by large numbers of visitors and are aimed at a certain sector of the market. For example, the Ideal Home Exhibition is held every September in the King's Hall, Belfast and attracts a large number of exhibitors showing household furniture, materials and equipment. People visit the exhibition to view the latest trends in house design.

The annual Motor Show, at the same venue, shows the latest models of cars and encourages the motoring public of Northern Ireland to order them.

Figure 4.14

Demonstrations by experts

This is a very effective method of advertising and is favoured by food manufacturers or manufacturers of kitchen utensils, for example. An expert is employed to give demonstrations using the product. The idea is then got across to the public that the product must be excellent if the expert uses it. In the following picture, Jenny Bristow is using Denny products and giving the public ideas on how those products may be used.

Mail shots

The term 'mail shot' covers all leaflets sent to people's homes. Mail shots are often used to inform people within a targeted area about the opening of a new store or about local special sale events. There is no guarantee that the mail shots will be read, and some people resent being sent what they consider to be junk mail.

Vehicles

Advertising on the sides of vehicles can be very effective because it may be seen by a large number of people in different parts of the country. This method is cheap if the business's own vehicles are used.

Advertising on public transport vehicles – such as buses – is popular but this must be limited to matters of interest in the area serviced by the public transport vehicle. As with hoardings, the message must be limited to a few words.

Shop window displays

These displays are very effective in attracting the passing public to enter the shop and make purchases. If the window display is good it will give the impression that the goods inside the shop are also good. One advantage of this method of advertising is that customers are likely to act immediately. On the other hand, the display is limited to people who are in that immediate area.

Carrier bags

Advertising on carrier bags is very cheap but effective because it is seen by large numbers of shoppers in the area of the shop. Very often, carrier bags are recycled, so the audience may be doubled.

Figure 4.15

ACTIVITY

Identify and write down the most appropriate methods of advertising to use in these particular circumstances.

a   A small shop, with very little money to spend on advertising, has a very attractive range of new clothes in stock. Few people know about the new range.

b   A village grocery shop has decided to remain open to 10.00 pm on six days per week.

c   A new household gadget is being launched on the market by a large company.

d   Your family has bought new furniture and wishes to advertise your old furniture for sale.

e   A large well-known ice-cream manufacturer wishes to improve sales of all types of ice-cream throughout the country.

f   A local jewellery business wants to tell the public about its excellent stock.

g   A craftsman, who makes wood carvings, is famous locally for his original designs and excellent workmanship. He would like to expand his market.

h   Organisers of a charity dance would like to make people aware of the event.

i   The Government wants to encourage people to travel by train.

j   A new, very expensive, perfume is being launched.

Legal Constraints on Promotion

The Government aims to protect consumers and to ensure that there is fair and honest trading in our fast-changing society. It is recognised that consumers are no longer able to rely on their own judgement when buying goods and services. A number of laws have been passed for these purposes, and they control the framework in which businesses operate.

It is interesting that the most common areas of consumer fraud investigated today are car clocking and trade mark infringement. In these cases, cars offered for re-sale are described as having low mileage, and, in the second type of fraud, counterfeit goods – mainly perfumes and cassettes – are described as being expensive brands.

Three pieces of legislation play a central part in constraining promotional activities:

Trade Descriptions Acts 1968 and 1972

These Acts were among the earliest pieces of legislation and still are the major tools used to guarantee fair practice in promotional activities.

The Trade Descriptions Acts prohibit the giving of false descriptions or the supplying of goods or services with false descriptions. This covers all information given on the goods about:

- their quantity or size
- their method of manufacture or testing
- the place and date of their manufacture
- the people who manufactured them.

The scope of the Trade Descriptions Acts is very wide and includes all forms of services as well as all types of goods. For example, some farmers were prosecuted for falsely describing their cattle as coming from a BSE-free herd.

In addition, these laws ensure that prices are genuine. If products are described as 'reduced' in a sale, they must have been on sale at the higher price in that shop for at least 28 consecutive days in the previous six months. Otherwise, sale bargains may only be described as 'special purchases' which indicates that those products were bought specially to offer to customers at a lower price. Sometimes the quality of special purchases is less high than that of the regular stock, and the law ensures that consumers are made aware of this possibility.

The Trade Descriptions Acts also state that the country of origin must appear on the packaging of all imported goods.

Descriptions may either be written, pictorial or oral, and any breaches of the Trade Descriptions Acts may incur fines of up to £5,000 sterling or imprisonment of up to two years.

Consumer Protection Act 1987

The Consumer Protection Act 1987 covers more than promotional activities but it is not appropriate, in this section on promotion, to examine any other aspect.

The Consumer Protection Act 1987 lays down rules to govern the use of such terms as 'sales price', 'reduced price' and 'bargain offer'. The point of the Act is to ensure that prices advertised in any of these ways are genuine reductions.

According to the terms of the Consumer Protection Act 1987, it is an offence to give misleading information regarding the pricing of any goods or services. All prices displayed must also include VAT.

The Consumer Protection Act also ensures that dangerous products such as poisons, medicines or solvents must show on the packaging that they are dangerous and must also include first aid procedures to follow if necessary.

Other Constraints on Promotion

> In addition to the legal constraints on promotion, several bodies have been established to give further protection to consumers in this area. In some cases these bodies have been set up by the Government, while in other instances, they are independent.

Advertising Standards Authority (ASA)

The Advertising Standards Authority is an independent body set up to monitor all advertisements which are not broadcast.

The ASA was formed in 1962 by the advertising industry itself, so it is self-regulatory, and this move prevented legal controls being established to govern advertising.

In 1995 the codes of the ASA were extended to cover sales promotion as well as advertising.

The Codes for the industry are written by the Committee of Advertising Practice (CAP).

The basic principles of the Advertising Standards Authority are to make sure that all advertisements are:

- legal, decent, honest and truthful
- prepared with a sense of responsibility to consumers and to society
- in line with the principles of fair competition.

The basic function of the Advertising Standards Authority is to ensure that the public is not misled or offended by advertisements. In order to fulfil this function, the ASA carries out spot checks on approximately 10,000 advertisements every week and will ask the company either to withdraw or to amend any advertisement which does not comply with its principles.

The majority of advertisers are so anxious not to offend the ASA's principles that many of them seek the Authority's advice before publication, which saves them the possible expense and bad reputation caused by having to withdraw an advertisement later.

If a company does not withdraw or amend its advertisement, the ASA does not have any legal power to make it do so. The ASA's main sanction is to ask publishers to refuse more space for an advertisement until its terms have been upheld. In the case of continued offences, the ASA will refer an advertiser to the Office of Fair Trading who can legally prevent similar advertisements being published in the future.

The Advertising Standards Authority also deals with complaints from members of the public who have felt misled or offended by an advertisement. On average the Authority deals with 12,000 complaints per year.

The Advertising Standards Authority regulates all advertising in non-broadcast media, which includes:

- Press — national, regional, magazines and free newspapers
- Outdoor — posters, transport and aerial announcements
- Direct marketing — direct mail, leaflets, brochures, catalogues and circulars
- Sales promotions — on-pack promotions, front page promotions, reader offers and competitions

- Internet
  banner and pop-up advertisements, commercial e-mails and on-line sales promotions
- Other electronic media
  advertisements on computer games, videos and CD-ROMs
- Cinema commercials
  shown at the beginning and end of films.

EXAMINATION QUESTION

What does 'ASA' stand for? Describe the work of the ASA.
(7 marks)

(CCEA Business Studies, GCSE, Paper 2 Higher Tier, 2001)

Tips for answering this question:

This is a very straightforward question but is valuable in terms of the number of marks it carries. All you have to do is to write down the full name of the ASA (1 mark) and then describe its work. You should describe three functions of the ASA, for which you would get 2 marks each. You are not asked for any opinions in this question, so do not waste time giving them.

PUTTING VIEWERS FIRST

Independent Television Commission (ITC)

The Independent Television Commission is another independent organisation and regulates commercial television services. The aim of the Independent Television Commission is to promote and safeguard the interests of all viewers.

Its basic principles are to make sure that all commercial television companies:

- adhere to rules on taste and decency
- are impartial
- do not give offence or cause harm
- support market growth and competition
- set high technical standards.

So, broadly speaking, its function for commercial television is very similar to the function which the Advertising Standards Authority has for advertising media.

The ITC monitors the content of programmes, advertising and technical quality on all commercial television channels, including cable and satellite services. In order to do this, the Independent Television Commission's work includes:

- issuing licences to television services
- setting standards for programme content as well as for advertising and for technical quality on commercial television and monitoring broadcast material
- making sure that viewers can receive television services at competitive rates
- investigating complaints from members of the viewing public.

OFFICE OF FAIR TRADING

Office of Fair Trading (OFT)

The Office of Fair Trading is an independent body which was set up in 1973 as a result of the Fair Trading Act.

Its basic function is to promote and protect the interests of consumers. To do this, the OFT ensures that businesses act fairly towards consumers and operate openly and in a competitive way. This includes making sure that consumers have as much choice as possible.

The Office of Fair Trading has two major aims:

1. to protect consumers and explain their rights
2. to ensure that businesses compete and operate fairly.

The main activities of the Office of Fair Trading are to:

- give advice to members of the public on consumer affairs
- enforce consumer protection laws, taking court action if necessary against businesses which do not behave properly
- investigate how markets are working
- fight against the abuse of market power
- investigate mergers that might lessen competition and cause monopolies.

ACTIVITY

Answer the following questions in your notebook:

a   What are the major principles of the Advertising Standards Authority?
b   How does the Advertising Standards Authority carry out its function?
c   Why do companies often seek the advice of the Advertising Standards Authority before they publish an advertisement?
d   What is the major difference between the work of the Advertising Standards Authority and the work of the Independent Television Commission?
e   What are the major principles of the Independent Television Commission?
f   What do the initials 'OFT' stand for?
g   Describe the function of the OFT.

Ethical and Moral Issues Relating to Promotion

The word 'moral' concerns the difference between right and wrong and concerns identifying the right thing to do. The word 'ethical' is similar and refers to the rules of conduct which should be applied.

In the area of promotion, the moral and ethical issues have largely been covered by legislation. Advertisers are legally prevented from acting immorally. They are not allowed to make false claims about their goods in advertisements and other promotional material. They must be truthful in their descriptions of the price, size, weight and all other details of their products.

The Trade Descriptions Acts also state that the country of origin must appear on the packaging of all types of imported goods. Some people do not wish to buy the products of countries which perpetuate practices they dislike. For example, at one time many people here refused to buy South African fruit because they were strongly opposed to the practice of apartheid in South Africa. Labelling the goods with the country of origin allows customers to make up their own minds on the issue and gives them the information to do so.

Some products, such as cigarettes, are proven to be health hazards. Morally, it is wrong to encourage people to purchase products which may ultimately affect their health. For this reason, the packaging of cigarettes must carry a health warning and advertising of cigarettes is not allowed on television.

The consumption of alcohol makes some people act in an unsocial way and is positively dangerous when driving. Expensive advertising campaigns by the Government have been mounted to inform drivers of the risks, and to discourage the practice. This is an aspect of promotion which is beneficial to the well-being of the community.

ACTIVITY

The following is a very poor answer written by a GCSE student on 'other constraints on promotion'. The student has made a large number of mistakes. You are asked to word-process the answer, correcting all the mistakes. All the answers are found in this unit.

The Advertising Standards Authority is not an independent body and monitors all advertisements whether they are broadcast or not. The Codes for the industry are written by the Committee of Public Practice (CPP).

The Advertising Standards Authority makes sure that all advertisements are legal and three other things which I can't remember.

The Advertising Standards Authority makes sure that the public is not misled or offended by advertisements and they sometimes take advertisers to court. Most advertisers do not care about this. On average the Authority deals with five hundred complaints per year.

The Independent Television Commission is also a dependent organisation. It examines radio services and make sure that no company is offended. It sticks to two rules which are (two things I can't remember).

The ITC also works with BBC1, BBC2 and satellite channels. They do not issue licences or investigate complaints from members of the viewing public.

The Office of Fair Trading was set up in 1998 as a result of the Fair Trading Act. It protects the interests of shop keepers. To do this, the OFT ensures that customers act fairly to businesses This includes making sure that consumers have as little choice as possible.

The main activities of the Office of Fair Trading are to give advice to shop-keepers on consumer affairs and enforce work protection laws. The OFT also investigates how markets are working and encourages mergers and monopolies.

R E V I S I O N

At this stage you should understand:

- sales promotion methods
- types and methods of advertising
- details of the Trade Descriptions Acts 1968 and 1972
- details of the Consumer Protection Act 1987
- the work of the Advertising Standards Authority (ASA)
- the work of the Independent Television Commission (ITC)
- the work of the Office of Fair Trading (OFT).

If you are uncertain about any of these topics, go over the unit again as revision.

The Marketing Mix – Place

You will recall that, in the introduction to this section, you learned that successful businesses are those who can get:

> **the right goods to the right place at the right time and at the right price.**

This unit is about getting the goods to the **place** where they are going to sell most successfully. This means that manufacturers must study carefully where to sell their products as well as how to get them, in good condition, to that place.

To do this, the business must consider:

- the most appropriate sales outlets for that product
- the most appropriate channel of distribution to use
- the most appropriate method of transport for that particular product.

> **Decisions about the type of sales outlet to use will depend on the type and value of the goods being sold and the socio-economic or cultural class of the area. The skill is in placing the appropriate goods in the most appropriate area.**

There is no point in placing very expensive goods in a poor area where people could not afford to buy them, nor is there any point in placing cheap goods in a wealthy area where people would not be interested in them.

ACTIVITY

State where you would place the following goods, giving reasons:

- pitchforks
- children's buckets and spades
- wallpaper
- jewish newspapers

- coffee
- expensive designer clothes
- shampoo
- second-hand furniture.

Parties Involved in Distribution

The following four parties are involved in distribution, and it is important to make sure that you understand the roles of all four before you study the various channels of distribution.

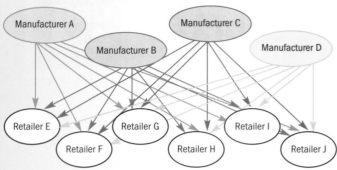

Transactions without a wholesaler

Manufacturer/Producer

The manufacturer or producer is the creator of goods in large quantities. In the case of goods such as furniture, cars etc. the manufacturer would be a factory owner. A farmer is also a producer – producing goods such as fruit, vegetables and meat. Similarly, a fisherman is also a producer.

Wholesaler

The wholesaler is the link between the manufacturer and the retailer. The wholesaler purchases goods in bulk from the manufacturer, and transports them to warehouses where they are stored. The goods are then available for sale to retailers in smaller quantities. This process is often referred as 'breaking bulk'.

The wholesaler provides a useful service for small retailers especially. Because of this service, retailers do not have to provide very large storage facilities nor do they have to buy and pay for large quantities of goods at one time. Instead, they can visit the local wholesaler on a regular basis and restock when necessary. In some cases the wholesaler offers a delivery service and often credit facilities are given to the retailer.

Transactions with a wholesaler

Wholesalers also provide important services for manufacturers, saving them the numerous transactions which they would have if they had to deal directly with retailers.

The following diagrams illustrate this point, using only four manufacturers, one wholesaler and six retailers. Imagine the number of transactions throughout Northern Ireland if manufacturers had to deal with every retailer!

The Holmes Group, with warehouses in Ballymena, Ballymoney, Belfast, Coleraine, Cookstown, Enniskillen, Londonderry, Lurgan and Omagh, is one example of a Northern Ireland wholesaler.

Retailer

The retailer is the final seller of the goods to the customer. Retailing is most frequently done in shops and they may range in size from very large supermarkets to very small village shops.

Whatever the scale on which they operate, they all provide a similar service to the customer. The retailer makes the goods available for the customer at a convenient place and also further breaks bulk of the products so that the customer is able to buy small amounts.

Consumer

The consumer – or customer – is the final user of the product. The consumer would buy small, usable amounts of the product and replace them frequently.

How bulk is broken (using soup as an example)

Refer to the two diagrams which illustrate the number of transactions which would be made with and without a wholesaler.

a   What environmental advantages would there be in having fewer transactions?
b   Name one social cost of closing wholesalers

Channels of Distribution of Goods and Services

A channel of distribution is the way in which the goods are passed from the manufacturer to the consumer.

The choice of channel of distribution depends on the:

- **type of goods** — If the product is a very specialised one, the manufacturer and consumer are likely to want to be directly in contact with each other. For example a shipping company would be in direct contact with its shipbuilders.

- **value of the goods** — Generally, the rule is that the more expensive the product is, the fewer the places which sell it. This maintains the expensive and elite image of the product. For example, it would be unusual to be able to buy a Rolex watch in very small towns.

- **life span of the goods** — If the product is perishable, it must be distributed widely so that people can get it quickly. Fresh fruit and vegetables would be in this category, and therefore are usually sold directly from producer to the retailer or even to the consumer.

- **costs involved** — The most cost-effective method has to be found. If the channel of distribution involves high costs it would be unsuitable for low-cost goods.

- **demand for the goods** — If the product is one which is used regularly by everyone, it must be distributed widely and be available immediately. For example, people expect to be able to buy shampoo almost anywhere.

- **competition for the goods** — Manufacturers need to beat the competition, and therefore they would distribute their products to the same places as are chosen by their competitors.

Explain the factors that might influence a business's choice of distribution channel.

(6 marks)

(Adapted from CCEA Business Studies, GCSE, Paper 2 Higher Tier, 2000)

Tips for answering this question:

In this question you should name any three things which help a business to decide how it will distribute its goods. This will earn you 3 marks. You should then explain those three factors in order to gain the remaining three marks.

There are three channels of distribution in common use:

1. From the manufacturer to the consumer via the wholesaler and the retailer.
2. From the manufacturer to the consumer via the retailer.
3. From the manufacturer directly to the consumer.

Channel 1 – From the manufacturer to the consumer via the wholesaler and retailer

This is the traditional channel of distribution and involves the product being passed through two middlemen before it finally gets to the consumer.

The product is first sold by the manufacturer to the wholesaler, then it is sold by the wholesaler to the retailer and, lastly, it is sold by the retailer to the consumer.

This channel of distribution is still widely used, particularly by small retailers who avail of the storage, bulk-breaking, credit and delivery services of the wholesaler. However this method is being replaced in the case of large retailers, as we shall see in our study of Channel 2.

Channel 2 – From the manufacturer to the consumer via the retailer

This channel distributes the goods from the manufacturer to the retailer who then sells the product to the consumer. This method is becoming more common and has been made possible for two reasons. Firstly, the growth of prepacked goods makes distribution easier, and, secondly, some retailers are so large that they can act as their own wholesalers.

Large companies such as Marks and Spencer, Sainsbury's, Tesco, Currys or Computer World all buy directly from manufacturers. They have the financial reserves necessary to do this, and their orders are so large that manufacturers find it easier to deal with them directly. Because these businesses deal with the manufacturers directly, placing very large orders, they earn large discounts and, as a result, they are able to sell the goods at a lower price to the final consumer.

Manufacturers feel that sometimes they can push sales of their products more forcefully if they deal directly with retailers rather than through a middleman. They also are now in more direct contact with retailers because they see the retailer as being close to the consumer, and this puts them in a better position to hear the views of consumers.

Finally, it is believed that direct contact between manufacturer and retailer builds up loyalty to the company and to its products.

Channel 3 – From the manufacturer directly to the consumer

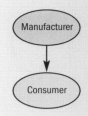

This channel distributes goods directly from the producer to the end-user. It is suitable for certain types of business – for example, businesses selling fresh produce, and businesses selling very exclusive, and therefore very expensive, goods.

Small craft industries often receive orders for items such as individually designed pieces of furniture, for example. The customer would have designed the item and then would liaise directly with the craftsman who has the skill to produce it.

Farmers often sell fresh fruit and vegetables at market stalls directly to their customers, and garden centres also sell their plants and flowers using this method.

Exclusive dress designers, such as Dior, also work in this way, directly consulting with their clients who are often film stars or royalty.

It is also possible to visit factory shops which are established by factories as outlets for their goods. One example of this practice is at Tyrone Crystal Ltd in Dungannon where the Visitors' Centre sells the factory's products. This factory also accepts orders for specially designed and engraved presentation pieces of crystal which is a further example of a direct transaction between manufacturer and consumer.

ACTIVITY

Maureen runs a restaurant in Tandragee. She has added a successful sideline to her restaurant by selling ready-made meals in shops in Tandragee, Richhill, Armagh and Portadown.

Maureen has carried out some market research and is certain that there would be a very good market for her ready-made meals among the elderly people in the area. Her plan is to sell complete dinners each day to the elderly people living in the local folds and sheltered accommodation.

Her accountant is unsure about cutting out the retailer and starting into direct selling to the consumer.

Maureen needs your help to persuade him about the benefits of her plan, and asks you to word-process the arguments she should use.

EXAMINATION QUESTION

Allsorts Suppliers Ltd, a large food manufacturer based in Lisburn, supplies and distributes goods to food retailers.

a   Which channel of distribution does Allsorts Suppliers use?

(2 marks)

b   Why do you think it uses that channel of distribution?

(4 marks)

c   Explain two costs involved in the distribution of goods.

(4 marks)

(CCEA Business Studies, GCSE, Paper 2 Foundation Tier, 2000)

Tips for answering this question:

Part A simply requires you to identify the channel used in this business, without any explanation.

In Part B you should give two reasons for the business's choice of channel. This is really asking you to give two advantages of that type of distribution. In a question like this, always take into consideration any details you know about the business described in the question.

In Part C you should name two costs but you are asked also to explain them. Say what the costs are and then give details of each one.

Figure 4.16

Changing Trends in the Distribution of Goods and Services

Looking at the three diagrams illustrating the channels of distribution will show how distribution has been simplified. Three stages in Channel 1 may be reduced to a single stage in Channel 3.

The present trend in home shopping is likely to continue because of the fact that the majority of women continue with their careers and have less time to shop. Long-established mail order catalogue companies such as Freemans remain popular for their convenience of home shopping and credit facilities. Many of the high street shops such as Next and Debenhams also have mail order services.

Shopping via the Internet is growing enormously in popularity, especially with its increased security of payment methods.

Increasingly, the trend is for large retailers to act as their own wholesalers and buy their goods directly from the manufacturers. Price savings made in this way allow the supermarkets to pass on these benefits to consumers in the form of lower prices. This stimulates trade even further for the retailing giants but causes greater difficulties for small retailers who cannot compete with the price reductions offered by the supermarkets.

Nevertheless, there will probably always be a place for small shops because of their long opening times, the convenience of their location and their personal service.

Implications of the Internet for Distribution

The Internet offers businesses of all sizes the possibility of world-wide trading. For the first time, traders now can be connected to customers in over 100 different countries, allowing them the chance to be literally in more than one place at the same time.

Recent surveys have estimated that there are 544 million people on-line worldwide. Just think of the vast opportunities all those people give businesses to expand their markets! The Internet enables everyone to sell directly to the public, bypassing all the middlemen.

The most suitable products for sale via the Internet are small items such as books and videos, low-cost items which people will take a risk on buying, or hard-to-find, unique items such as crafts products.

While the overall trading opportunities are immense, distribution of products to a world-wide market can be a problem.

Implications for distribution of Internet sales:

- Products have to be delivered in safe condition, cheaply and on time.

  Small items can be posted using either surface mail or air mail. Larger items must be shipped to their destination. International trade is therefore dependent on existing carrier and postal services.

- Matters involving customs and excise, import and export regulations and shipping laws must all be observed.

- Internet sales service must be accompanied by a fleet of delivery vehicles.

  The use of the Internet should not be seen as being only for international trade. Local marketing is also one of its features. More and more large supermarkets are offering on-line shopping with a delivery service.

ACTIVITY

Norman is a retired gentleman and an excellent craftsman. As a hobby, he makes wooden items such as ornaments, picture frames, small pieces of furniture, carved boxes and wooden bowls. Although this work started off as a hobby, people regularly ask him to supply goods for them to give as presents.

His work is so good and his designs so original that you are sure they would sell very well to a wider market.

Norman has never had to use a computer in his life and does not understand how the Internet would help him.

Write, or word-process, a short account of how the Internet could help his business.

Methods of Transport Used to Distribute Goods

Distribution involves transporting the goods to their final destination. The choice of transport method depends on the answers to the following questions:

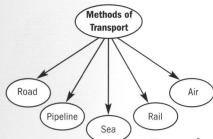

Methods of Transport
- Road
- Pipeline
- Sea
- Rail
- Air

- Is the product valuable?
- Is the product perishable or breakable?
- What is the weight of the product?
- How quickly is the product required?
- How much does the method of transport cost?

Various methods of transport are available:

Road transport

In Northern Ireland, road is the most commonly used method of transport and we depend on it for our supplies. Road transportation is mainly by lorries and vans which are generally owned by the traders and manufacturers themselves. Containerisation is a feature of road transport which allows lorries to make excellent use of their space.

Road transport is suitable for all types of goods and is used for bringing new stock to businesses in Northern Ireland as well as for transporting its exports to the ports.

Figure 4.17
Lorries are the most frequently used method of transport in Northern Ireland

Advantages of road transport

- It is a very adaptable system and permits door-to-door delivery.
- It can be used at any time of the day or night, and is not dependent on timetables.
- In some circumstances, return loads can be organised which reduces the cost.
- Road transport is more secure than some methods of transport because the goods are always accompanied by a driver.

Disadvantages of road transport

- Buying and maintaining the vehicles, and paying fuel costs and drivers' wages are all very expensive.
- Congestion on the roads can sometimes lead to delays.

Rail transport

Northern Ireland is poorly serviced by railways and many areas are too far from the existing lines to make any use of them.

Altogether, Northern Ireland has 210 miles of railway. This operates from Belfast to Dublin, from Belfast to Coleraine and Londonderry with a branch line from Coleraine to Portrush, and suburban routes from Belfast to Portadown, Bangor and Larne.

Advantages of rail transport

- Rail transport is cheaper than road transport.
- It is also faster in larger countries where long distances may be travelled.

Disadvantages of rail transport

- Rail transport needs road transport to take the goods to the railway station and from the station to their final destination.
- The goods are handled by more people, which has implications for their safety and security.

Air transport

Northern Ireland is served by two main airports – Aldergrove International Airport and Belfast City Airport. In Northern Ireland, many business and other people depend on air transport in order to attend meetings in England.

Advantages of air transport

- It is very fast which makes it most suitable for small, light products, especially if speed is important.
- It is a very secure method of transport.

Disadvantage of air transport

- Air transport is very expensive and those costs are then passed on to the consumer.

Sea transport

Sea transport is the principal method of transport used for international trade.

Figure 4.18

Advantages of sea transport

- It is much cheaper than air transport.
- Its economy makes it suitable for heavy goods and large quantities which are not required very quickly.
- Using the roll-on roll-off system, fully loaded lorries are driven straight on to the ships and straight off again at the end of the journey. This allows the goods to remain undisturbed and their good condition is assured.

Disadvantage of sea transport

- Sea transport really only works in conjunction with road transport which is essential to continue the journey of the goods to their final destination.

Pipeline transport

This method of transport is associated with the transportation of oil and gas over long distances. For example, oil from the oilfields in

Figure 4.19
Phoenix Natural Gas pipes being laid in Belfast area

the Middle East is piped hundreds of miles to the docks for export. Using road transport for this purpose would be extremely expensive and inconvenient.

In Northern Ireland, Phoenix Natural Gas has laid 600 kilometres of natural gas pipeline to distribute gas around the Greater Belfast area. In addition, the company has installed 500 kilometres of 24-inch sub-sea pipelines across Belfast and Larne Loughs to bring gas from England to the province.

ACTIVITY

Copy the following table and complete the boxes on the right-hand side to show the type of transport which is most suitable in each example.

Product	Appropriate Method of Transport
Fresh flowers coming from Jersey to Northern Ireland	
Jam being distributed from a warehouse in Belfast to a shop in Islandmagee	
Petrol being distributed to filling stations throughout Northern Ireland from Belfast	
Daily newspapers coming from England to Northern Ireland	
A human heart needed for a transplant operation in London, coming from Templepatrick	
Oil from oilfields in the Middle East to the nearest port	
Twice weekly supplies to Tesco in Northern Ireland from its central stores in England.	
Taking live sheep from a farm to the local market	

REVISION

At this stage, make sure that you understand:

- The relationship between the manufacturer, retailer and consumer in distribution
- Details of the three channels of distribution in common use
- Changing trends in distribution
- Implications of the Internet for distribution
- Details of the methods of transport used to distribute goods.

The Marketing Mix – Product

> The fourth and final part of the marketing mix which we will study is the product – possibly the most important element of all. After all, if there is no product, there is nothing to market.

Let's be clear, before we go any further, what exactly 'product' is. Products are not only goods but may also be services. A product may be defined as the commodity which the business is offering for sale.

A car is obviously the product of a company such as Ford, a holiday is the product of any hotel or travel agency, a band's product is a concert, an operation or other treatment would be a hospital's product while legal advice from a solicitor is also a product.

A product is the commodity which the business is offering for sale.

Product Life Cycle

All products have a lifespan. Some products, such as mustard, seem to have a very long lifespan while other items are crazes for a period of time but tend to go out of fashion equally quickly.

However, even products such as mustard have had to change over the years in order to maintain their places in the market. For example, originally mustard was manufactured in powder form. Later it was developed in its ready-made form and, even later, a variety of flavours were added to give us the range of mustards we can buy today.

Colman's English Mustard: a product with a very long lifespan

The concept of the lifespan of a product is illustrated by the product life cycle, which shows the path of a product from the very beginning through to its withdrawal from the market. This identifies six separate stages in the life cycle of a typical product:

1. research and development
2. introduction or launch
3. growth
4. maturity
5. saturation
6. decline.

ACTIVITY

Use a dictionary to look up the meaning of these six terms. Copy the following table and complete it with the definitions you have found. It is important that you apply the definitions to a market situation.

Life Cycle Stage	Definition
Development	
Introduction	
Growth	
Maturity	
Saturation	
Decline	

Stage 1 – Research and development

This stage takes place before the product is put on the market at all. During the research and development stage, market research would be carried out on the product and it would also be tested, particularly in the case of mechanical or scientific products.

This stage would be very lengthy for expensive products such as cars, and could last as long as 10 years. By contrast, this stage would last a very short time in the case of fashion items where the producer would be anxious to get the product ready for the market as quickly as possible while the fashion lasted.

Stage 1 is an expensive stage for the producer. Research is expensive and no income is being received, so the product is in a loss-making position at the research and development stage.

Stage 2 – Introduction or Launch

In the introductory stage of the life of a product, emphasis is placed on marketing and promotion in order to make the public aware of the product and to create a desire to buy it.

At this point, sales would be slow at the beginning for all goods but would increase rapidly for low cost goods such as detergents if the marketing activity had been successful. In the case of high-fashion goods, sales would also be fast because people would want to have the item as quickly as possible. Sales would be slower for expensive products such as cars, because most people would not spend so much money on a product which had not proved its reliability.

The product would still not be in a profit-making position at this introductory stage because sales would not yet be great enough to cover the costs incurred in the first research and development stage.

Stage 3 – Growth

At this stage, sales grow rapidly as most people would be aware of the product by now, many would have tried it and it would be starting to achieve a degree of customer loyalty.

At the growth stage, sometimes prices can be reduced especially if other producers start to provide competition by putting similar products on the market.

The increased sales will put the product into a profit-making position at this stage as the income from sales covers the initial costs of research and development.

Stage 4 – Maturity

At the maturity stage, sales levels are maintained and the product has an established place in the market. However, the competition becomes very intense at this stage and it is more difficult to increase the volume of the product's sales any further. In an attempt to do so, the product will be advertised intensively once again.

The maturity stage is usually a lengthy one in household products but would last for a very short time in fashion items as the next new craze takes over.

Profits at this stage are at their highest because sales have stabilised.

Nevertheless, an astute business would realise at this stage that it needs to begin to research and develop a second product to have ready to replace its first product when it reaches the later stages in the cycle.

Stage 5 – Saturation

The saturation stage is the highest point in the life of the product. Although competition is intense, there are unlikely to be any new competitors at this stage.

Sales have been pushed as far as possible and new customers cannot be found. Some may be attracted to the product because of decreased prices or extra advertising. At this stage the weakest products will drop out of the market which may prolong the saturation stage of the others for a period of time.

Profits would still be good at the saturation stage, but not growing.

Stage 6 – Decline

The decline stage is the final stage in the life of a product. Sales have fallen to such an extent that they are not covering the manufacturing costs and the product is therefore unprofitable.

Further advertising or price reductions would not be successful and the product should be withdrawn from the market when this stage is reached.

However, this decline stage can be lengthy for some products. For example, some bed-time drinks appear to be less widely used now than previously and less advertising is done. However, these products still have a good place on the market because there is still a sufficient number of customers to sustain them.

Other, short-life products – like last year's high fashion – simply cannot be sold at any price, and so their decline stage is exceptionally short.

The business which has prepared for this stage will have a second product ready for introduction to the market to replace the declining product.

ACTIVITY

Think of any five products which are at the following stages of the product life cycle at the present time, and write their names in the table below.

Product	Stage
....	is at the introduction stage
....	is at the growth stage
....	is at the maturity stage
....	is at the saturation stage
....	is at the decline stage

Illustration of the product life cycle

The product life cycle is illustrated on a graph. By now, you will have realised that the length of the different stages will vary according to the type of product being manufactured and sold. For this reason, the shape of the graph will be different for various products.

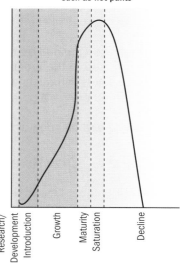

Typical product life cycle of detergent

Typical product life cycle of a fashion item such as hot pants

ACTIVITY

Place the following products on the product life cycle at the stage you think is most appropriate:

- computers
- ice-cream
- internet telephones
- mobile telephones
- bed-time drink

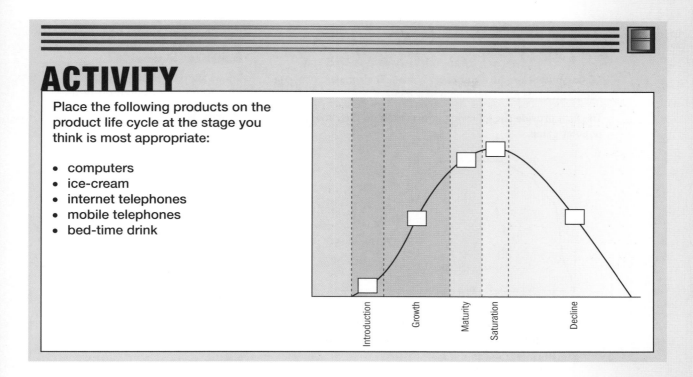

Strategies Used to Extend the Product Life Cycle

Businesses aim to prolong the life of their products as long as possible in order to maximise profits. This is frequently done by making minor alterations to the product, which makes people want to have the latest variety or model. For example:

- sales of Flash cleaners have been expanded by introducing a variety of Flash for the bathroom, for the kitchen etc
- popular drinks such as Coca-Cola, Club Orange and Lilt have introduced 'lite' varieties so that people on diets would continue to buy them
- new, updated editions of books are introduced to maintain sales when previous editions are becoming out of date and sinking into the decline stage
- car manufacturers bring out new designs to their cars on an annual basis, sometimes involving only minor modifications. In each of these cases, the new model or 'improved formula' product is re-launched to persuade consumers to buy it.

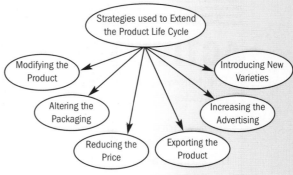

In other cases, packaging of the product is altered to give an updated appearance to the product while promotion and advertising are obvious methods by which to extend the product's life cycle. This is done at stages in the product's life when sales need to be stimulated.

A price reduction is another strategy frequently used to encourage sales and combat competition.

In other cases manufacturers may reconsider the place in which they are selling the product and may decide to introduce it to the export market in order to improve sales.

EXAMINATION QUESTION

CC Computers produce computer games. Their major competitor has just launched a new game.

The firm provide the following information on their most popular game.

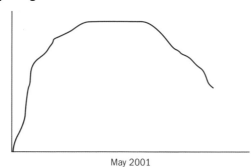

May 2001

a   Identify the stage of the game's life cycle reached in May 2001 and discuss possible reasons why the game has reached this stage.

(5 marks)

b   Recommend two strategies to CC Computers for extending the life cycle of their most popular game.

(4 marks)

(Adapted from CCEA Business Studies, GCSE, Paper 2 Higher Tier, 2001)

Tips for answering this question:

a   1 mark is allocated for the correct identification of the stage. You are asked to 'discuss' the reasons why it has reached that stage. This means that you must give a few points of view and then draw a conclusion about the most likely reason. For 4 marks you should give two reasons.

b   In this case, you are asked to 'recommend' so you must name the two strategies which you think are best in these circumstances, and give your reasons.

ACTIVITY

The following products have reached the saturation level of the product life cycle. How would you extend their lives and prevent them going into the decline stage?

a   A window cleaning cream which has had a very reliable reputation for a long time but is losing out to newer competing products.

b   A high-fat chocolate bar which is no longer popular because of a recent healthy living campaign.

c   A computer which is very cheap but is not suitable for e-mailing or using the Internet.

d   A fizzy drink which has been packaged in the same way for 50 years.

How the Product Life Cycle Assists a Business in Decision Making

A successful business needs to understand the stage in the life cycle which its product has reached. If it does, it will then be able to make decisions which either might prolong the life of the product or have another product ready for the market at just the right time.

The product life cycle informs the business of the stage its product has reached. The business can then react by readjusting its use of the elements of the Marketing Mix. A successful business applies the elements of the Marketing Mix in exactly the most appropriate proportions.

If the product is in the **introduction** stage:

the business needs to make sure that it is being offered for sale in the most appropriate place and using the most appropriate pricing policy which would be either skimming or penetration pricing. At this stage, the business will also decide to advertise widely to create an awareness of the product. The product will be made in low quantities at this stage until sales have improved.

If the business is in the **growth** stage:

less advertising would be required because sales are growing, but the business would decide to produce in greater quantities in order to meet the demand. Competitive pricing would also have to be introduced if other producers had brought similar products to the market. At this growth stage, a forward looking business would consider marketing abroad and would be exploring opportunities through the Internet.

If the product has reached the **maturity** stage:

sales would not be increasing so the business would stabilise production levels because it would not want to have excessive stock. The business would also decide to increase its advertising and change the style of advertising to persuasive advertising in order to encourage the public to buy the product. Although profits at this maturity stage would be very high, a successful business would realise that it should begin to research and develop a second product. Alternatively, it might take the opportunity to slightly alter minor aspects of the product and re-launch it as 'new' or 'improved'.

If the product is at the **saturation** stage:

intensive advertising would be continued and the business might decide to reduce the price of the product or to engage in sales promotions such as offering free gifts or 'buy one get one free'.

If the product has reached the **decline** stage:

the business would try to extend this stage as long as possible but at least until the remaining stock had been sold. The appeal of the product at this stage is only either to those who have a loyalty to the product, or to those who are slow to try new ideas. If the product is one which is likely to have a short decline stage, an immediate decision to stop production would be made, and no further advertising would be undertaken. Price reductions

Figure 4.20

or other sales promotions would be offered only if large stocks remained, in which case strategies such as 'buy three for the price of two' would be used to clear them. At this decline stage, the business would decide to introduce its new product to the market.

It can be seen, therefore, that information obtained from the product life cycle does assist a business in its decision making.

Depending on the type of product, and on its stage in the cycle, the business would decide to change the balance of its marketing mix by making alternations to:

• the product itself
• the place in which it is sold or
• the style of promotion.

ACTIVITY

Complete the following table to show the level and type of each element of the Marketing Mix which it is appropriate to use at each stage of a product's life.

Price	Promotion	Place	Product
Introduction			
Growth			
Maturity			
Saturation			
Decline			

Legal Constraints on Products

The Government has imposed a number of legal constraints on products which are designed mainly to protect consumers.

However, it is recognised that the law also acts as a useful framework for business and, in the vast majority of cases, businesses are anxious to treat customers fairly and to produce goods which are of high quality. They want to deal with complaints in a proper manner because poor quality goods or poor service gives the business a poor reputation and ultimately affects sales.

Nevertheless, it is impossible for the law to cover every eventuality. Consumers still need to exercise common sense and caution when buying goods. If a stranger offers you a brand new, very modern car with luxurious extras for £1,000, your common sense should tell you to walk away from what is obviously an illegal deal.

This is summed up in the Latin words 'caveat emptor' which means 'let the buyer beware'. This is exactly what the buyer should do by taking time to read the fine print on packaging, for example.

Let the Buyer Beware!

The following four Acts or Orders provide the main legal framework in the area of production in Northern Ireland.

Sale and Supply of Goods and Services Act 1994

This Act ensures that goods and services supplied by a business are 'of satisfactory quality'. This means that goods must be:

- properly and safely manufactured and of satisfactory quality
- as they are described on the packaging
- fit for the purpose for which they were sold.

In order to comply with the Sale and Supply of Goods and Services Act 1994, manufactured goods are expected to be made in a way which complies with safety regulations. For example, toys must not have small parts which a baby could easily remove and choke on.

Goods are also expected to be as they are described, so the contents of a tin of biscuits, for example, must be like the illustration on the outside of the tin.

Figure 4.21
These tins should contain the type of biscuits illustrated

Goods must also be fit for their purpose, so a waterproof coat, for example, must keep out the rain. However, it is important that the customer looks at the labels carefully. In the example of the coat, if the label described the coat as being 'showerproof', the manufacturer intended it to withstand rain showers rather than downpours. The consumer would not have a justifiable complaint if he/she used it for any other purpose – such as going out in heavy rain.

If manufactured goods do not comply with the above details, the consumer is entitled to a full cash refund. An offer to repair the goods instead, does not have to be accepted.

The Sale and Supply of Goods and Services Act does not cover goods which have been bought privately.

Consumer Protection Act 1987

The Consumer Protection Act 1987 is designed to protect consumers from products that do not reach a reasonable level of safety. Any product not achieving the level of safety which consumers are entitled to expect is said to be defective.

Any person injured by a defective product is entitled to sue the producer or manufacturer for damages. However, if unsafe goods have been supplied, under the terms of this Act, an offence would also have been committed even if no one were injured by those goods.

In the case of foreign goods which were imported to this country, the consumer may take action against the importer, or against any business which had branded the goods with its own name. Wholesalers or retailers are not liable under the terms of this Act.

The consumer is expected, as in the case of the previous Act, to use the product responsibly. Warnings and instructions given with the product should be obeyed, and the product should be used with reasonable care. Therefore, if the manufacturer could show that the product became defective because of the way in which the consumer used it, then the consumer would have no right to claim against the manufacturer. Any action against a manufacturer must be taken by a consumer within three years of the injury.

Certain products are not covered by the Consumer Protection Act 1987. Those goods not covered are:

- growing crops
- water
- food
- aircraft
- motor vehicles
- tobacco.

The Consumer Protection Act 1987 is enforced by the trading standards officers of local authorities. They have the power to test products and suspend the sale of items which they believe contravene safety legislation.

In the case of imported goods, Customs officers have the power to hold goods at the port for up to two days in order to make enquiries about their safety.

ACTIVITY

You have been asked to sit on a panel to answer consumers' questions. The following questions have been sent to you in advance, and you will have to answer them when the panel meets.

Use a computer to prepare your written answers now.

1. I bought a shirt but when I arrived home I changed my mind. I took it back to the shop the next day but the staff would not give me a refund. Can they do this?
2. I bought new shoes recently but the heel of one shoe broke the second time I wore them. The shop is offering to repair them. Do I have to accept this offer?
3. My new toaster has never worked properly. The shop manager told me to send it back to the manufacturer as the fault had nothing to do with the shop. Is this correct?
4. Recently I bought an electric cooker privately from a neighbour. What are my rights?

Food Safety (Northern Ireland) Order 1991

The Food Safety (Northern Ireland) Order 1991 is enforced by environmental health officers, and aims to make sure all food offered to the public is safe to eat and is properly described.

This Order makes it an offence for caterers to sell food that is unfit for human consumption, is contaminated, or is falsely or misleadingly presented.

All premises used by food businesses must be registered with their local district council. This includes vehicles selling hot dogs or ice-cream.

The Food Safety (Northern Ireland) Order 1991 requires people who handle food to have received practical hygiene training appropriate to their job. This is to ensure that people have the practical skills and knowledge they need.

Figure 4.22
All food businesses need to be registered

Weights and Measures (Northern Ireland) Order 1981

Enforcement of the Weights and Measures (Northern Ireland) Order 1981 is the responsibility of the Trading Standards Service in Northern Ireland, and is a major part of the work of the trading standards officers.

The provisions of the Weights and Measures (Northern Ireland) Order 1981 are:

- it protects goods from being sold which are under weight or in short measure
- it ensures that the scales or other equipment of measurement are accurate.

EXAMINATION QUESTION

Samuel and Frances have recently got part-time jobs. Samuel has started to work in a local coffee shop and Frances will be working with environmental health officers in the local authority.

a   Examine the relevance of the Food Safety Order to environmental health officers and to the coffee shop.

(4 marks)

b   Analyse the implications of the Consumer Protection Act 1987 for the coffee shop.

(6 marks)

(Adapted from CCEA Business Studies, GCSE, Paper 2 Foundation/Higher Tiers, 2001)

Tips for answering this question:

Part A must be answered from the point of view of both the environmental health officer and the coffee shop. The total of 4 marks would be divided into 2 for each of these two points of view. For 2 marks each, you should give full details of one way in which the Order affects the work of both the officer and the shop.

In Part B you are expected to 'analyse' which is a more difficult command word and therefore worth 6 marks. In a question like this, you should break down the various parts of the Act and say how these affect the work of the coffee shop. Make sure that your answer is related to the coffee shop.

Other legislation that helps consumers

Unsolicited Goods and Services (Northern Ireland) Order 1976

This Order protects consumers from having to pay for goods which they did not request.

Unsolicited goods (goods which you did not ask for) should be kept for six months, ready for collection by the sender. If, after six months, they have not been collected, they become the property of the person who received them.

Consumer Credit Act 1974

This Act ensures that consumers are told the annual percentage rate (APR) when they borrow money or purchase goods on credit. This is very important because it enables consumers to compare the cost of the credit facilities with those offered in other shops.

Other Constraints on Production

Consumer protection, in the area of production, is provided via a number of channels other than the law.

In some cases, the Government has established agencies for the purpose of consumer protection while, in other cases, local authorities provide this service and do regular checks on products. Some industries themselves have established voluntary codes in the interests of consumers, and there are also other independent organisations which take on this role.

The Consumers' Association

The Consumers' Association was set up in the 1960s to improve the standards of goods and services available to the public in the United Kingdom. It provides a valuable service giving advice and information to consumers on a wide range of products and services.

The Association is the largest independent consumer organisation in Europe, and is totally funded by subscriptions from members.

The Association carries out testing of consumer products and reports on their findings. For example, their work on washing machines put the machines of a large number of manufacturers through rigorous tests, compared the results, decided on the washing machine which was the best value in terms of money and performance, and reported the results in its magazine *Which?*

Adverse reports in *Which?* are so disliked by manufacturers that they frequently modify the product and have it retested. Consumers are able to consult the magazine and get impartial information before making a purchase.

Figure 4.23

Another valuable function of the Consumers' Association is its role as a pressure group to draw attention to, and try to stop, any business practices which are unfair to consumers. Such practices are also reported in their magazine *Which?* and this publicity helps to stop these practices.

ACTIVITY

a   Name any large product – such as a television or washing machine – your family is thinking of buying soon.

b   Then visit your nearest library and ask to see some past issues of the magazine *Which?*

c   Use the magazines to research the price and make of the recommended model of whatever product you intend to purchase.

The British Standards Institution

The British Standards Institution (BSI) is an entirely independent organisation which carries out tests on products in order to make sure that they meet the BSI standard for reliability, quality and safety.

The Institution awards its kitemark to a product which passes its tests. The kitemark is understood by the public to be a sign of good quality, and therefore any product displaying it sells well in the shops.

For this reason, manufacturers are eager to have the kitemark awarded to their products. The kitemark is also a guarantee for the consumer that the product is a good buy.

ACTIVITY

Visit as many furniture and hardware shops as you can, and make a note of the number of times you see the BSI kitemark, and the types of products which have the kitemark. Look to see if those products bearing the kitemark are manufactured by a range of companies or just a few. Also note if those products bearing the kitemark are more or less expensive than other competing products.

Copy and use the following table to record your information.

Name of Product	Name of Manufacturer	Price

You may also like to explore the work of the following organisations:

- **British Electro–Technical Approvals Board (BEAB)**
  Checks electrical items to make sure that they are safe for consumers to use.
- **Association of British Travel Agents (ABTA)**
  Provides safeguards against being sold a holiday which is below the expected standard and it is worth checking that your travel agent is a member of the Association.
- **National House Building Council (NHBC)**
  Provides similar safeguards in house building and it is advisable to check that your builder is a member of the Council.
- **General Medical Council (GMC)**
  Will listen to and investigate allegations of careless or incompetent treatment by doctors.
- **Citizens Advice Bureaux**
  Are all independent charities which provide free, confidential advice on consumer affairs and many other issues. There are Citizens Advice Bureaux in many towns throughout Northern Ireland and their addresses and telephone numbers can be found in the *Yellow Pages* or at www.adviceguide.org.uk.

Environmental health officers

Environmental health is controlled by the local district councils in Northern Ireland. The work of Environmental Health Officers falls into four areas:

Food control

Environmental health officers are concerned with ensuring the safety of food, at all stages of production, storage, distribution, and sale until it reaches the consumer.

It is the responsibility of environmental health officers to enforce the Food Safety (Northern Ireland) Order and, in doing so, they inspect food premises and give advice on hygiene and safety matters. These inspections may be as a result of a complaint from a member of the public.

During the inspection they can take samples, inspect records, and take photographs. As a result of their inspections of food premises officers may take various actions, depending on the severity of the situation. They may take legal action by serving an improvement notice or, in extreme cases, they may recommend a prosecution or forbid the further use of the premises or equipment until the health hazards are rectified.

Health and safety at work

Environmental health officers are responsible for enforcing the Health and Safety at Work Act in commercial and recreational premises. They inspect premises and advise on how to protect employees and members of the public using the premises. They also investigate accidents since their main concern is that conditions at work or in leisure facilities should not be detrimental to health.

Housing

Environmental health officers monitor housing standards and can take action to ensure that repairs to properties are carried out in order to make houses suitable for human habitation. This applies particularly where large houses have been divided into bedsits. Environmental health officers are responsible for ensuring that people are protected from fire and public health hazards.

Figure 4.24

Pollution and environmental protection

The work of environmental health officers also includes monitoring and controlling pollution levels and educating the public in protecting the environment. This is because high levels of pollution put the health of members of the public at risk.

ACTIVITY

Imagine that you are an environmental health officer. James, a GCSE Business Studies student, has written to ask you about your work because he is thinking of a career in environmental health.

Write a letter to him, giving an outline of your work.

EXAMINATION QUESTION

Outline the work of an environmental health officer.

(2 marks)

(CCEA Business Studies, GCSE, Paper 2 Foundation Tier, 2001)

Tips for answering this question:

This is a simple, knowledge-based question which requires a brief outline of one function of the officer. There are only 2 marks allocated to the question, so do not spend a lot of time giving a long list of his functions.

Trading standards officers

In Northern Ireland the Trading Standards Service is separate from the local authorities. This is different from the situation in England where the service is the responsibility of the local authorities.

The aim of the Northern Ireland Trading Standards Service is to promote a fair trading environment in which consumers are protected against malpractice, and responsible business activity is actively encouraged. This body aims to provide a fair and impartial service, and offers advice and assistance to both consumer and trader.

Trading standards officers are responsible for enforcing a wide range of approximately 38 consumer protection laws. The main ones are:

- Trade Descriptions Act 1968
- Prices Acts 1974 and 1975
- Unsolicited Goods and Services (Northern Ireland) Order 1976
- Weights and Measures (Northern Ireland) Order 1987
- Fair Trading Act 1973
- Consumer Credit Act 1974.

Trading standards officers investigate complaints by members of the public against traders. Complaints may be in relation to weights and measures, false or misleading descriptions of goods and services, misleading price indications, credit transactions, counterfeit goods, video recordings, package travel, and labelling of electrical appliances.

In addition, trading standards officers carry out tests and regular inspections on weighing and measuring equipment. These tests are carried out in shops, petrol stations, supermarkets, pubs, and restaurants. The officers then apply a stamp to show that the equipment has passed the accuracy test.

Trading standards officers also work with packers and importers to ensure that pre-packed goods contain the marked weight and that the necessary information is clearly marked on packs.

This work by trading standards officers gives consumers confidence that the goods they buy are correctly weighed or measured and ensures that they get a fair deal when buying goods or services.

Figure 4.25

ACTIVITY

Imagine that you are a trading standards officer. Marie, a GCSE Business Studies student, has written to ask you about your work because she needs the information for her coursework.

Write a letter to her, giving an outline of the work of a trading standards officer.

EXAMINATION QUESTION

Describe the work of a trading standards officer.

(2 marks)

(CCEA Business Studies, GCSE, Paper 2 Foundation and Higher Tiers, 2001)

Tips for answering this question:

This is a simple, knowledge-based question which requires a brief outline of one function of the Officer. There are only 2 marks allocated to the question, so do not spend a lot of time giving a long list of his functions.

What Do You Do if You Have a Complaint?

The answer to this lies very much in the type of complaint you have.

- *If you have been sold faulty goods which are not fit for the purpose you intended them for:*
  The best thing to do is to return to the shop. Always bring the receipt for the goods because it is unreasonable to expect the shop to remember either you or the particular sale. Explain the problem clearly and calmly. In the vast majority of cases, the shop will give you a refund or replace the goods, solving the problem immediately.
  However, if the shop assistant is not helpful, ask to see the manager and again explain the problem. If the problem is not solved by the manager then you have to take the matter up with one of the outside agencies.
- *If the problem is about unsafe or unfit goods, or goods which have been inaccurately described:*
  You may contact the Trading Standards Service. Their headquarters are in Belfast and they have regional offices in Armagh, Ballymena, Enniskillen and Londonderry.
- *If the problem is related to wrong weights or measures:*
  Also contact the Trading Standards Service.
- *If the problem is a matter of environmental health:*
  Such as being served food in unhygienic conditions, you should contact the Environmental Health Department in the headquarters of your local authority
  In all of these cases, the nearest office of the Citizens' Advice Bureau will give advice.

At this stage you should understand:

- the stages of the product life cycle
- how to illustrate the product life cycle on a graph
- strategies used to extend the product life cycle
- how the product life cycle assists a business in decision making
- the terms of the Sale and Supply of Goods and Services Act 1994
- the terms of the Consumer Protection Act 1987
- the terms of the Food Safety (Northern Ireland) Order 1991
- the terms of the Weights and Measures (Northern Ireland) Order 1981
- the work of the Consumers' Association
- the work of the British Standards Institution
- the work of environmental health officers
- the work of trading standards officers.

You should also know the meaning of:

Product	Reseach/Development	Launch/Introduction
Growth	Maturity	Saturation
Decline		

As revision, look each one up in the Glossary at the end of the book.

International Marketing

International marketing is marketing which takes place between different countries.

If successful, international marketing should result in international trade which is the buying and selling of goods from and to foreign countries.

It is impossible for any country to be totally self-sufficient and to be able to meet all its own needs. This is particularly true in the case of a small country such as Northern Ireland, and is the reason why international marketing is actively encouraged by the Government.

Benefits and Drawbacks of Marketing Abroad

Benefits

- **Increased market and profits**

  By marketing abroad, a business can sell its goods in increased quantities. This situation leads to increased profits for the business.

- **More employment**

  Increased sales lead to higher levels of production in the business. This situation gives employment to a greater number of people

- **Economies of scale**

  Increased production creates opportunities for economies of scale. This ultimately results in higher profits for the business.

- **Greater variety**

  Marketing abroad increases the variety of goods available for consumers. This generally creates a better standard of living in the country.

  Figure 4.26

  For example, the climate in Northern Ireland is unsuitable for the cultivation of citrus fruits, tea and coffee and, without foreign trade, these goods would not be available in Northern Ireland.

  Martin Luther King had this in mind when he once said, 'Before you've finished your breakfast this morning, you'll have relied on half the world.'

- **Political reasons**

  The Government encourages international marketing and trade because it establishes and develops good relations with other countries.

Drawbacks (or difficulties)

- **Competition**

  When a business enters the international market, it will meet stiff competition because there are so many more producers trying to sell their goods.

  To succeed, a business's marketing and product have to be better than those of its competitors.

  - **Production**

    Increased markets and increased production may require capital investment and recruitment of additional staff. Accommodation and financial arrangements would have to be made available to undertake this.

    The business has to be aware of its capacity for production. If this capacity is exceeded, it will have to make sure that the increased investment would be economical and viable (see Unit 3.1).

  - **Distribution**

    Distribution on an international scale is much more difficult than for a business which is marketing and selling to the domestic market only.

  Secure packaging and efficient transport systems all have to be in place. The business would need to employ agents in the foreign country or else set up a base in the foreign country.

- **Documentation**

  Businesses marketing internationally have to be familiar with the documentation required for sending goods abroad. Within the European Union, documentation has been simplified, but the problem remains in trade with other countries outside the European Union such as America or the Far East.

- **Language**

  Businesses which market internationally must have at least some members of staff who are capable of speaking, writing and translating the language of the country in which the marketing is taking place.

Figure 4.27

- **Currency**

  Businesses need to be familiar with the currency of the foreign country and be able to market their products in that currency. Within Europe, this problem has been eased somewhat recently, since many European countries have adopted the Euro as its currency.

- **Promotional activity**

  Increased promotional activity may be required abroad and the promotional material must also be modified to suit the foreign country.

- **Cultural differences**

  Exporters have to be conscious of the values and traditions of the country to which they are selling. It is vital that those values and traditions are respected.

  (You should refer to the final section of this unit for further consideration of the cultural dimension.)

The products of the fibreboard plant owned by Balcas are fibreboard pre-primed internal components for the architectural and housebuilding sectors. These consist of architectural mouldings – wall panels, skirting boards, architraves, window boards and dado rails – and are marketed under the name 'Fable'.

The company produces approximately 50,000 linear metres per day – enough for 200 houses. Of this total, 86% is exported while 14% is sold within Ireland. International business is obviously of great importance to the company.

Balcas has experienced many benefits as a consequence of international marketing. The fibreboard plant has increased its workforce by 500% over the past 10 years while its production level has risen due to the installation of a second production line at a cost of £1.2 million. Increased use of automation has resulted in better, and more economical, use of equipment and the plant is now organised on a two-shift system. This increased production has led to economies of scale which are reflected in the company's profits.

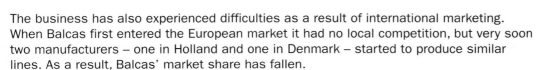

The business has also experienced difficulties as a result of international marketing. When Balcas first entered the European market it had no local competition, but very soon two manufacturers – one in Holland and one in Denmark – started to produce similar lines. As a result, Balcas' market share has fallen.

A second problem is that many European customers see Ireland as remote and communication can become a difficulty. To overcome this, Balcas set up Freephone lines by which customers, at any location, could access the company easily and at no expense. In addition, Balcas is careful to maintain direct and personal contact with its customers by regular visits from the Managing Director and the Sales Manager. In this way, agents are no longer required abroad yet a personal service, and a high level of customer care, are maintained.

Since all Balcas trade is within the European Union, documentation is not a problem, and, in order to remove a potential barrier, the company supplies quotations and invoices in the customer's own currency. While this makes trade easier for the customer, it does expose the business to some risk due to variations in the exchange rate.

English is used by Balcas in all transactions since it is spoken as a second language throughout Europe. However, the company has explored the possibility of trade with the Middle and Far East and acknowledges that the idea would not be feasible without the relevant language skills.

Some interesting regional differences in tastes have become apparent. For example, Balcas has found that wall panelling is very popular in Holland while, in Germany, the style of panels produced by Balcas is not popular. Distinct building traditions have also emerged, and the company has found that window boards must be wider for the southern English market than for the northern English market as a result of traditional differences in building techniques.

ACTIVITY

Read the case study on Balcas and answer the following questions:

a   Why is international marketing very important to Balcas?
b   Name two advantages which Balcas has gained through international marketing
c   Why did Balcas' market share fall in Europe?
d   Why is it so important for Balcas to maintain a high level of personal service and customer care?
e   Why is documentation not a problem for the company at present? How might this situation change?
f   Name two cultural differences which Balcas has met.
g   Explain how Balcas may be at risk by trading in the customer's own currency.

EXAMINATION QUESTION

CC Computers produce computer games. It is thinking about marketing its new game abroad.

a   Explain how this might affect the business.

(6 marks)

b   Give two reasons why it should market its products abroad.

(4 marks)

(CCEA Business Studies, GCSE, Paper 2 Higher and Foundation Tiers, 2001)

Tips for answering this question:

a   In this 6-mark question you should name and give details of three effects on the business. Those effects may be either advantages or disadvantages to the business.

b   In Part B you are really being asked for two advantages or positive reasons, and they must be seen from CC Computers' point of view.

Implications of the Global Market for Businesses in Northern Ireland

> The 'global market' simply refers to trading on a world-wide scale (around the globe).

Every business, no matter how small, can now think of the whole world as being its marketplace if its product is the type of product which is demanded in other countries. The present situation has been thought of as a second industrial revolution.

Many of Northern Ireland's businesses are small. Previously those smallest businesses had a narrow market base and would not have considered exporting to be a viable option. The global market now presents that opportunity.

Globalisation has been made possible partly by:

- the lifting of import controls between countries
- the advances of modern technology in general but especially due to the continuing development of the Internet.

It is estimated, that the Internet population has doubled each year since 1988, and in February 2002, there were thought to be 544 million people on-line throughout the world.

Other components of modern technology which have also played a part are e-mail, electronic data exchange, CD-ROM, video conferencing, mobile communications, networked computers and digital television.

Northern Ireland is a small country and, as part of an island on the extreme western side of Europe, it is geographically remote. These facts present difficulties for businesses in Northern Ireland which do not have to be considered by businesses in other, more central locations. Technology succeeds in reducing the effects of that remoteness and offers connection with potential customers in over 100 different countries.

> **The global market provides many challenges for businesses in Northern Ireland, but it also presents definite opportunities. The questions now are 'How can those opportunities be grasped?' and 'How can the difficulties be overcome?'**

The implications of the global market for Northern Ireland as a country are:

- the need for the cultivation of a wide vision

  The Report by the Economic Development Strategy Review Group 'Strategy 2010' recommends that students should have language skills in a variety of languages and should have opportunities to participate in international exchanges. The Report also stresses the value of town twinning arrangements which develop opportunities for exports and joint ventures as well as other inward investment projects and links. These are seen by the Review Group as being ways of widening the vision of Northern Ireland's population.

- businesses need training and practical experience

  Training and practical experience of export marketing is required in order to be able to avail of marketing opportunities abroad.

- business in Northern Ireland needs to be able to use the available technology competently

  In 2000, a Chamber of Commerce study concluded that few businesses in Northern Ireland were using modern technology fully. It was found that Northern Ireland was using technology at a lower level than any of the other 12 regions of the United Kingdom. The practical implications of this fact are capital investment in technology which would need to be accompanied by training.

- stiffer competition for businesses in Northern Ireland

  This could result in the closure of some manufacturing companies and the redundancy of employees. On the other hand, stiffer competition could have beneficial results for businesses in Northern Ireland. It could be fought with the use of advanced technology and skills, and could result in increased trading and employment. The outcome of competition is largely determined by how globalisation is regarded and the degree to which it is welcomed.

- the opportunity for Northern Ireland to trade equally with all other countries

  Using modern technology, communication is equally easy throughout the world. Trading opportunities are equally available everywhere.

If those trading opportunities are taken up, they will result in Northern Ireland having more investment and employment which will lead to improved living standards and a growth in national wealth.

Opportunities and Competition in International Marketing Created by Technology

Modern technology has created both opportunities and competition for existing businesses. Whether traders are able to grasp the opportunities or succumb to the competition is largely due to their own circumstances.

The greatest opportunity which the business is presented with is that of expanding its market throughout the world. To be able to grasp that opportunity, the business has to be prepared in advance. This means it needs to:

- research the market abroad to discover if its product has to be modified
- decide on suitable forms of transport for the goods
- cater for the type of packaging required
- understand the documentation required for sending goods abroad
- ensure that its employees are properly trained to undertake extra commitments
- train some staff to speak the foreign language required
- research the political and legal system of the foreign country concerned
- make sure that its machinery and equipment are capable of coping with increased demands
- examine the culture of the foreign country concerned
- put in place a suitable pricing policy
- make provision for the return of goods.

Modern technology has also opened up opportunities for every other business as well, and this results in a situation of increased competition. Where there is competition, producers have to compete to persuade consumers to buy their products. The reality is that only the best survive.

In order to combat the competition and keep ahead, the business has to:

- innovate by changing its product in a way which makes it unique and more desirable than other products in the same market
- make sure that the quality of the product is of the highest possible standard
- reduce its prices below the level of the competitors
- offer special inducements with the sale
- supply the goods in the shortest possible time.
- offer a personal service.

The business which can overcome the competition will survive and its market will continue to expand. This will result in increased employment and further opportunities.

The business which cannot overcome the competition will fail and result in redundancies for its employees.

However, it may be beyond the scope of small businesses to respond positively to the competition. For this reason, mergers of businesses into larger units may be the answer to the need for increased capital in order to take advantage of economies of scale.

In order to make their products recognisable all over the world, some large businesses adopted single names for their products. Do you know what these were originally called in this country?

Present Name	Former Name
Oil of Olay	....
Snickers	....
Starburst	....

Cultural Dimension of International Marketing

Any business which is trading internationally needs to have an appreciation of the traditions, culture and legislation of the countries with which it is dealing. It is important that those aspects of the foreign way of life are respected.

- **Language**

    A knowledge of the foreign language is a basic requirement. This is needed for complete understanding of the transaction taking place, and also for the correct translation of instructions on the packaging of the product.

- **Traditions**

    It is important that local traditions, beliefs and customs are not offended. For example, some Indians do not regard black clothes as being fashionable, as is the case in this country. Instead, they connect black with evil spirits and therefore would not wish to wear black. This fact has to be understood if successful trade is to be completed.

- **Religion**

    The religious culture of a country needs also to be understood and respected. A practice in McDonald's illustrates how one company does this.

    In McDonald's restaurants in Israel, Big Macs are served without cheese in order to separate meat and dairy products. This separation is required in kosher restaurants in order to fulfil the requirements of Jewish law.

Figure 4.28

- **Hours of trading**

  Climatic conditions are very different abroad and this results in variations of trading hours. For example, it is too hot to work in the afternoon in Italy and shops are closed from 1.00 pm to 5.00 pm. Contact with Italian businesses has to be avoided during those times.

- **Commercial and technical requirements**

  Technical specifications, particularly in electrical goods, differ throughout the world. Products may have to be modified for use abroad.

- **Local legislation**

  Laws vary from country to country. It is important to understand these thoroughly so that they are not broken.

- **Local economy**

  It would be impossible to set a price for a product and sell it at the same price in every country. What the local market would bear and what the local people could pay must be considered.

  McDonald's are found throughout the world offering the same products for sale. However the price at which those products are sold varies according to what local people could spend, and also according to the price charged by their competitors in that particular country.

ACTIVITY

Copy the following table and match the parts of the sentences appropriately.

Knowledge of a foreign language is needed	must be respected in international trade
Prices vary throughout the world	differences in trading hours
Local traditions, beliefs and customs	particularly in electrical goods
Climatic conditions cause	to suit the religion of the other country
Products may have to be modified	to suit the local economies
Technical specifications differ throughout the world	to understand the transaction taking place

ACTIVITY

In the following wordsearch, find the words shown in the list. The words can be read in straight lines, horizontally, vertically or diagonally, either backwards or forwards. There is no overlap of words in the grid.

Marketing
Abroad
International
Culture
Global
Compete
Expand
World
Language
Local
Merger

```
W M H G I N T E R N A T I O N A L
G U Q P J W E N G A D A O R B A K
A P W I E R C M P Z A T K M C U T
S W A L I U A A S B R O C H S K G
A L Z M D U R R C B B E I C K I L
D A U X S L E K C C G T I C M P O
N L O C B E M E Z X I E B Y R S B
A U P E N C T T P Q I P Y C M U A
P X Y E P T M I L A Y M M V Y U L
X O D E D R Y N N H S O M T D E I
E R Y L B U O G Q B U C T I K L S
E B R V Y T I O I U Q B T U E M I
S O E E R B T H V M Y I L G R P L
W E I I X A I P R T U E M A U T U
E G A U G N A L B P Q Q W U C N Y
P X C V B E U F H H K J L I O O B
C U L T U R E F I R E G R E M U L
```

R E V I S I O N

At this stage you should understand:

- benefits of marketing abroad
- drawbacks of marketing abroad
- what the global market means for businesses in Northern Ireland
- what makes the global market possible
- how modern technology creates opportunities
- how modern technology creates competition
- how culture and tradition affect international marketing.

You should also know the meaning of:

International marketing   Global market

As revision, look each one up in the Glossary at the end of the book.

SECTION FIVE

Finance and accounting

Learning Objectives

To develop a knowledge and critical understanding of:

- business financial needs
- the sources, uses and management of finance
- the interpretation and analysis of financial information
- business costings
- the significance of break even and the margin of safety
- forecasting and the importance of adequate cash flow
- how financial information is used as an aid to decision making.

Business Financial Needs

A business may need money (also referred to as finance) for many different reasons. Some of those reasons may require large sums for a long period of time while, in other cases, the money may be required in small amounts and for a short time.

The time for which the finance is needed may be:

Short Term	Medium Term	Long Term
up to 1 year	1–5 years	over 5 years

Types of Capital

It is important for you to know the meaning of 'capital'. Capital can be thought of as the money invested in a business when it is first opened. That money is then used to buy whatever machinery, equipment or other items which are needed in the business.

These items become part of the assets of the business. For example if the new business is a shop, the owner will need to buy equipment such as display cabinets and cash tills before the shop can be opened.

There are three types of capital:

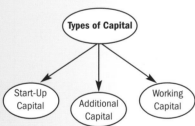

Start-up capital

Start-up capital is the finance needed to get a business started. At the very beginning of its life, the business needs capital to get 'off the ground'.

For example, the owner of any new business must be able to either buy or rent premises, to buy the basic equipment necessary for that particular type of business and to buy stock in order to trade.

Additional capital

Most businesses need additional (or more) capital at some stage. For example if the business is successful, the owner may decide to expand it. In order to expand, the owner would have to purchase more assets such as vehicles or machinery, and recruit more employees.

Additional capital might also be required to extend a business into different areas or to start trading in new lines of goods. Other reasons for needing additional capital are the rebuilding or refurbishment of premises, or perhaps the decision to purchase premises which have previously been rented.

Working capital

Working capital is necessary to pay for the day-to-day running expenses of the business and to pay bills such as electricity and telephone.

If a business does not have sufficient working capital it will have cash-flow problems which could cause its total failure.

Lack of working capital would mean that the business could not pay its bills and eventually its creditors (people to whom it owes money) would have to take legal action to get their money. In extreme cases, the court would have the business wound up and its assets sold in order to raise money to pay the creditors.

EXAMINATION QUESTION

Explain the difference between start-up capital and working capital.

(4 marks)

(CCEA Business Studies, GCSE, Paper 2 Foundation Tier, 2002)

Tips for answering this question:

You are asked to 'explain' the difference. To do this, you should first explain what start-up capital is. This will earn you 2 marks. You should then explain what working capital is in order to earn the remaining 2 marks. Your answer should show that you understand the difference between the two types of capital.

ACTIVITY

Copy out the following table and say which type of capital would be appropriate in each case. The first one is done for you.

Money to develop a new market	Additional capital
Money to buy stock to start trading	
Money to pay creditors	
Money to pay the rates bill	
Money to replace the computers	
Money to redecorate the offices	
Money to pay the suppliers	

Sources of Finance

There are several methods by which businesses may raise necessary finance. The method which they choose depends on how much they wish to borrow and how long they wish to borrow it for.

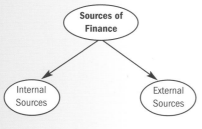

Money can be raised both internally – inside the business – or externally – from sources outside the business.

Internal Sources of Capital

There are five major internal sources – that means the money is raised *inside* the business. This is the cheapest method of raising finance because there are no interest charges.

Owner's own capital

In this case, the owners draw on their own private financial resources and invest more of their private money into the business.

Using the owner's own capital has the advantages of remaining private and does not have to be repaid. On the other hand, not all owners have additional capital to call on.

This method would be used if the money were required long term.

Retained profits

Sometimes the owners may decide to 'plough back' profits from previous years instead of taking them out of the business for their own use.

This method also has the advantages of remaining private and does not have to be repaid. However not all businesses make enough profit to be able to keep it in the business.

Retained profits would be used if the money were required in the medium or long term.

Sale of fixed assets

Businesses have large sums of money invested in their fixed assets and sometimes choose to sell some surplus assets – perhaps a machine – in order to raise money. However, new or small businesses are unlikely to have any surplus assets to sell and even a business which has surplus assets would find the method slow. There is also a limit to the number of assets which a business can sell before it starts to affect its production.

Selling fixed assets would be done if the money were required in the medium term.

Sale of stocks

Every manufacturing business and every shop has stocks of goods which have not been sold. The business can raise finance quickly by holding a sale and offering the goods to the public at a discount. In this way the business gets its money quickly and can use this money to manufacture or buy new stock. We are all familiar with the January sales in shops which clear the winter stock, and also raise money and create space for the new spring stock.

Selling stock would be done if the money were required in the short term.

Figure 5.1

Debt collection

Most businesses have debtors – people who have bought goods and have not paid for them. It is common practice for businesses to allow 30 days' credit although all the large supermarkets sell only for cash. The money which is owing by debtors is not working for the business, so the business has to have a system of credit control to chase debtors and get the money it is owed.

Debt collection is useful if the money were required in the short term.

EXAMINATION QUESTION

The company wishes to purchase a new machine costing £10,000. Give reasons for using internal sources of finance to buy the machine.

(4 marks)

(CCEA Business Studies, GCSE, Paper 1 Higher Tier, 2001)

Tips for answering this question:

In this question you would be expected to give two reasons for using internal sources. It is really asking you to give advantages of internal sources but does not require you to go into details about the different sources.

ACTIVITY

Name one advantage and one disadvantage of each of the sources of finance named.

SOURCE OF FINANCE	ADVANTAGE	DISADVANTAGE
Owner's own capital		
Retained profits		
Sale of fixed assets		
Sale of stocks		
Debt collection		

External Sources of Capital

There are nine major external sources – that means the money is raised *outside* the business. External sources are more expensive than internal sources and incur interest charges.

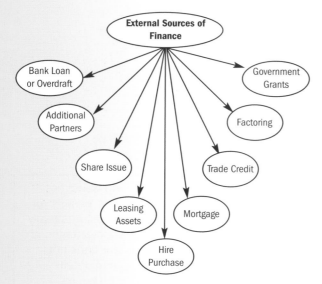

Bank loan or overdraft

A bank loan is suitable as a medium or long-term source of finance. The bank agrees to lend the business a set sum of money for an agreed period of time. In return the bank charges interest at a rate which is fixed for the entire period of the loan. For this reason a bank loan can be an expensive way to raise finance.

The bank requires security for its loans. This means that the bank has the right to sell an asset belonging to the business if the loan is not repaid within the agreed time.

A bank overdraft is a short-term means of finance. This is an arrangement with the bank whereby the business is allowed to pay cheques from its bank account beyond the amount which has been lodged in the account.

Interest is paid on the amount actually overdrawn each day and therefore getting a bank overdraft is usually cheaper than a bank loan which has a fixed rate of interest.

ACTIVITY

A bank is unlikely to give a loan to a business without knowing more about the business.

a What document would you advise a person seeking a loan to show to the bank?
b Explain how this document would help in securing the loan.

Additional partners

If a partnership needs extra finance, the partners can agree to invite an additional partner to join the partnership.

The new partner will contribute capital which can be used to finance the purchase of assets or whatever the extra finance is required for in the business. However the new partner is entitled to a share of the profits of the business.

Figure 5.2

Share issue

In the case of a limited company, extra finance may be raised by issuing new shares in the company and inviting members of the public to become shareholders.

This is a long-term source of finance for the company and no interest is payable although all shareholders are entitled to dividends (share of the profits).

Leasing assets

Leasing is a method of acquiring assets and is a medium-term method of finance. Leasing is similar to renting and the business does not have to pay a lump sum as it would have to do if it was buying the asset.

The lease is arranged by a finance company and the business makes regular payments to it for the use of the asset. These payments can be very high because they include profits for the finance company. The asset remains the property of the finance company which is another disadvantage of leasing.

Despite these disadvantages, leasing is commonly used in business because it enables businesses to have the use of up-to-date equipment and they are able to get the asset immediately.

Hire purchase

Hire purchase is another method of medium-term finance which is used for the purchase of assets. In the case of hire purchase, the business pays a deposit on the asset and agrees to pay off the balance in equal instalments over an agreed period of time. The business has the use of the asset while it is paying it off – or hiring it.

The major difference between hire purchase and leasing is that in the hire purchase system, the business eventually becomes the owner of the asset once it has paid off all the instalments.

Hire purchase is a popular method of buying assets because the business can have very modern equipment without having to part with a large sum of money at the outset, and it will eventually own the asset.

The major disadvantage is that the total cost of the asset is much higher than if it were bought for cash.

ACTIVITY

Andrew owns an earth-moving business and is hoping to buy a new digger soon. He is unsure whether to use hire purchase or leasing and has come to you for advice.

Complete the following table to show Andrew the advantages and disadvantages of both hire purchase and leasing to help him to decide which of these two sources of finance would be best for him to use.

Advantages of Hire Purchase	Disadvantages of Hire Purchase	Advantages of Leasing	Disadvantages of Leasing

Mortgage

A mortgage is a very long-term method of raising finance and is most often used to help in the purchase of premises.

The mortgage is arranged over a long period of years (usually 20 to 25) and the sum borrowed, plus interest charges, has to be repaid in instalments over that period. This makes the purchase more expensive than if it were bought for cash. The premises act as collateral which means that the premises can be taken and sold by the mortgage company should the business fail to make repayments.

The big advantage of a mortgage is that the business has the use of the premises from the beginning and can carry on its work there while making repayments. Another advantage is that the premises eventually become the property of the business when all the payments have been made

Figure 5.3

Trade credit

Trade credit is a short-term means of finance, and is where suppliers allow their customers to have a period of time (usually 30 days) in which to pay for the goods they have received.

Trade credit gives an advantage to buyers because they have the immediate use of the goods. This would help the working capital of a small shop, for example, because the shop could buy the goods on credit, and then sell them and raise money from them before having to pay the supplier.

Trade credit has the added advantage of being free. However, suppliers usually give discount for cash payment which would be lost by using the trade credit facility.

Factoring

Factoring is also a short-term source of finance and is a service, offered by banks, to help businesses to collect debts from customers who are not paying their accounts.

The bank 'takes over' the debt and pays the business 80% of the total debt immediately. The bank then takes responsibility for recovering the remainder of the debt. When it recovers the remaining amount it makes another payment to the business but charges a fee of 5% of the total amount of the debt.

Factoring is expensive and, therefore, is more frequently used by large businesses. It has the advantage of letting the business have immediate cash.

Figure 5.4

EXAMINATION QUESTION

The company wishes to purchase a new machine costing £10,000. Some of the directors wish to continue the policy of self-financing while others would like to use factoring as a source of finance. Advise the company how factoring could help it to raise the finance.

(4 marks)

(CCEA Business Studies, GCSE, Paper I Higher Tier, 2001)

Tips for answering this question:

This question is really asking for the advantages of factoring. For 4 marks you would be expected to name and give details of two reasons in favour of factoring. There would not be any extra marks for giving disadvantages of factoring.

Government grants

Several systems of government grants apply in Northern Ireland to assist businesses financially (see Section 1 for more details).

Such grants usually do not have to be repaid although they usually do have conditions. It is common, for example, that the Government would specify the location of the business so that some of the unemployment problems in a certain area might be solved.

EXAMINATION QUESTION

Denise Nelson, an artist who set up her own business 18 months ago, needs a loan from the bank to buy additional equipment for her studio.

If Denise does not get the bank loan, suggest two other sources of finance that might be available to her and explain the advantage of each.

(6 marks)

(CCEA Business Studies, GCSE, Paper 2 Foundation Tier, 2002)

Tips for answering this question:

This question carries a high number of marks and 3 marks would be awarded for each of the two suggested sources. For those 3 marks you should name the source and say why it would be suitable for Denise's business. In answering this question it is important that you take the type and size of the business into consideration when suggesting the sources.

ACTIVITY

In each of the circumstances described here you are asked to identify the most appropriate source of finance to use. Write down your answer in your notebook and give reasons for your choice of source.

a A company wishes to purchase five new cars for its sales representatives.
b A small shopkeeper needs to increase his working capital temporarily.
c A business needs short-term help to buy extra stock for the Christmas market.
d Elaine and Martin cannot raise enough money for their business to be able to compete with other businesses in their area.
e A limited company wishes to expand its market and needs more long-term capital.
f A company is having difficulty in getting its debtors to repay the large amounts they owe.
g A large company needs to update its machinery but does not have enough money available immediately.
h A business has plans to buy modern premises which would allow it to expand production.
i A French company is planning to set up a new business in Northern Ireland in an area where there is high unemployment.

REVISION

At this stage you should also understand the details of:

Capital	Start-up capital	Additional capital
Working capital	Owner's own capital	Retained profits
Sale of fixed assets	Sale of stocks	Debt collection
Bank loan	Bank overdraft	Additional partners
Share issue	Leasing assets	Hire purchase
Mortgage	Trade credit	Factoring
Government grants		

As revision, look each one up in the Glossary at the end of the book.

Final Accounts and Balance Sheet

Final Accounts

Purpose of the final accounts

There are two accounts which are collectively called the 'final accounts'. They are the trading account and the profit and loss account.

> Accounts can be described as a story in figures! The story which the final accounts tell is about the result of the year's work in the business and the amount of profit made.

As you can guess from their name, the final accounts are worked at the end of the trading year – which does not have to be at the end of the calendar year.

The purpose of the trading account is to find the gross profit (or gross loss), and the purpose of the profit and loss account is to calculate the net profit (or net loss) for the year.

These profits will be explained more fully later in the unit, so just remember their names for now.

Final Accounts

Trading Account → Gross Profit/Loss

Profit and Loss Account → Net Profit/Loss

The Trading Account

As you have already learned, the purpose of the trading account is to find the gross profit.

How to find the gross profit

Gross profit is the difference between the money the business makes from the sale of goods (sometimes called the turnover) and what the goods cost the business to manufacture or buy as well as the expenses of selling them. These costs are known as the cost of sales.

Therefore, if a business has sales of £100,000 and the cost of sales is £75,000, the gross profit would be £25,000. However, if the sales are £100,000 and the cost of sales is £110,000 then the business would make a gross loss of £10,000.

> **Gross Profit = Sales (or Turnover) – Cost of Sales**

ACTIVITY

Copy out the following table and, from the details given, calculate the gross profit or gross loss for five different years for a carrier business called Speedy Service.

Answer the questions at the end.

	Year 1	Year 2	Year 3	Year 4	Year 5
Sales	£120,000	£140,000	£155,000	£160,000	£185,000
Cost of Sales	£83,000	£ 97,000	£115,000	£165,000	£165,000
Gross Profit					

a   In which year did Speedy Service have the worst trading result?
b   What do you think may have caused this poor result?
c   If you were the owner of Speedy Service, what would your reaction be to these results?
d   What would you advise the owner to do?

How to find the cost of sales

In order to sell goods, the business has to purchase them. These new purchases will be added to the opening stock which is the stock of goods already in the business. At the end of the year some stock will be left unsold. The stock which is left is called the closing stock and will be kept for the next year.

> **Cost of Sales = Opening Stock + Purchases − Closing Stock**

If a business has opening stock valued at £9,000, purchases of £15,000 and closing stock of £3,750 then its cost of sales would be £20,250.

In the trading account, this information is displayed in the following way:

				£	£
Cost of Sales:					
Opening Stock	..	..	..	9,000	
Add: Purchases	..	..	..	15,000	24,000
Less: Closing Stock	..	..			3,750
Cost of Sales	..	..	..		£20,250

Returns inwards and returns outwards

Some goods may have to be returned perhaps because they have been broken or the wrong goods have been delivered. Those returns are known as **returns outwards** (because they are going out from the business) and they reduce the total amount of the purchases.

Some of the goods sold may have to be returned for similar reasons. Those are known as **returns inwards** (because they are coming back in to the business) and they reduce the total amount of the sales.

Let us suppose that the above business had returns outwards of £500.

In the trading account, the returns outward would be displayed like this:

			£	£
Cost of Sales:				
Opening Stock	..	..		9,000
Add: Purchases	..	..	15,000	
Less: Returns Outwards	..		500	14,500
				23,500
Less: Closing Stock	..	..	..	3,750
Cost of Sales	..	..	..	..	£19,750

ACTIVITY

Compare the first calculation of the cost of sales with the second calculation which included returns outwards.

a   What effect have returns outwards had on the cost of sales?

b   Why have the returns had this effect?

The trading account records:

Now to summarise all the above information!

1. The total earned from sales over the year – also known as the turnover.
2. The cost of sales.
3. Any expense incurred in selling the goods, e.g. wages of sales staff.

The title of the trading account must show the name of the business and the end-of-year date.

Display of the complete Trading Account
The following trading account is displayed for 'Sounds Good to Me!' – a music shop.

Trading Account of Sounds Good to Me! for the year ended 31 December 20..

				£	£	£
Sales	..	..	..	..	..			27,500
Less: Returns Inwards	..	..			1,000
						26,500
Less: Cost of Sales:						
Opening Stock	..	..		9,000	
Add: Purchases	..	..	15,000		
Less: Returns Outwards ..	..	500	14,500	
				23,500	
Less: Closing Stock	..	..	..	3,750	
Cost of Sales	..	..	..	..			19,750
GROSS PROFIT	..	..	..			£6,750

ACTIVITY

Copy the following account and complete the spaces.

Trading Account of Michael's Mechanics for the year ended 31 December 20..

	£	£	£
Sales			35,000
Less: Returns Inwards			[ ]
			33,000
Less: Cost of Sales:			
Opening Stock		[ ]	
Add: Purchases	18,000		
Less: Returns Outwards ..	350	17,650	
		25,150	
Less Closing Stock		4,750	
Cost of Sales			[ ]
GROSS PROFIT			£12,600

The Profit and Loss Account

The purpose of the profit and loss account is to find the net profit which is the true profit of the business at the end of each trading year.

To find the net profit

Net profit takes into consideration all the running expenses which have to be paid by the business. Examples of a business's expenses are rent, rates, electricity, telephone, salaries, depreciation and heating. Net profit is the amount of money remaining after these expenses have been paid out of the gross profit.

Therefore, if a business has a gross profit of £15,000 and its expenses are £9,000, the net profit would be £6,000. However, if the gross profit is £15,000 and its expenses are £19,000, the business would have a net loss of £4,000.

Net Profit = Gross Profit – Expenses

ACTIVITY

a   Copy out the following table and, from the details given, calculate the Net Profit for The Bookworm, a bookshop and The Fish Tank, a fish shop.

b   What advice would you give the owner of The Fish Tank?

	The Bookworm	**The Fish Tank**
Gross Profit	£20,000	£14,000
Expenses	£14,505	£15,210
Net Profit/Loss		

Additional received income

Sometimes a business may receive small amounts of income which are not related to its main work. A shop, for example, may have unused rooms at the top of the building which it rents out as offices.

The rent received from the offices would be additional income for the shopkeeper, and would be added on to the gross profit in the profit and loss account.

> Now to summarise the above information on the profit and loss account!

The profit and loss account records:

1. the gross profit (transferred from the trading account)
2. all running expenses
3. any additional income.

The title of the profit and loss account also must show the name of the business and the end-of-year date.

Display of the complete profit and loss account

The following profit and loss account is displayed for 'Sounds Good to Me!' – a music shop.

Profit and Loss Account of Sounds Good to Me! for the year ended 31 December 20..	£	£
Gross Profit		6,750
Add: Rent Received		2,000
		8,750
Less: Electricity	510	
Stationery	125	
Rates	756	
Interest on Loan	159	
Advertising	845	
Insurance	545	
Sundry Expenses	124	
Telephone	400	3,464
NET PROFIT		£5,286

ACTIVITY

Study the above account and answer the following questions:

a Make a list of four other expenses which you think Sounds Good to Me! might have.
b Suggest two ways in which this business might improve its net profit.
c Sounds Good to Me! could reasonably expect to increase its net profit in the following year. State why this is so.

ACTIVITY

Copy the following account and complete the spaces.

Profit and Loss Account of Michael's Mechanics for the year ended 31 December 20..

			£	£
Gross Profit				☐
Add: Rent Received				2,500
				15,150
Less: Electricity..			630	
Stationery			190	
Rates			☐	
Advertising			500	
Insurance..			700	
Postage			79	
Telephone			239	3,138
NET PROFIT				£ ☐

EXAMINATION QUESTION

Explain why gross profit is normally greater than net profit.

(2 marks)

(Adapted from CCEA Business Studies, GCSE, Paper 2 Foundation Tier, 2000)

Tips for answering this question:

Only one reason is required for 2 marks in this question.

Trading and Profit and Loss Account for the year ended 31 December 20..

	£	£
Sales		69,456
Opening Stock	450	
Add: Purchases	21,000	
	☐	
Less: Closing Stock	461	
Cost of Goods Sold		☐
Gross Profit		☐
Administration	900	
Rent and Rates	3,600	
Wages	32,000	
Bad Debts	416	36,916
Net Profit		£11,051

Complete the spaces above.

(3 marks)

(Adapted from CCEA Business Studies, GCSE, Paper 2 Foundation Tier, 2000)

Tips for answering this question:

Each of the answers gains 1 mark. When you have completed all three boxes, add the entire account again to check your work.

Distribution of profits

At the end of the year it is usual for a business to have to use the net profit in various ways before giving the remainder to the owners. The following diagram shows ways in which the net profit is distributed.

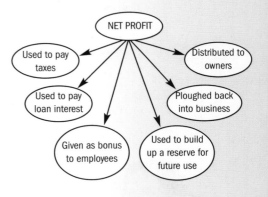

How the distribution of profits to the owners is shown in the profit and loss account

Figure 5.5

A sole trader needs no further account because all the profit goes to the owner.

The financial affairs of a partnership or a company are more complicated and both these organisations need to work an appropriation section in the profit and loss account.

The appropriation section goes after the part you have already learned about and simply shows how the profit is shared or appropriated – hence its name! You should study the two following examples.

<table>
<tr><td colspan="3">Profit and Loss Account (Appropriation Section) of Jack and Jill for year ended 31 December 20..</td></tr>
</table>

	£	£
Net Profit		10,000
Share of Profit:		
Jack	5,000	
Jill	5,000	
	£10,000	£10,000

<table>
<tr><td colspan="3">Profit and Loss Account (Appropriation Section) of The Ballymena Bread Company Ltd for year ended 31 December 20..</td></tr>
</table>

	£	£
Net Profit		110,000
Taxation	27,500	
Dividends paid	32,500	
Retained profit	50,000	
	£110,000	£110,000

ACTIVITY

Examine the above appropriation section of the Ballymena Bread Company Ltd and answer the following questions.

1. What is the percentage rate of tax which this company is paying?
2. What percentage of the total net profit has been distributed as dividends?
3. How might the Ballymena Bread Company Ltd use the retained profit?

The Balance Sheet

assets   liabilities

The purpose of the balance sheet is to show the accurate value of the business on any given date.

The balance sheet is not actually an account. It is a list showing all the assets and liabilities. It also shows the owners' original capital investment and any profits they are entitled to receive as well as their drawings (money they have taken out of the business for their own private use).

> The balance sheet lists assets and liabilities.

> So what are assets and liabilities?

> Assets are items owned by the business, and liabilities are items owed by the business.

ACTIVITY

Use a computer to copy the following list and show whether each item is an asset or a liability.

Money in the bank   ....

Money owing to suppliers   ....

Machinery   ....

Money owing by customers   ....

Office equipment   ....

Bank overdraft   ....

Unpaid telephone bill   ....

Premises   ....

Assets are divided into **fixed** and **current** assets:

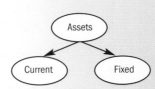

- Current assets   – Those assets which can quickly be exchanged for cash. An example is stock.

- Fixed assets   – Those assets which will be more permanent in the business. An example is machinery.

Liabilities are divided into **long-term** and **current** liabilities:

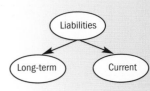

- Current liabilities   – Those liabilities which must be paid immediately. An example is creditors.

- Long-term liabilities   – Those liabilities which are borrowed for a longer time. An example is bank loan.

Working capital

Working capital is also displayed in the balance sheet. Working capital is the term given to the money which is needed for the day-to-day running of the business.

Working capital is used to pay bills such as creditors and wages, as well as expenses like electricity or telephone. It is also used to buy goods for resale in a shop or raw materials in a factory.

It is important for a business to keep working capital at the correct level because, if it is too low, the business will not be able to pay its debts and is said to have a cash flow problem. However if the level of working capital is too high the business is not using its money in the most profitable way.

Working capital is calculated by subtracting the total of the current liabilities from the total of the current assets.

> **Working Capital = Current Assets – Current Liabilities**

Now to summarise the above information on the balance sheet:

The balance sheet records:

1. the business's assets – divided into current assets and fixed assets
2. the business's liabilities – divided into current and long-term liabilities
3. the owner's capital and drawings
4. the net profit (transferred from the profit and loss account).

The title of the balance sheet must show the name of the business and the date it is being worked.

The following complete balance sheet is displayed for 'Sounds Good to Me!'

Balance Sheet of Sounds Good to Me! as at 31 December 20..			
	£	£	£
FIXED ASSETS			
Premises		80,000	
Recording Equipment		13,200	
Motor Van		8,700	101,900
CURRENT ASSETS			
Cash in Hand	970		
Cash at Bank (Current Account) ..	10,050		
Stock	3,750		
Debtors	1,750	16,520	
CURRENT LIABILITIES			
Creditors		9,000	
Working Capital			7,520
			£109,420
LONG TERM LIABILITIES			
Capital		80,000	
Add: Net Profit		5,286	
		85,286	
Less: Drawings		14,866	70,420
Bank Loan			9,000
Mortgage			30,000
			£109,420

In the above balance sheet you should note that:

a the fixed assets are listed first, followed by the current assets
b the current liabilities are subtracted from the current assets to find the working capital
c the working capital is added to the total of the fixed assets
d the total of the long-term liabilities must equal the total found in step c above.

ACTIVITY

Copy the following balance sheet on the computer and complete the spaces.

Balance Sheet of Michael's Mechanics as at 31 December 20..

	£	£	£
FIXED ASSETS			
Premises		☐	
Machinery		4,300	45,300
CURRENT ASSETS			
Cash in Hand	☐		
Stock	4,750		
Debtors	750	6,020	
CURRENT LIABILITIES			
Creditors	800		
Bank Overdraft	1,200	2,000	
Working Capital			☐
			£49,320
LONG-TERM LIABILITIES			
Capital	35,848		
Add: Net Profit	☐		
	47,810		
Less: Drawings	2,490		45,320
Bank Loan			4,000
			☐

ACTIVITY

Answer the following questions in your notebook.

a   Explain the difference between fixed and current assets.
b   From the above balance sheet, complete the following formula.
    Working capital = ... less ....
c   Why do you think that capital is classified as a long-term liability?
d   Define a current liability.
e   What do you understand by 'drawings'?

EXAMINATION QUESTION

The following information has been extracted from Denise's balance sheet.

Current Assets		Current Liabilities	
Stock	600	Creditors	2000
Debtors	800		
Cash	2200		

Use the information above to calculate the working capital for Denise.

(2 marks)

(CCEA Business Studies, GCSE, Paper 2 Foundation Tier, 2002)

ACTIVITY

This activity is based on work in Units 5.2 and 5.3.

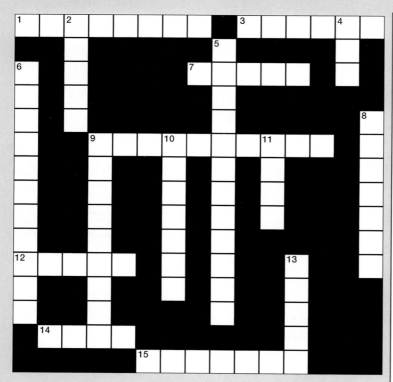

Clues Across:
1 Another name for sales (8)
3 Name given to things owned (6)
7 Purchases plus profit equals this (5)
9 Each partner gets a ... of the profit (10)
12 Name for trading and profit and loss accounts (5)
14 Acid .... (4)
15 People who owe you money (7)

Clues Down:
2 Proportion (5)
4 Number of types of profit (3)
5 List of assets and liabilities (7,5)
6 Type of profit before expenses are paid (5, 6)
8 Type of capital (7)
9 Goods bought (9)
10 Original investment in the business (7)
11 First word of one of the ratios (4)
13 Another word for expenses (5)

REVISION

At this stage you should understand and be able to interpret:

- a trading account
- a profit and loss account
- a vertical balance sheet.

You should also understand the meaning of the following terms:

Gross profit	Net profit	Cost of sales:
Returns inwards	Returns outwards	Assets
Liabilities	Fixed assets	Current assets
Long term liabilities	Current liabilities	Working capital

As revision, look each one up in the Glossary at the end of the book.

UNIT 5.3 Interpretation of Accounts

Now that you understand the final accounts and balance sheet, you can start to interpret them and to extract information from them.

So who would be interested in this information?

Obviously, the owners and managers need to study the accounts. The business's bank would also be interested. Tax authorities and the employees of the business all have their own reasons for watching its progress.

ACTIVITY

Copy the following list, and put in one reason why each of these groups would be interested in the trading results of a business.

Owners   ....

Managers   ....

Tax authorities   ....

Employees   ....

By reading the final accounts and balance sheet it is easy to see the level of profit which the business has made and the size of its turnover. However, this does not tell us enough to enable us to assess the true performance of the business.

There are a number of ratios and percentages which help us to get an accurate calculation of the performance of the business and also enable us to compare its performance from year to year. These calculations all use figures which are shown in the final accounts and balance sheet.

Gross Profit Percentage

This calculation shows the amount of gross profit which a business has made on sales. It is a measure of the business's trading efficiency – the higher the percentage figure is, the better the trading performance.

Figure 5.6

The formula for finding the gross profit percentage is:

$$\text{Gross profit percentage} = \frac{\text{Gross profit}}{\text{Sales}} \times 100$$

For example, if a business has sales value £68,740 and its gross profit is £29,500:

$$\text{Gross profit percentage} = \frac{29,500}{68,740} \times 100$$

Gross profit percentage = 42.9%

This result means that for every £1 of sales, this firm makes almost 50p gross profit – an excellent result!

EXAMINATION QUESTION

	Year 1	Year 2	Year 3
Sales	£54,706	£63,750	£70,322
Gross Profit	£41,030	£45,900	£49,225
Net Profit	£9,300	£10,200	£10,900
Gross Profit Percentage			

Calculate the gross profit percentages and show your calculations. (3 marks)

(Adapted from CCEA Business Studies, GCSE, Paper 2 Foundation Tier, 2000)

Tips for answering this question:

In this question, it is essential that you know the formula for gross profit percentage. Write down the formula (this will earn some marks) and then substitute the appropriate figures for each of the years. Make sure that you show your answers as percentages

Net Profit Percentage

This calculation shows the amount of net profit which is made on sales. It measures the business's efficiency not only in trading but also in keeping its expenses down – the higher the percentage figure is, the better the overall performance.

If a business succeeded in keeping its gross profit percentages steady from year to year but found that its net profit percentages were going down, it would have to examine its expenses.

The formula for finding the net profit percentage is:

$$\text{Net profit percentage} = \frac{\text{Net profit}}{\text{Sales}} \times 100$$

For example, if a business has sales value £68,740 and its net profit is £13,500:

$$\text{Net profit percentage} = \frac{13,500}{68,740} \times 100$$

Net profit percentage = 19.6%

This means that for every £1 of sales, this business makes 19.6p profit – an average result!

EXAMINATION QUESTION

	Year 1	Year 2	Year 3
Sales	£54,706	£63,750	£70,322
Gross Profit	£41,030	£45,900	£49,225
Net Profit	£9,300	£10,200	£10,900
Net Profit Percentage			

Calculate the net profit percentages and show your answers in the spaces. (3 marks)

(Adapted from CCEA Business Studies, GCSE, Paper 2 Foundation Tier, 2000)

Tips for answering this question:

The tip for the previous examination question also applies to this question.

EXAMINATION QUESTION

Trading and Profit and Loss Accounts for the year ended 31 March 20..

	£	£
Sales		14,500
Less: Cost of Goods Sold		7,500
Gross Profit		7,000
Less: Rent	3,400	
Heat	120	
Sundry Expenses	880	4,400
Net Profit		£2,600

Using the above information, calculate the net profit percentage.

(2 marks)

(CCEA Business Studies, GCSE, Paper 2 Higher Tier, 2002)

Tips for answering this question:

In calculating the net profit percentage, you should show where you substitute the figures into the formula, (1 mark) and then work out the answer on a separate line. The final correct answer will gain 1 further mark. In any calculation question it is always important to show every step of the work.

Stock Turnover Rate

This calculation shows the number of times in a year that the business is able to sell the value of its average stock. It is, therefore, another measure of the business's trading efficiency – the higher the rate is, the better the business activity.

A business's turnover rate depends on the type of goods it sells. If its goods are high-value goods – jewellery, for example – it will make fewer sales but each sale is likely to be for a large amount of money. A jeweller may only replace stock once or twice a year.

On the other hand, if the business deals in goods which are low value – vegetables, for example – it will make a large of number of sales but each sale would be for a small sum. Stock of perishable vegetables would be replaced every working day.

The formula for finding the stock turnover rate is:

$$\text{Stock turnover rate} = \frac{\text{Cost of goods sold}}{\text{Average stock}}$$

For example, if the trading account shows that a business's cost of sales is £13,800 and its average stock is £2,010. (Average stock is: opening stock plus closing stock divided by 2):

$$\text{Stock turnover rate} = \frac{13,800}{2,010}$$

Stock turnover rate = 6.9 times

Figure 5.7

This result means that the business sells out its stock almost seven times each year.

ACTIVITY

Trading Account of Sounds Good to Me! for the year ended 31 December 20..

	£	£	£
Sales			27,500
Less: Returns Inwards			1,000
			26,500
Less: Cost of Sales:			
Opening Stock		9,000	
Add: Purchases	15,000		
Less: Returns Outward	500	14,500	
		23,500	
Less: Closing Stock		3,750	
Cost of Sales			19,750
GROSS PROFIT			£6,750

Using the details in the above account, calculate the stock turnover rate for the music shop 'Sounds Good to Me!'

Return on Capital Employed (ROCE)

This calculation shows the net profit which the owner has received on the capital invested. The owner should compare this result with the profit which would have been received if the money had been invested in shares in other businesses or deposited in the bank, for example.

The formula for finding return on capital employed is:

$$\text{Return on capital employed} = \frac{\text{Net profit}}{\text{Capital employed}} \times 100$$

For example, if the capital invested in the business is £80,000 and the net profit is £13,500:

$$\text{Return on capital employed} = \frac{13,500}{80,000} \times 100$$

$$\text{Return on capital employed} = 16.8\%$$

This result means that the owner is making almost 17% profit on his/her investment.

EXAMINATION QUESTION

a   Caroline wishes to calculate the return on capital employed. Show her the formula she should use.
(2marks)

b   How could Caroline use the return on capital employed figure to help her to decide whether to become a partner in a business?
(4 marks)

(Adapted from CCEA Business Studies, GCSE, Paper 2 Foundation Tier, 2000)

Tips for answering this question:

a   In the first part, you should simply write down the formula for ROCE.

b   In the second part, for 4 marks, you would be expected to state two uses of the return on capital figure. These would be awarded 2 marks each if they were fully explained.

Current Working Capital Ratio

This ratio is also sometimes referred to as the **current ratio** and shows the relationship between a business's current assets and current liabilities. The current working capital ratio measures the business's ability to pay its current debts such as creditors.

The formula for finding the current working capital ratio is:

$$\text{Current working capital ratio} = \frac{\text{Current assets}}{\text{Current liabilities}}$$

For example, if a business has current assets value £74,375 and its current liabilities are £36,200:

$$\text{Current working capital ratio} = \frac{74,375}{36,200}$$

$$\text{Current working capital ratio} = 2.05:1$$

ACTIVITY

Balance Sheet of Sounds Good to Me! as at 31 December 20..

	£	£	£
FIXED ASSETS			
Premises		80,000	
Recording Equipment		13,200	
Motor Van		8,700	101,900
CURRENT ASSETS			
Cash in Hand	970		
Cash at Bank (Current Account) ..	10,050		
Stock	3,750		
Debtors	1,750	16,520	
CURRENT LIABILITIES			
Creditors		9,000	
Working Capital			7,520
			£109,420
LONG-TERM LIABILITIES			
Capital		80,000	
Add: Net Profit		5,286	
		85,286	
Less: Drawings		14,866	70,420
Bank Loan			9,000
Mortgage			30,000
			£109,420

Using the details in the above balance sheet, calculate the current working capital ratio.

Acid Test Ratio

This ratio measures whether a business is able to pay its current debts without having to sell some of its stock. For this reason, the acid test ratio does not include stock in its calculation. It is agreed that an acid test ratio of 1:1 is safe.

The formula for finding the acid test ratio is:

$$\text{Acid test ratio} = \frac{\text{Current assets} - \text{Value of stock}}{\text{Current liabilities}}$$

For example, if a business has current assets value £34,900, if its stock value is £20,100 and its current liabilities amount to £18,000:

$$\text{Acid test ratio} = \frac{34,900 - 20,100}{18,000}$$

Acid test ratio = 0.82:1

EXAMINATION QUESTION

The following information has been extracted from Denise's balance sheet.

Current Assets		Current Liabilities	
Stock	600	Creditors	2000
Debtors	800		
Cash	2200		

Show Denise the formula she should use to calculate the acid test ratio and work out the ratio for her.

(5 marks)

(CCEA Business Studies, GCSE, Paper 2 Foundation Tier, 2002)

Tips for answering this question:

a   You are asked to 'show' the formula. That means that you have only to write it down – not explain it. There are 2 marks for the formula.

b   In calculating the ratio, you should show where you substitute the figures into the formula (2 marks for this part) and then work out the ratio on a separate line. The final correct answer will gain 1 further mark.

c   In any calculation question it is always important to show every step of the work.

REVISION

At this stage you should know, understand and be able to use the formula for:

- gross profit percentage
- net profit percentage
- stock turnover rate
- return on capital employed (ROCE)
- current working capital ratio
- acid test ratio.

Businesses cannot avoid costs but they are always anxious to minimise them wherever possible in order to maximise their profits (make them as big as possible). Costs can be classified as either fixed or variable.

Fixed Costs

Fixed costs are those costs which are not affected by the quantity of goods produced or sold or by the scale of services rendered. They are called 'fixed' because they do not alter regardless of the volume of work done in the business. For example, factory rent is a fixed cost because it will have to be paid in full whether the factory is manufacturing goods at full capacity or at a reduced level. Other examples of fixed costs are rates, administrative costs, cleaning and insurance. Sometimes fixed costs are referred to as 'overheads' or 'indirect costs'.

On a graph, fixed costs would be shown as a straight horizontal line as is shown here. You can see that the fixed costs stay on one level regardless of the number of units produced. You should also notice that the fixed costs are at that level even if there are no units being produced.

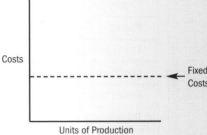

Variable Costs

Variable costs are those costs which vary – or change – according to the level of work being done in the business. For example in a factory, wages will increase if the factory is working at full production level but will decrease if production is reduced and some employees have to be made redundant. Electricity usage will vary for the same reasons as will the purchase of raw materials.

On a graph, variable costs would be shown as a straight diagonal line because they rise in direct proportion with the rise in production. Notice that there are no variable costs at the point of no production.

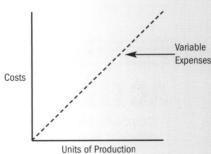

Total Costs

The total costs of the business are found by adding the variable and fixed costs together.

> **Total Costs = Fixed Costs + Variable Costs**

On a graph, total costs are shown as a diagonal line but notice that the total costs line starts at the level of fixed costs. This is because, even at the point of no production, the business has incurred total costs equal to the fixed costs.

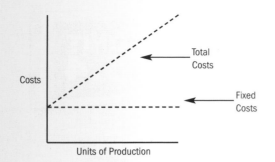

Costs

Total Costs

Fixed Costs

Units of Production

Drawing these graphs will be important when you learn about break even and you will get practice then in drawing them yourself.

ACTIVITY

Copy the following table and tick the appropriate spaces to show whether each cost listed is fixed or variable.

Cost	Fixed	Variable
Mortgage		
Depreciation		
Rates		
Transport of goods		
Machinery repairs		
Advertising		
Telephone		
Electricity		
Loan interest		
Postage of goods		

ACTIVITY

Complete the following table with the missing amounts of costs which were extracted from four different years' final accounts of Fivemiletown Flowers – a small florist shop.

Year	Fixed Costs	Variable Costs	Total Costs
1	£8,000		£13,500
2		£6,000	£14,500
3	£9,000		£15,350
4	£9,500	£9,000	

Activity continues on the next page

> a Name two fixed costs which Fivemiletown Flowers might have.
> b Explain the steady increase in fixed costs over four years.
> c Name two variable costs which Fivemiletown Flowers might have.
> d Give one possible reason why the variable costs have risen sharply in Year 4.

Break Even

> A business's break-even point is where its total costs equal the total of its sales income.

The break-even point is the minimum point at which the business can survive. At this point the business is making neither a profit nor a loss – it is simply covering its costs.

If it can sell more goods than the level of break-even it will make a profit. However, if its sales fall below the break even level, then the business would be in a loss-making situation.

Significance of the break-even Point

The concept of 'break even' is extremely important in business because it can show:

- the amount of goods which need to be sold in order to make a profit
- the level of costs which can be borne
- the price which needs to be charged for goods
- how price changes would affect the business's profits.

How is the break-even point worked out?

The most usual method of finding the break-even point is to work a graph. It is also possible to calculate the break even point using a formula. Either method needs to have information on both the business's total costs and its revenue (income) from sales.

Calculating break-even by formula

The formula for calculating break even is:

$$\text{Break even} = \frac{\text{Total fixed costs}}{\text{Selling price per unit} - \text{Variable cost per unit}}$$

Study the following example:

Jim Lindsay owns a bookshop in Omagh. He needs help to calculate his break-even point but knows that his total fixed costs are £4,000 per month, each book sells on average at £7 and his variable costs are £2 per book.

$$\text{Break even} = \frac{4{,}000}{7-2}$$
$$= \frac{4{,}000}{5}$$
$$= 800$$

This means that Jim must sell 800 books every month in order to break even. He says that he would find this difficult to do so he decides to increase the price of his books from £7 to £9. The new calculation would be:

$$\text{Break even} = \frac{4{,}000}{9-2}$$

$$= \frac{4{,}000}{7}$$

$$= 571.4 \ (572)$$

After the price increase, Jim must sell 572 books every month in order to break even. He feels he can manage this level of sales but knows that he cannot increase his prices again or else his customers will begin to go to other bookshops.

ACTIVITY

a   Helen owns a bakery in Toomebridge. Her total fixed costs are £2,100 per month, her variable costs are £1 per unit on average and she sells each cake for £4 on average.

b   Calculate Helen's break-even point.

c   Helen gets the bad news that her rent is being increased by £100 per month. What is her new break-even point?

d   Create a spreadsheet for Helen to display the above information. Use it to find Helen's new break-even point if:

   i.   she increased the average price of her cakes from £4 to £5

   ii. her rates increased by £50 per month

   iii. she employed a schoolgirl to help her on Saturdays. This would increase her variable expenses from £1 per unit to £1.10 per unit.

ACTIVITY

Complete the following table for Tom who is the manager of a toy factory in Magherafelt. The fixed costs of the factory amount to £500 per week and the variable costs are £2 per toy. Each toy is sold for £4. The table is started for you.

Activity continues on the next page

Activity continued

Number of Toys Sold	Total Income From Sales	Fixed Costs	Variable Costs	Total Costs	Profit/Loss
0	0	500	0	500	−500
25	100	500	50	550	−450
50					
75					
100					
125					
150					
175					
200					
225					
250					
275					
300					

Calculating break-even graphically

A break-even graph is used to illustrate the:

- profit or loss of a business
- relationship between total costs and sales
- relationship between fixed and variable costs.

Break-even graphs do have some limitations which you should be aware of:

- Perhaps not all the goods will be sold.
- Fixed costs are assumed to never change. This is not always the case. Some circumstances such as greatly increased production might mean taking on new premises which would increase the rates, for example.
- Sales are not always made at a constant level. Businesses sometimes have to offer discounts to clear their stock.

Before beginning to draw a break even chart, it is essential to have details of the business's sales, as well as details of its fixed and variable costs.

Worked example of a break-even chart

In this example we will work a break-even graph for David Williams who is the owner of a factory in Larne which manufactures small items of office equipment.

He needs your help in finding the break-even point for a new stapler which is just ready to be put on the market.

His fixed costs in the factory amount to £500 per week and his variable costs are £6 per stapler. Each stapler is going to be sold for £11.

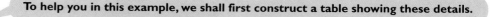

To help you in this example, we shall first construct a table showing these details.

Number of Staplers Sold	Total Income From Sales	Fixed Costs	Variable Costs	Total Costs	Profit/Loss
0	0	500	0	500	−500
20	220	500	120	620	−400
40	440	500	240	740	−300
60	660	500	360	860	−200
80	880	500	480	980	−100
100	1100	500	600	1100	0
120	1320	500	720	1220	+100
140	1540	500	840	1340	+200
160	1760	500	960	1460	+300

We can then use the table to construct the graph and read off the break-even point.

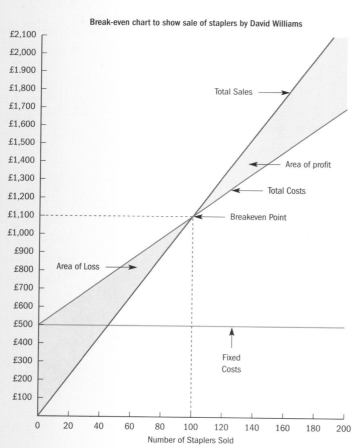

Break-even chart to show sale of staplers by David Williams

Note the following:

- the total income from sales and total costs should be able to be read off the vertical axis
- it should show the total units of sales – staplers, in this case – on the horizontal axis
- the fixed costs should be plotted first
- next plot the total costs
- finally, plot the income from sales
- always remember to put on all labels
- the break-even point should be shown with a broken line drawn to the horizontal axis.

The break-even point is 100, therefore David Williams must sell 100 staplers per week in order to cover his costs of £1,100

ACTIVITY

You should now return to the table which you completed for Tom.

a   Use the information in the table to draw a break-even graph for Tom's toy factory in Magherafelt, and indicate the break-even point on the graph.

b   Read the graph and answer the following questions.
  i.   What would be the result if Tom sold 300 toys?
  ii. What would be the result if he sold 200 toys?

EXAMINATION QUESTION

The following details were provided by an artist who runs her own business.

Fixed costs per month   ..   £500
Variable costs per month ..   £50 per picture
Selling price   ..   ..   ..   £100 per picture

a   Using the information, draw and label a graph to show the break-even point.

                                                (6 marks)

b   Her variable costs are high. What might be causing this?

                                                (4 marks)

(Adapted from CCEA Business Studies, GCSE, Paper 2 Higher Tier, 2002)

Tips for answering this question:

a   It is easy to gain full marks for Part A if you work the graph carefully and label all parts. The 6 marks for this question are allocated like this: vertical axis (1 mark), horizontal axis (1 mark), total costs line (1 mark), fixed costs line (1 mark), total sales line (1 mark), break-even point (1 mark).

b   Part B is a straightforward question which is asked in order to see if you understand variable costs. Think of two variable costs which the artist would have and then say why she may be paying too much for them.

The margin of safety

One of the main aims of a business is to make a profit and expand its market. No business therefore would be content to operate at the break-even point for long, so once the business has found its break-even level it then attempts to exceed it and plan for a higher level of sales. This higher level then becomes its 'selected operating point'.

The difference between the selected operating point and the break-even point is known as the margin of safety. So:

> The margin of safety is the amount which a business sells in excess of its break-even point.

Let us return to the graph for the sale of staplers where the break-even point was 100. David Williams now tells us that he plans to sell 140 staplers per week.

Study the following graph to see how the margin of safety is illustrated.

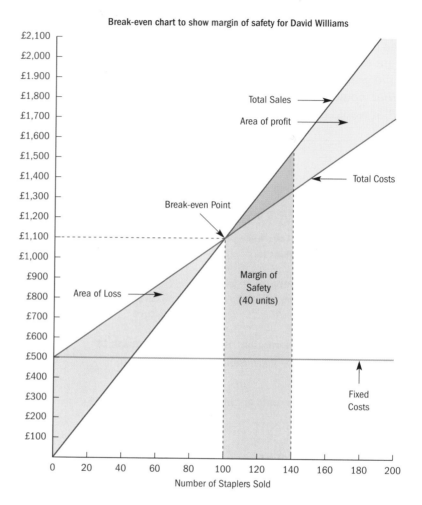

Break-even chart to show margin of safety for David Williams

The margin of safety is 40 because David Williams plans to sell 140 staplers per week which is 40 more than the break-even point.

EXAMINATION QUESTION

The following information was provided by JP Ltd:

Monthly Costs of Production of a new Toy

Fixed costs	£2000
Labour	£6 per unit
Materials	£4 per unit
Production capacity and expected sales	450 units
Selling price	£15

a Explain why it is important for a business to calculate the break-even point

(4marks)

b Calculate how many units JP Ltd need to produce and sell in order to break-even

(3 marks)

c What do you understand by the term 'margin of safety'?

(2 marks)

d What margin of safety would JP Ltd have for this product?

(I mark)

e Consider the implications for JP Ltd if labour costs increased to £7 per unit

(5 marks)

(CCEA Business Studies, GCSE, Paper 2 Foundation and Higher Tiers, 2001)

Tips for answering this question:

a Two reasons would be expected to be given for full marks

b In this type of question it is always advisable to show every step of your work. 1 mark is given for stating the formula, 1 mark is given for substituting figures into the formula and the third mark is for the final answer. Even if your final answer is incorrect, you could get some marks for the process.

c This question only requires a straightforward definition of 'margin of safety'. Keep your answer short.

d For 1 mark you should simply write down the number of units

e When you are asked to 'consider' it means that you must look at the situation from different viewpoints and see the difficulties as well as the advantages. In this instance you need to show the change in the break-even point and what changes this will mean in production. Be careful to take into consideration the factory capacity of 450 units

REVISION

At this stage you should understand the meaning of the following terms:

Fixed costs	Variable costs	Total costs
Margin of safety	Break-even point	

As revision, look each one up in the Glossary at the end of the book.

Forecasting

What is a forecast?

You are well used to hearing the weather forecast on the radio or television. It predicts what the weather will be like for the following few days and is very useful to people such as farmers who can then plan their outdoor work around those conditions.

A cash flow forecast acts in exactly the same way for a business. It predicts – or forecasts – the level of spending and level of income which the business will have during the following period of time. Always remember that a forecast is for the future.

The big difference is of course, that no one can do anything to alter the weather, whereas the business owners and managers have some control over the timing of the flow of money in and out of the business.

So What is Cash Flow?

> 'Cash flow' is the term used to describe the flow of money into and out of a business.

Importance of Adequate Cash Flow

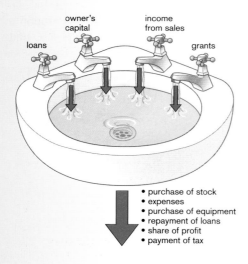

Figure 5.8

It is important for a business to maintain an adequate level of cash flow. This is because:

- an even cash flow ensures that the business would never suffer from a shortage of ready money. This shortage would arise if the bills had to be paid at regular intervals but the income was coming in irregularly
- the business must ensure that there is a steady supply of money coming in so that it is able to pay its essential debts such as creditors and wages
- without adequate cash flow the business could be forced to close because suppliers would no longer trade with a business which could not pay for its purchases
- employees would not continue to work for the business if their wages were not being paid
- it would save the business from having to borrow money which would incur interest charges
- if the business has a good cash flow, it could take advantage of cheaper stock offers. Taking advantage of offers enables the business to re-sell the goods more cheaply and thus attract customers.

You can see that a cash flow problem would be created if the goods were not sold quickly and cash was not received in order to pay the expenses or pay the suppliers for the goods.

This situation is known as a liquidity problem and many businesses have had to close for this reason.

The following diagram illustrates the constancy of the flow of cash in and out of the business:

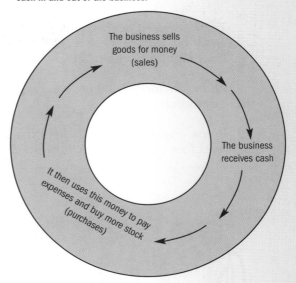

The business sells goods for money (sales)

The business receives cash

It then uses this money to pay expenses and buy more stock (purchases)

EXAMINATION QUESTION

Why is it important for a business to have adequate cash flow?

(3 marks)

(CCEA Business Studies, GCSE, Paper 2 Foundation Tier, 2001)

Tips for answering this question:

A question which starts with 'Why' is asking you to give a reason for something. In this case, the examiner wants you to give a reason (or reasons) why it is important to have adequate cash flow. You may approach this in two different ways – you may state three reasons why adequate cash flow is important, or you may state one reason and then go on to explain the details of that reason. Either approach could gain full marks.

ACTIVITY

You are the Financial Director of The Plastic Products Company – a business which manufactures all forms of plastic containers.

The factory is very well equipped with state-of-the-art machinery and has a highly trained workforce. Business has been very good for many years and The Plastic Products Company is well established in the market. One new business has come into the plastics market recently and is keen to get new orders.

Activity continues on the next page

The Plastic Products Company has experienced some minor cash flow difficulties in the past, and a board meeting has been called to consider ways in which the business might reduce the risk of future, larger cash flow problems.

As the Financial Director, you have been asked to speak at the meeting and to lead the discussion.

Prepare your speech now in preparation for the meeting. You would be expected to have at least four suggestions of how the risk might be reduced.

One of the ways to control cash flow is to prepare a cash flow forecast.

Purpose of a Cash Flow Forecast

There are six main reasons for constructing a cash flow forecast:

1. **It enables the owner or manager to plan the business's expenditure**

   Perhaps a machine has to be replaced during the year while other expenses such as electricity always have to be paid at regular intervals. Recording all forecasted expenditure enables the business to see if these payments would result in cash shortages at certain times.

2. **It shows the amount required and when it is needed**

   Any business wishing to borrow money will see from the cash flow forecast exactly how much needs to be borrowed and exactly when the extra cash is required. This prevents the payment of interest for longer than necessary.

3. **It shows when loans could be repaid**

   Presentation of a cash flow forecast would show the bank or other lender if, and when, the business would be able to repay the loan. This would encourage the bank to give a loan.

4. **It inspires confidence and acts as a check on spending**

   A cash flow forecast gives the owner confidence, and shows if the business's financial plans are being maintained.

5. **It supports the business's business plan**

   A cash flow forecast is required as part of the business's business plan and can be used to support it

6. **It sets targets for the business**

   A cash flow forecast sets targets for the business to work towards and, at the end of the period, it shows what actually happened in the business. These actual results can then be compared with the forecast.

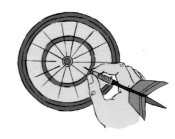

The difference between what actually happened in the business and the forecasted performance is known as the **variance** and owners would have to investigate the cause of large variances.

Consequences of Incorrect Forecasting

There are two main consequences:

1. **It would cause a shortage of working capital**

   If a business failed to forecast its income and spending accurately it would experience a shortage of working capital.

   (You have already learned that working capital is used to pay for the running expenses of the business. It follows therefore that if incorrect forecasting resulted in a shortage of working capital, the running expenses could not be paid.)

2. **Some of the business's assets may have to be sold**

   If a business forecasts incorrectly and runs short of cash, it may be forced to sell some of its assets. This could affect its production if, for example, machinery were sold.

Display of a Cash Flow Forecast

A cash flow forecast records:

- Receipts — the total money received from sales or other means over the period – these are the receipts. These are recorded as separate items and the totals are also shown.
- Payments — all payments made over the period of the forecast are recorded separately.
- Balances — the opening and closing balances each month.

The following cash flow forecast is displayed for six months for Mary Little who owns and runs a small hairdressing salon in Bangor. Mary set up her business on January 1 with her own capital of £8,000. She forecasts that for each of the first three months she will make £1,000 in cash sales which should rise to £2,000 per month in April when she has become established.

She will have to buy shampoo and other supplies of £500 per month during the first three months, rising to £1,000 per month for the next three months. She will pay herself £600 per month and pay £400 per month to one assistant. During January she plans to buy extra equipment costing £3,000. Mary's rent has been agreed at £400 per month. Electricity costing £180 is due to be paid in March and June and telephone bills of £100 also have to be paid in March and June. £300 for insurance will be paid in January.

Cash Flow Forecast for Mary Little from 1 January to 30 June 20..

RECEIPTS	January	February	March	April	May	June	Total
Sales	1,000	1,000	1,000	2,000	2,000	2,000	9,000
New Capital	8,000	8,000					
Total Receipts	9,000	1,000	1,000	2,000	2,000	2,000	17,000
PAYMENTS							
Purchases	500	500	500	1,000	1,000	1,000	4,500
Salary	600	600	600	600	600	600	3,600
Wages	400	400	400	400	400	400	2,400
Equipment	3,000						3,000

Table continues on the next page

Table continued

RECEIPTS	January	February	March	April	May	June	Total
Rent	400	400	400	400	400	400	2,400
Electricity			180			180	360
Telephone			100			100	200
Insurance	300						300
Total Payments	5,200	1,900	2,180	2,400	2,400	2,680	16,760
Opening Balance	0	3,800	2,900	1,720	1,320	920	10,660
+ Receipts	9,000	1,000	1,000	2,000	2,000	2,000	17,000
	9,000	4,800	3,900	3,720	3,320	2,920	27,660
−Payments	5,200	1,900	2,180	2,400	2,400	2,680	16,760
Closing Balance	3,800	2,900	1,720	1,320	920	240	10,900

ACTIVITY

RECEIPTS	Jan	Feb	March	April	May	June	Total
Sales	2,000	2,000	2,000	3,000	5,000	5,000	19,000
Total Receipts	2,000	2,000	2,000	3,000	5,000	5,000	19,000
Rent	300	300	300	300	300	300	1,800
Wages	500	500	500	500	1,000	1,000	4,000
Electricity			150				150
Advertising			500	500			1,000
Equipment	4,000						4,000
Total Payments	4,800	800	1,450	1,300	1,300	1,300	10,950
OpeningBalance	0	−2,800	−1,600	−1,050	650	4,350	−450
+ Receipts	2,000	2,000	2,000	3,000	5,000	5,000	19,000
2000		−800	400	1,950	5,650	9,350	18,550
- Payments	4,800	800	1,450	1,300	1,300	1,300	10,950
Closing Balance	−2,800	−1,600	−1,050	650	4,350	8,050	7,600

Activity continues on next page

Study the cash flow forecast opposite and then answer these questions:

1. Choose one type of business from the following list which the cash flow forecast might be for.

   Garden Centre   Toy Shop   Hairdresser

2. Choose one type of business from the same list which the cash flow forecast would not be for.

3. Justify your choice of business in Number 2.

4. How could the owner have prevented the low balances during the first three months?

5. State one disadvantage of that course of action.

6. What comment would you make about the overall performance of this business?

ACTIVITY

Cecil put £17,400 into the bank as his own capital on 1 January to open a small café in Portrush.

He forecasts that his sales will be £500 for each of the first two months, rising to £1,000 in March. Easter is in April and the day trippers start coming then so he anticipates his sales will be £3,000 in April and May and will rise again to £4,000 in June when the town has more visitors.

Cecil has calculated that his purchases will be £300 in January and February, £500 in March, £700 in April and May and £1,000 in June. Cecil plans to employ one part-time waitress in January, February and March. For April and May he will employ a second part-time waitress, and will take on a third part-time person for June. Each part-time employee will be paid £250 per month. Small items of new machinery are to be bought in January and April costing £400 each time. Cecil's rent has been agreed at £400 per month. Electricity costing £150 is due to be paid in March and June and telephone bills of £100 will be paid in March and June.

You should now design a cash flow forecast for six months from January to June on a spreadsheet for Cecil using the details given here.

EXAMINATION QUESTION

Cash Flow Forecast – Jan to March 2001

RECEIPTS	January	February	March
Opening Balance	55,000	22,000	a
Sales	42,000	41,000	46,000
Total	97,000	63,000	b
EXPENSES			
Creditors	10,000	9,000	5,000
Purchases	22,000	11,000	10,000
Heat	3,000	0	0
Wages	40,000	41,000	38,000
Machinery	0	0	2,000
Total	75,000	61,000	55,000
Closing Balance	22,000	2,000	c

a Examine the cash flow forecast for the beginning of the year. Complete boxes a, b, and c.

(3 marks)

b Study the closing balance for March. Advise the business on what action it should take.

(4 marks)

(CCEA Business Studies, GCSE, Paper 2 Foundation Tier, 2001)

Tips for answering this question:

As in all mathematical questions, check your work carefully in Part A. 1 mark is given for each correct answer. In the second part, make sure that your advice is related to what the business should do in the future to improve the balance. You would be expected to offer two pieces of advice to gain 4 marks.

REVISION

At this stage you should:

- understand the purpose of forecasting
- know the importance of cash flow
- be able to interpret a cash flow statement
- understand the consequences of incorrect forecasting.

If you are unsure, you should go over the unit again as revision.

Command Words Used in the GCSE Business Studies Examination

Both the Foundation and Higher Tiers of the GCSE examination must examine four assessment objectives. A variety of key terms – known as command words – is used to do this. It is important to understand what the command word in a question is asking you to do. Unfortunately, many candidates lose marks because they do not do what the question requires.

This list is presented to show the exact requirements of each term used. You will notice that there is some overlap between the terms used to examine different assessment objectives.

It is important that candidates present their answers clearly and write in complete sentences.

AO1

In the first assessment objective, the examiner is finding out if the candidate knows and understands the content of the specification. AO1 questions usually are short and carry few marks.

Define The candidate has to explain the meaning of a term precisely. An example should also be given.

Explain The candidate must give the details of a topic to show that he/she understands its meaning. An example makes the explanation clearer.

Give The candidate is being asked for examples or a list. The answer does not have to be written in sentences nor does it require any explanation.

Identify This command is similar to the last one. The candidate has to name or list the required information.

List This command is the same as 'give'.

Name This command is the same as 'give' or 'list'.

Outline The candidate is asked to write a short description or a brief summary.

Show your calculation In questions requiring mathematical calculations, the candidate should show the steps leading to the final answer.

State This command is the same as 'give', 'list' or 'name'.

What is/are This command is asking for an explanation so the candidate should give the details of the topic being questioned.

AO2

In the second assessment objective, the examiner is finding out if the candidate can use knowledge and understanding by applying them to a given situation to solve a problem.

Apply The candidate should show that he/she can apply his/her knowledge of the subject to a given situation. An example should be given.

Comment on The candidate has to write an explanation or to make remarks on the situation.

Calculate The candidate is being asked to work out the answer to a mathematical question. The formula should be written down, then the appropriate figures should be substituted and finally the answer should be given.

Demonstrate The candidate has to show that he/she understands the business concept being discussed. Examples are required in this type of question.

Describe The candidate is required to write about the main features of the topic in order to show knowledge of it. No explanation is needed.

Distinguish between In this type of question the candidate is being asked to show the difference between two terms.

Examine This type of question requires an investigation into a situation. The candidate has to look closely at the facts and interpret them. Some questions may mean that the candidate would have to give reasons why some of the facts are more important than others in that situation.

Explain As for AO1.

Give an example Here the candidate is being asked to name an example of something – perhaps from his/her own knowledge or perhaps selected from a piece of given material.

How This command is similar to 'explain'. The candidate would have to apply a business concept to a situation or problem.

Show This command is similar to 'demonstrate'. The candidate has to show understanding of the business concept named in the question. Examples are required.

Suggest Here the candidate is being asked to give views on reasons why something has occurred or perhaps on ways to solve a problem. The candidate's views should be backed up with examples.

Use the data etc. The candidate has to select the required data and apply it to the question asked.

Which In this type of question the candidate has to choose the best option.

Why This command is similar to 'explain' and requires the candidate to give details of a topic to show understanding of its meaning.

AO3

In the third assessment objective, the examiner is finding out if the candidate can analyse and interpret information from a variety of sources.

Advise This type of question is asking the candidate to give ways in which a problem might be solved or to show the best way to do something. If there is a high number of marks being awarded, the candidate should give details of several courses of action. The candidate has to choose the best course of action and must give reasons for that choice.

Analyse This question requires the candidate to show understanding of the topic by breaking it down into parts or essential features. The question is asking why something happened so the candidate has to show the events or reasons which led to that situation. A thorough explanation is necessary but a conclusion is not.

Calculate As for AO2.

Compare/contrast In this type of question the candidate has to consider the similarities and differences between two options. To do this involves looking at the points for and against each option.

Describe As for AO2.

Discuss In this type of question, the candidate should investigate or examine the topic, giving reasons for and against it. It is necessary for the candidate to come to a conclusion and give his/her opinion of the issue.

Examine This instruction is similar to 'analyse'. The topic has to be broken down and looked at in depth but a conclusion is not required.

Explain As for AO1 and AO2.

How As for AO2.

Illustrate This command word requires the candidate to clarify the topic by means of either an example or visual material such as a diagram.

Interpret This command word asks the candidate to examine the data and see how it could be applied to the situation being discussed.

Organise The candidate has to select relevant information and to put it in order – perhaps of importance, for example.

Select In this case the candidate has to choose from a variety of alternatives and to pick out the most relevant.

Show As for AO2.

Use the data etc. As for AO2.

Which As for AO2.

Why As for AO2.

AO4

In the last assessment objective, the examiner is finding out if the candidate can make judgements by weighing up both sides of a situation. This Assessment Objective also shows if candidates are capable of making decisions and judgements, drawing conclusions and making recommendations. These are high-level skills and therefore AO4 questions carry more marks.

Advise As for AO3.

Analyse As for AO3.

Assess This command is asking the candidate to make an informed judgement about how good or how effective something is. The candidate must show both the strengths and the limitations but must end with a definite judgement with reasons.

Compare/contrast As for AO3.

Consider Here the candidate has to weigh up the arguments for and against two courses of action.

Criticise This type of question also makes the candidate weigh up the strengths and weaknesses of a situation. To do so, the candidate has to consider all the evidence.

Decide This command word requires a decision or judgement between the alternatives being discussed. The candidate's decision must be supported with reasons or evidence.

Discuss As for AO3.

Do you agree/think This command makes the candidate think whether a statement is correct. A judgement is required so the candidate has to look at all the alternatives and to decide whether he/she agrees with the view expressed. The decision must be supported with reasons.

Evaluate This is similar to 'criticise' and 'assess' and requires the candidate to make an appraisal of a situation or to judge its value. To do this, the candidate must weigh up both the strengths and weaknesses of something and to reach a conclusion, stating reasons.

Explain As for AO1, AO2 and AO3.

Give reasons for This command word is similar to 'why' and requires an explanation.

How well In this case the candidate has to make a judgement on the success of a certain course of action, for example.

In your view/opinion Here the candidate has to make a personal judgement. To do this, he/she must consider the positive and negative points and then reach a conclusion, which should be supported by reasons.

Judge This command word is very similar to the last one. The candidate has to make a personal judgement based on evidence and backed up with reasons.

Justify This command word requires the candidate to consider the grounds for a decision. He/she must not only make a decision but must then show that it is the best decision in the circumstances.

Predict This implies forecasting or saying what will happen in the future. The candidate has to consider the data available and then make a judgement about the consequences.

Recommend This also implies a judgement and a choice saying which is best. The recommendation made must be supported by evidence and reasons.

Show As for AO2 and AO3.

Suggest This invites the candidate to state ways in which something should be done or improved. This requires judgement on the part of the candidate and should be supported by reasons for the suggestion.

Which As for AO2 and AO3.

Why As for AO2 and AO3.

GLOSSARY

A

Accounts The records of the financial transactions of a business.

Acid test ratio Shows a business's ability to pay its current debts without having to sell some of its stock.

Additional capital Extra capital brought into a business, perhaps for expansion.

Amalgamation A voluntary and agreed joining of two or more businesses in order to form one large business. Can also be known as a merger.

Annualised working hours A system in which workers are contracted to work a given number of hours in a year rather than a given number of hours in a week.

Appraisal The process of assessing an employee's performance in his/her job.

Appraisee The person who is being appraised.

Appraiser The person who is carrying out the appraisal.

Arbitration The second stage of a process in which the Labour Relations Agency provides a solution to the parties in a dispute.

Articles of association A legal document used in the setting up of a limited company.

ASA Stands for 'Advertising Standards Authority' which is a body set up to monitor all advertising which is not broadcast.

Asset An item owned by a business, such as premises or vehicles.

B

Balance sheet Is a list of assets and liabilities and shows the accurate value of a business on any given date.

Batch production A method of production in which several of the same product are made at one time.

Bonus An extra payment made to employees who work well and help the business to achieve its objectives.

Break-even point The point at which a business's total costs equal the total of its sales income. It is the minimum point at which the business can survive.

BSI The British Standards Institution is a body which tests products to ensure that they are reliable, safe and of good quality.

Business growth Any form of expansion of a business.

Business plan A detailed description of what a business hopes to do over a future period of usually one to five years.

C

Capital The factor of production which is contributed by the owners and is wealth which is invested in order to create further wealth.

Cash flow The flow of money into and out of a business.

Cash flow forecast A prediction of the level of spending and level of income which a business will have during the following period of time.

CBI Stands for 'Confederation of British Industry' which is an organisation for employers and acts as a pressure group.

Chain of command Is the route by which orders and decisions are passed downwards through an organisation.

Channel of distribution The means by which goods are passed from the producer to the consumer.

Charter mark An award for public service organisations which provide the highest quality service.

Closed shop An agreement that all employees in a business organisation would belong to a trade union.

Collective bargaining A process whereby trade union officials represent all union members to negotiate agreements with management, usually on pay and conditions of service.

Command economy See *planned economy*.

Commission An extra financial reward for sales staff. It is usually expressed as a percentage of sales.

Communication The passing of information from a sender to a receiver.

Competition Act Passed in 1998, this Act is the major anti-competition legislation and brings our law into line with European Union law.

Competition Commission An independent body set up in 1999 for the purpose of investigating mergers and monopolies.

Competitive marketing Any market in which there are many businesses competing for customers.

Competitive pricing See *market-led pricing*.

Conciliation The first stage of a process in which two parties in a dispute are brought together by the Labour Relations Agency in order to solve the dispute.

Conglomerate Is where a number of businesses merge but their products are totally unrelated.

Consultation Is the process by which management discusses with employees and seeks their views.

Consumer A person who is the final user of the product.

Consumers' Association A body which gives advice and information to consumers and aims to improve the standard of goods and services.

Consumer Protection Act Passed in 1987, this Act lays down rules which ensure that prices advertised are genuine, and also is designed to protect consumers from unsafe products.

Contract of employment It is an agreement between the employer and the employee and its main purpose is to define the rights and duties of both parties.

Cost-based pricing A pricing policy which is based on the business's total fixed and variable costs plus a percentage profit.

Cost of sales A business's opening stock plus purchases less closing stock.

Craft union A trade union of employees who all work at the same craft.

Current assets Items owned which can be quickly exchanged for cash, for example stock.

Current liabilities Amounts owing which must be paid immediately, for example to creditors.

Current working Shows the relationship between a business's current assets
capital ratio and its current liabilities.

Curriculum vitae A list of a person's qualifications, work and achievements which is used as a method of selection.

D

Decline The sixth and final stage of the product life cycle, when sales have fallen and the product is unprofitable.

Deed of partnership A legal document which may be drawn up for business partners to replace the Partnership Act.

De-industrialisation A situation where there is a decline of manufacturing industries in an area.

Delayering Refers to the modern practice of reducing the number of levels in a business in order to give all employees a greater say in its decision making.

Demand The quantity of goods which will be bought at a given price.

Desk research See *secondary research*.

Destruction pricing A pricing policy which is designed to destroy competitors' sales and drive them out of the market.

Director A person who is appointed to a company's Board and has responsibility for the running of the company.

Disability Discrimination Act Passed in 1995, this Act makes it unlawful to treat disabled people less favourably than other people in employment.

Discount A sales promotion method in which a percentage is taken off the price of the product.

Diseconomies of scale The opposite of 'economies of scale', where a business becomes too large to run efficiently.

Dismissal Is where an employer discontinues an employee's work because of incompetence or dishonesty.

Division of Labour A type of specialisation in which the manufacture of a product is divided into a number of small stages.

E

E-commerce Stands for 'electronic commerce' which is buying and selling via the Internet.

Economies of scale Economies which are gained when an increase in production causes a decrease in production costs.

Entrepreneur A person who has a business idea and is willing to take a risk in order to make it work.

Equal Pay Act Passed in 1970 and amended in 1984, this Act states that men and women performing the same, or similar, work must be paid the same and must be given the same conditions of service.

Equality Commission Is the body which has responsibility in Northern Ireland for implementing the fair employment legislation and creating a more equal society in Northern Ireland.

External business growth Growth which takes place outside the business. This may be by takeovers or amalgamation, for example.

External recruitment A system in which advertising for new employees invites applications from people who do not work in the business.

F

Factoring A short-term method of finance in which the bank takes responsibility for the collection of the debts of a business.

Factors of production Four resources of land, labour, capital and enterprise which must be present before production can take place.

Fair Employment Order Passed in 1998, this Order ensures that people of all religious beliefs and political opinions have equal opportunities in employment.

Field research See *primary research*.

Financial economies Economies which are gained in situations where a business can obtain finance by cheaper methods.

Fixed assets Items owned by a business which are more permanent, for example machinery.

Fixed costs Costs which are not affected by the quantity of goods produced or sold, or by the scale of services rendered.

Flat structure A modern type of organisational structure which has few levels but has a greater number of people working at each level. It is the opposite of a hierarchical structure.

Flexitime A system of employment which gives the employee some choice of when to start and finish work, as long as the total hours required per week are worked.

Flow production A method of production in which one product is made continuously and in large numbers. Also known as mass production.

Food Safety Order Passed in 1991, this Act ensures that all food offered to the public is safe to eat and is properly described.

Franchise A system in which a business idea is hired out to other businesses.

Franchisee A person who buys a franchise.

Franchiser A person or company who sells a franchise.

Fringe benefit Is a non-financial method of motivation and includes such perks as company cars, pension schemes, private health care and free housing.

Full-time employment A system in which an employee is engaged to work the total number of specified hours per week.

G

General union A large trade union whose members are workers in one area of work but come from a wide range of industries.

Generic advertising A method of advertising which advertises a whole industry or a particular type of goods regardless of where the goods are sold.

Global market Trading on a world-wide scale.

Go slow A form of industrial action in which workers slow down production without actually going on strike.

Gross profit The difference between a business's income from sales and the cost of sales. It is found in the trading account.

Gross profit percentage The amount of gross profit which a business has made on sales. It measures a business's trading efficiency.

Growth The third stage of the product life cycle, when sales are growing rapidly.

H

Health and Safety Order Passed in 1978, this Order sets out the responsibilities of both employers and employees to ensure that the work environment is safe.

Hierarchical structure A type of management structure which has one person at the top and a large number of employees at the bottom. It is the opposite of a flat structure.

Hire purchase A medium-term method of finance used for the purchase of assets. A deposit is paid at the beginning and the remainder paid in instalments while the business uses the asset.

Horizontal integration Is the joining together of two businesses which are at the same level of production and work with the same type of product.

I

Induction Is the training given to new employees and is designed to make them fit into their new workplace easily.

Industrial union A trade union whose members all work in one industry but may do different types of work within that industry.

Informative advertising A type of advertising which is intended to give information.

Internal business growth Growth which takes place inside a business such as ploughing back profits. Also known as organic growth.

Internal recruitment A system in which advertising for new employees is done inside the business.

International marketing Marketing which takes place between different countries.

Interview A method of appraisal in which a one-to-one discussion takes place between the appraiser and the appraisee.

Invest NI Northern Ireland's economic development agency which was created in 2002.

Investors in People An award given to a business organisation which has invested in the training of the people working there.

ITC Stands for 'Independent Television Commission' which is a body set up to regulate commercial television services.

J

Job analysis A process in recruitment where the employer identifies the duties and needs of a given post.

Job description A document used in the recruitment process to define the duties and responsibilities of the post being offered.

Job enlargement A method of motivation in which extra tasks are given to an employee.

Job enrichment A method of motivation in which extra responsibilities and jobs requiring higher level skills are given to an employee.

Job production A method of production in which one single item is made at a time – often to a customer's individual specification.

Job rotation A system in which employees move between different jobs in order to avoid boredom.

Job satisfaction Is the degree of fulfilment and happiness which an employee gets from his/her work.

Job sharing A system in which two employees undertake one job and share its duties between them.

Just-in-time production A method of production and stock control in which products are manufactured just in time for them to be sold.

L

Labour Relations Agency An independent body in Northern Ireland which provides impartial advice and assistance on industrial relations.

Large enterprise A business which has more than 250 employees.

Launch The second stage of the product life cycle, when the product is introduced to the market.

Leasing A medium-term method of finance used for acquiring assets. Similar to renting, the business makes regular payments for the use of the asset.

Liabilities Amounts owed by a business, for example to creditors.

Liquidity The ability of a business to pay its debts.

Long-term liabilities Amounts owed by a business which may be owed over a longer period of time, for example a mortgage.

Loss leader A sales promotion method in which the price of one or two products is reduced to a very low level in order to attract customers to the shop.

Loyalty cards A sales promotion method in which each purchase in the store earns points which can be exchanged later for cash or Air Miles.

M

Manager A person on the second layer of authority in a business who has responsibility for its day-to-day running.

Manufacturer See *producer*.

Margin of safety The amount which a business is able to sell in excess of its break-even point.

Market economy An economic system in which there is total private ownership and entrepreneurs take responsibility for decision making.

Market-led pricing A pricing policy in which a business accepts the price which competitors are charging and prices its product at the same level. Also known as 'competitive pricing'.

Market research The collection of information from consumers to find out if they like, or will buy, certain products.

Market segmentation The selection of groups of people with similar tastes who would be most interested in a particular product. Segmentation may be by age, gender, background, class or geography.

Marketing The process which identifies, anticipates and satisfies customers' requirements profitably.

Marketing economies Economies which are gained in situations where a business can save in expenses associated with marketing.

Marketing Mix All the key activities which are used in marketing a business's goods – price, promotion, place and product.

Mass production See *flow production*.

Maturity The fourth stage of the product life cycle, when sales levels are maintained and the product has become established on the market.

Memorandum of association A legal document used in the setting up of a limited company.

Merger See *amalgamation*.

Micro business A business which has fewer than 10 employees.

Mission statement A statement of a business's main aims and objectives.

Mixed economy An economic system in which there are privately and publicly owned businesses and the government and business people have decision-making responsibilities.

Monopoly A situation in which one business controls more than 25% of the market.

Mortgage A long-term method of finance often used for the purchase of premises.

Motivation The way in which a person can be encouraged to make an effort to do something.

Municipal undertaking An activity organised by a local authority.

N

Needs analysis The first stage in the recruitment procedure where the employer decides exactly what the business needs from new employees.

Net loss Arises when a business's expenses exceed its gross profit.

Net profit The true profit of a business which is found in the profit and loss account by subtracting all expenses from the gross profit.

Net profit percentage The amount of net profit which a business has made on sales. It measures a business's trading efficiency and also its ability to keep expenses low.

Northern Ireland Act Passed in 1998, this Act ensures equality in the public sector in all employment issues.

O

Observation A method of appraisal in which the employee is watched doing his/her work.

OFT Stands for 'Office of Fair Trading' which is an independent body set up to promote and protect the interests of consumers.

Off-the-job training Training which is provided by a specialist outside the employee's normal place of work.

On-the-job training Training which is given at the employee's normal place of work.

Operative Is a shop floor worker and is responsible for making the business's product.

Organic growth See *internal business growth*.

Organisational structure The way in which a business is organised. It may be structured by product, by function or geographically.

Overdraft A short-term means of finance in which the business is allowed to write cheques beyond the amount of the balance in the account.

Overtime ban A form of industrial action in which workers refuse to work any hours beyond the length of their normal working day.

Owner A person who has invested money in a business.

P

Partnership A business which has between two and 20 owners and is most often found in professional businesses and those giving a service.

Partnership Act Passed in 1890, this Act governs the formation and running of business partnerships.

Part-time employment This is where an employee works less than a full week – three mornings per week, for example.

Penetration pricing A pricing policy in which a low price is set at the beginning. The price is increased when the product's place in the market has been secured.

Permanent employment Is where an employee is contracted to work for a business until he/she leaves because of retirement, resignation, redundancy or dismissal.

Person specification A document drawn up as part of the recruitment procedure to identify the qualities, skills and experience which an ideal applicant for the post should have.

Persuasive advertising A method of advertising which is intended to create a need and to encourage members of the public to purchase the advertised product.

Picketing A form of industrial action in which workers on strike stand with placards outside the workplace to discourage other workers from going to work.

Piece work A system of payment in which employees are paid according to the number of products they make.

Planned economy An economic system in which there is public ownership and the government takes responsibility for decision making.

Ploughed back profit See *retained profit*.

Price war A pricing policy which cuts the price of some products to a very low level in order to attract customers.

Primary production The first stage of production, which is extracting raw materials and using the earth's resources to grow crops.

Primary research A method of market research which collects original information and is carried out by making direct contact with consumers and members of the public. Also known as 'field research'.

Private-sector businesses Businesses which are owned by private people.

Private limited company A company which cannot sell its shares on the Stock Exchange. Its shares are owned by a small group of people.

Producer A person who manufactures goods or services.

Product The goods or services which a business is offering for sale.

Product life cycle The lifespan of a product showing the path from the beginning of the product to its withdrawal from the market.

Profit and loss account One of the final accounts. Its purpose is to find net profit.

Profit sharing A financial method of motivation whereby employees receive a share of the profit made by the business.

Promotion (in employment) Is where an employee has been given a job at a higher level in the same business.

Promotion (in marketing) All methods by which businesses inform customers about their products and encourage them to buy those products.

Public corporation A government-controlled market body.

Public limited company The largest type of private sector organisation. Its shares are traded on the Stock Exchange.

Public private partnership A business activity organised and funded jointly by a public body and a private company.

Public relations Any activity where the public's awareness of a business is raised and the business is seen to be generous and public spirited.

Public-sector businesses Businesses which are owned by the country and run by the government.

Q

Quality assurance The need to achieve constant, high standards in all that customers require.

Quality circles A similar system to team-working. Employees are organised into groups and meet regularly to examine the quality of what they are doing and try to find ways of improving it.

Questionnaire A means of primary research and is a list of written questions which members of the public are to be asked in order to find information.

Quota sampling A method of sampling in which interviews are held with a set number of people who fall into pre-determined categories, e.g. male or teenager.

R

Race Relations Order Passed in 1997, this Order states that people of all races, colours, nationalities and ethnic origin must be treated equally in employment, recruitment and training.

Random sampling A method of sampling in which people are randomly selected and questioned.

Recruitment Is the employment of new workers.

Research and development The first stage of the product life cycle, which takes place before the product is put on the market.

Resignation Is where an employee leaves a business voluntarily because he/she has decided to give up work or is leaving to go to a different job.

Retailer The shopkeeper who is the final seller of goods to the consumer.

Retained profit Profit which the owner re-invests in the business. Also known as 'ploughed back' profit.

Retirement Is where an employee leaves a business because he/she has reached the end of his/her working life.

Return on capital employed Shows the net profit which the owner of a business has received on the capital invested.

Returns inward Goods which are subtracted from sales because they have been sent back to the business by another business.

Returns outward Goods which are subtracted from purchases because they have been sent back by the business to another business.

S

Salary Payment given to an employee in return for work done. Usually paid monthly.

Sale and Supply of Goods Passed in 1994, this Act ensures that goods and services
Services Act supplied by a business are of satisfactory quality.

Sales promotion See *marketing promotion*.

Sampling A method of primary research which questions a sample of people as being representative of the whole population. Sampling may be random, quota or target.

Saturation The fifth stage of the product life cycle, when sales are at their highest and new customers cannot be found.

Secondary production The second stage of production, which works on raw materials to manufacture finished goods.

Secondary research A method of market research which uses published statistics, data and other information all of which have been collected previously. Also known as 'desk research'.

Self-appraisal The process of assessing one's own work to find ways of improving its quality.

Self-employment An employment system in which a person sets up his/her own business and works for himself/herself.

Sex Discrimination Order Passed in 1976 and amended in 1988, this Order states that men and women should have equal treatment and opportunity in employment and recruitment.

Shareholder A person who has invested money in a limited company by buying shares. This makes the shareholder a part-owner in the company.

Short-term contract Is a system of temporary employment in which the employee is engaged to work for a short period – over Christmas, for example.

Single-union agreement An agreement that management in a business organisation would negotiate with only one named union.

Skimming A pricing policy which sets a relatively high price initially in order to skim the market. The price is reduced later when other businesses enter the market.

Sleeping partner A partner who contributes capital to a partnership business but does not work in it or take part in its organisation.

Small enterprise One which has fewer than 50 employees.

SME Stands for 'small- to medium-size enterprise', being one which has between 50 and 250 employees.

Sole trader A person who owns and runs his/her own business.

Span of control This refers to the number of people over whom a manager or supervisor has direct control.

Sponsorship A method of promotion in which a company meets the costs involved in running an event or providing a service.

Stakeholder A person who has an interest in the activity.

Start-up capital The capital needed to get a business started.

Stock Exchange The place where shares in companies are bought and sold.

Stock turnover rate The number of times in a year that a business is able to sell the value of its average stock. It measures a business's trading efficiency.

Strike action A form of industrial action in which workers refuse to work.

Supervisor A supervisor is on the lowest level of management in a business and has direct contact with the workforce.

Specialisation Is when an employee concentrates on one particular operation and does it all the time. Specialisation may be by product, process, function or country.

T

Takeover Is when one business buys over the control of another business.

Target sampling A method of sampling in which people from only a particular market segment are interviewed.

Team working A system in which employees are grouped together in teams, making sure that each team has the full range of skills and abilities required to carry out the task.

Technical economies Economies which are gained in situations where a business can cut its production costs by introducing upgraded technology or by altering its production methods.

Teleworking Is a form of homeworking which has been made possible by advances in technology. The employee works at home but keeps in touch with the business by computer.

Temporary employment A system in which an employee is engaged to work for a specified period of time – one year, for example.

Tertiary production The stage of production which provides services to members of the public and to other industries.

Total costs The sum of a business's fixed and variable costs.

Trade Descriptions Acts Passed in 1968 and 1972, these Acts prohibit the giving of false descriptions of goods and service for sale.

Trade union An organisation which represents the interests of workers.

Trades Union Congress An umbrella organisation which speaks on behalf of the entire trade union movement.

Trading account One of the final accounts. Its purpose is to find gross profit.

Training Is the acquisition of knowledge and skills which can be applied to a particular job.

V

Variable costs Costs which change according to the level of work being done in the business.

Vertical integration Is the joining of two businesses which are at different levels of production but are in the same industry. Vertical integration may be either backwards, forwards or lateral.

W

Wage Payment given to an employee in return for work done. Usually paid weekly.

Weights and Measures Order Passed in 1981, this Order protects consumers from being sold goods which are underweight.

White collar union A trade union whose members are non-manual workers and work in technical, clerical, supervisory or managerial jobs.

Wholesaler The wholesaler purchases goods in bulk from the manufacturer, stores them, and sells them to retailers in smaller quantities.

Work to rule A form of industrial action in which workers observe every rule in an exaggerated way, which disrupts production.

Workers' co-operative A business organisation formed by workers, often in an attempt to keep a business open and save jobs.

Working capital Capital required to pay the day-to-day running expenses of the business.

Index